Silent Saboteurs

The Collusion That Almost Broke Me

Jeanine Orzani

Dedication

To the people who saved my life.

To two people who will not be named, who reached out when I was suicidal and ready to disappear, after I posted a single word: "Bye."

You spoke to me when I could not speak for myself.

You helped bring me back when it felt like there was no way forward.

You know who you are.

And to Sarah Gleeson.

To the woman who recognised me when others tried to diminish me.

Who called me in one of those moments, asked where I was, and stayed when I told her I was sitting on the beach, contemplating walking into the water and swimming until I couldn't swim anymore.

Who understood that sometimes survival begins with someone refusing to let you sit alone at the edge.

You didn't just help me choose to live.

You sat with me at the table when it mattered, and helped light the fire that followed.

I am still here because of you.

Acknowledgements

A lot of what's in this book started on my social media. Posts where I was just trying to make sense of things out loud. I've taken those pieces, added context, and woven in what I've learned along the way.

I used AI tools to help shape the structure and tighten up the writing, but the heart of this book - the stories, the truths, the pain, and the persistence - that's all of me. The words are mine. The experiences are mine. The fight is mine.

I've done my best to be accurate and fair, but if there are any mistakes or things I got wrong, that's on me. Be gentle. This wasn't easy to write.

This book is, in many ways, a response to the people who tried to take me down. People who lied, who manipulated, who underestimated me.

I'm still here.

More than that, this is a thank you to the people who helped me get through.

To my mentor, your guidance helped me hold it together when everything felt like it was falling apart.

To my family, yes, it's messy and complicated, and there's been more than our share of dysfunction, but I still love you.

To the friends who checked in, your messages and calls meant more than you know.

To my therapists, thank you for listening, believing, and helping me make sense of the chaos.

And to the strangers who reached out with encouragement, your kindness landed at exactly the right time...

Anyone who really knows my story understands how much it has taken to bring these truths to light. It's been exhausting, painful, and often isolating. But I kept going, because the truth matters and so does accountability.

I don't claim to be a writer. I'm just someone with a story that needs to be told. If my way of doing this ruffles feathers in the writing world, I get it, but I had to do it my way.

To anyone still fighting in the shadows, you're not alone. Keep going. There's light ahead, even if you can't see it yet.

Contents

About the author — 1

Author's Note — 5

Preface — 7

1. Where It Began — 9

2. Lived Experience — 21

3. Mentor — 35

4. Power and Control — 43

5. Nepotism — 69

6. Collusion — 83

7. Journey of Discovery — 95

8. Critical Incidents — 113

9. Mobbing — 137

10. The Red Haired Renegade — 149

11. Profile — 157

12. Neurodiversity — 167

13. Speaking Truth to Power — 181

14. Creating Accountability — 191

15. Credibility   209

16. Choices   225

17. Duty of Care   245

18. Upstander vs Bystander   259

19. Reclaiming My Power   273

20. Recovery   291

21. I'm No Angel   303

22. The Future   323

23. Taking Out The Trash   333

24. Activism   351

Breaking The Code   377

About the author

Hi, I'm Jeanine.

For those who don't know me, I'm a former union official. For those who do, well, you know I've lived through some very heavy moments.

These harrowing experiences weren't accidental. They were designed to derail me.

But anyone who truly knows me also knows this: I'm a fighter.

Many of you have followed my journey and know I've shared a lot of information about narcissism.

I made a decision some time ago to put that knowledge to good use and shine a light on the darkness, not just for myself, but for others, too.

I believe there's no such thing as a bad experience, not if you're given the space and opportunity to transform it.

For context:

"There is a prime bully or bullies, a known quantity you'd recognise.

But what you don't know is that they've recruited others to target you, too.

These are the 'flying monkeys,' like those sent by the Wicked Witch of the West in The Wizard of Oz.

They do her bidding, no questions asked."

Victims of narcissistic abuse often hear things like:

- *"Get over it."*

- *"Just forget about it."*

- *"Why don't you move on?"*

- *"Think positive, it'll be fine."*

- *"If you stop thinking about it, they don't exist."*

- *"Stop living in the past."*

- *"Hope you find peace."*

These statements may be well-intentioned, but they are incredibly damaging. In psychology, they're known as toxic positivity, a form of emotional invalidation that causes more harm than good. These responses also assume the narcissist has let you go.

Let me be clear:

They never let you go.

On the upside, every time someone tells me to "move on," I gain even more motivation to speak up. I've been fighting for change in this space for a long time, because someone had to say: **ENOUGH is ENOUGH.**

It's time to change the rules.

Don't you think?

As we say in the union world:

"Do nothing, nothing changes."

What can I say?

They taught me well.

"You can take the ACTIVIST out of the union, but you can't take the ACTIVIST out of the woman."

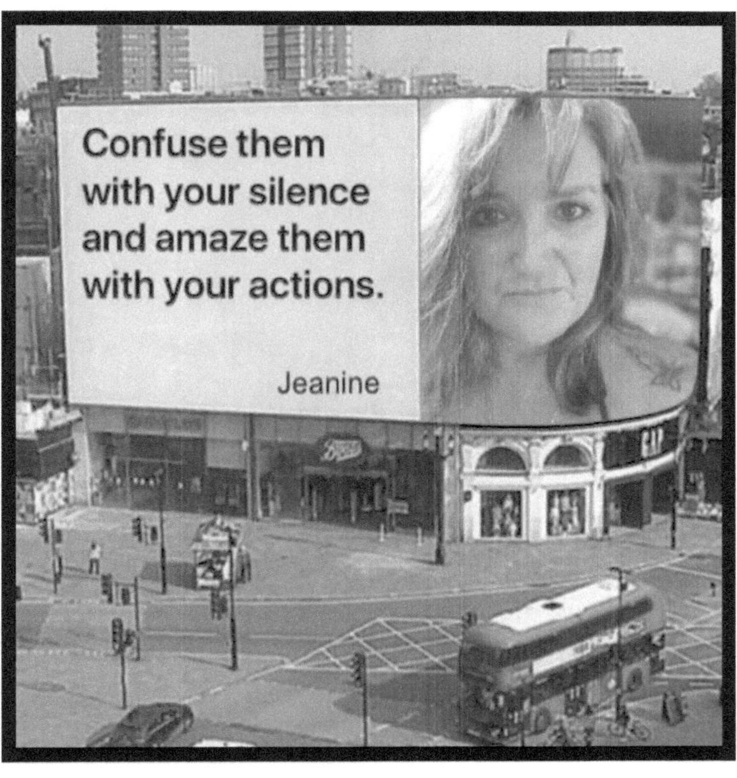

Author's Note

This is the story I carried in silence for far too long.

It's the weight of what was done, what was allowed, and what was ignored.

It's the ache of being disbelieved.

The sting of professional sabotage disguised as procedure.

The quiet complicity of those who knew better and did nothing.

I didn't write this for revenge.

I wrote it to reclaim my voice.

To speak the truths that were buried under layers of gaslighting, power games, and institutional apathy.

Some names appear in these pages because the silence around them enables harm.

Others have been withheld, not to protect them but to protect myself.

Where relevant, parts of this story fall under the protections provided by Chapter 11, Part 4A of the *Fair Work (Registered Organisations) Act 2009 (Cth)*.

I've spoken out in good faith, grounded in my lived experience, supported by evidence, and driven by a need for justice, not just for me, but for others still navigating the same darkness.

This book is the result of years of trying to make sense of the senseless, to find meaning in the betrayal, and to build something out of the ruins.

I offer it as both a record and a reckoning.

To anyone who has been silenced, sidelined, or shattered, I see you.

This story is mine, but you may find pieces of yourself in it, too.

Moral of the story:

When power protects the abuser, justice must speak louder.

Preface

In workplaces across the globe, bullying and harassment are not just issues of personal distress; they are systemic problems that can undermine the integrity of entire organisations.

This book delves into the often-overlooked forms of mistreatment that occur within the most unexpected spaces: union environments.

For many, unions represent solidarity, support, and collective strength. However, behind closed doors, those very environments can harbour toxic behaviours; bullying, harassment (in all its forms - including sexual harassment and the worst case sexual assault), exclusion, discrimination, passive aggression, gossip, micromanagement, and favouritism. All perpetuated by colleagues, counterparts, and delegates, including members of the management team and respective executives.

This book is not just an examination of these harmful practices but a call to action. It seeks to raise awareness, offer support, and provide strategies for addressing and preventing the silent epidemic of mistreatment within unionised settings.

Whether you're a rank-and-file member, a union leader, or an ally, this work is meant to empower you to stand up against any form of workplace abuse, no matter the source or position.

It is time to reimagine union solidarity. One rooted in the dignity and well-being of every member, without exception.

Together, we can begin to break the silence, hold perpetrators accountable, and build a stronger, healthier future for unions and those they represent.

Through firsthand accounts, expert analysis, and practical guidance, the reader will explore the complexities of bullying and harassment that often go unreported in unionised workplaces or are simply brushed under the carpet.

By sharing stories and insights, I hope to foster an environment where solidarity truly means mutual respect and fairness, ensuring that unions are not only a force for workers' rights but also a safe and supportive space for all.

It's the fact that they all KNOW employment law, but some break it - AGAINST their OWN EMPLOYEES - while running campaigns that promote workers' rights.

It begs the question:

When the leaders exhibit these behaviours, where's the actual integrity?

It's an appalling and sadly not uncommon contradiction: organisations or individuals in positions of unyielding power champion workers' rights, yet exploit their own employees.

It's not just hypocrisy. It's a profound betrayal of trust and of values, especially for those who genuinely believe in the cause.

Moral of the story:

"DO NOTHING, NOTHING CHANGES"

Where It Began

The seeds of bullying and harassment in unionised environments, like in many institutions, are often sown in the spaces where power dynamics remain unchecked.

While unions were created to protect workers from exploitation and ensure fair treatment, their foundational ideals are sometimes compromised when internal conflicts arise.

For many, the concept of solidarity is meant to unify and empower; yet, within the very structures that are supposed to protect workers, divisions can form, and toxic behaviours can flourish.

In the early days of labour movements, unions were born out of the need for collective strength in the face of systemic oppression.

Workers, often facing long hours, low wages, and dangerous conditions, found solidarity in one another, demanding better treatment and securing essential rights.

But as unions grew in size and influence, the challenges of maintaining a cohesive and respectful community within such a diverse group has become more complex.

In some cases, union leadership has become a source of power, and as with any system, power can corrupt.

What began as a movement for equality has sometimes become a breeding ground for the very behaviours it was meant to combat.

Personal rivalries, differences in opinion, and political ideologies have turned colleagues into adversaries, making union spaces feel hostile rather than supportive.

From my own observations, over time, it would appear some individuals within unions began to exploit their roles for personal gain, bullying and harassing others to assert control, maintain influence, or stifle dissent.

This often went unnoticed or unchallenged, as members were hesitant to speak out against the very people who were supposed to represent their interests.

The close-knit nature of unions meant that disputes could be magnified, and sometimes conflicts were resolved through intimidation or manipulation rather than dialogue and resolution.

In many ways, the history of workplace bullying within unions mirrors broader societal struggles with power, hierarchy, and inequality.

What began as a struggle for justice and fair treatment became marred by the same issues that affect any group with power structures: exclusion, discrimination, and toxic behaviour.

By understanding where it began, we can better address the problem and restore the union movement's core mission of mutual respect, fairness, and equality for all.

For those asking:

How did it get so bad?

The answer:

It always was. It's not all black-and-white. It's all shades of grey.

But through some very controversial online activism and this book, as a victim-survivor of abuse within the union environment, I hope to:

Bring the darkness into the light, so we may, really and truly, make ***REAL CHANGE*** begin.

My story is no secret.

Despite the perpetrators' attempts to keep it "in-house" under the guise of protecting me, the reality was quite different.

They were protecting themselves. That strategy ultimately backfired, as I refused to stay silent about what had been done to me.

Once I fully grasped the extent of the abuse, my voice only grew louder.

I made it well known that I'd had enough of the patriarchy.

I'd had enough of males objectifying, gaslighting, abusing, and being downright disrespectful to women in the workplace.

I was called deluded.

I was told to calm down.

I was told to let it go.

They suggested I needed to be quiet if I wanted to continue having a relationship with them.

It's been a long journey, and one that I am still clearly on; to ensure integrity, accountability, and transparency are cultivated, not just with lip service.

On behalf of all victims of workplace abuse:

- I will continue to call out gender bias and inequality.

- I will continue to challenge gender stereotypes and discrimination.

- I will continue to help create a more inclusive world.

- I will continue to celebrate women and their achievements.

- I will continue to lift other women up (not tear them down).

- I will continue to seek justice.

The truth is, abusive people enjoy the framing game.

Abusive people provoke their chosen target for a reaction, then claim it as evidence of mental instability, evil-mindedness, or something else that implies it is the victim who is at fault.

Abusive people divert all attention away from their own behaviour, and they seek support from others, turning them against their target.

It can be devastating for an individual who is already suffering from mistreatment to then be blamed, slandered, rejected, and also isolated.

The abuser enjoys the sense of power and control they derive from tormenting with impunity, the positive attention they get from playing the victim, and fishing for sympathy.

It is an effective method of intimidating the target from attempting to speak up and expose the truth.

Tactics used by an abusive person, such as belittling, silencing, punishing, coercing, gaslighting, harassing, or humiliating, can seriously affect a target's well-being.

Past behaviours are the best predictors of future behaviours.

To work out what they'll do next, look at the patterns from the past.

The take-home message:

Nobody deserves to be abused at work.

It's All Just A Facade.

The fact is that certain individuals become leaders of organisations in our communities and in the public arena.

Then, promote themselves as having high moral values of equality, social justice, dignity & respect for others, and maintain a false veneer of trustworthiness and integrity.

These individuals are highly skilled at portraying a persona of being caring human beings, yet can perform horrid, defamatory, heinous acts on unsuspecting victims.

Then, when challenged, they will lie to save themselves and call the victims crazy, even delusional.

Which brings me to the topic of values. In particular, union values.

What are the values of unions?

Let's explore more of that.

According to the Department of Education, Employment and Workplace Relations, it's about:

- Social Justice

- Collectivism

- Unity

- Fairness

- Equality

- Opportunity

- Progression

- Betterment of society, and

- A decision-making mechanism, which is democratic and accountable.

Furthermore, union values aspire to "ensure behaviours in others that are contradictory to furthering the principles and values of collectivism are challenged appropriately."

As for ideal union leadership values, well, that's simple. They are:

- Education and empowerment

- Development

- Clear communication

- Vision

- Empathy

- Humility

- Commitment

- Patience

- Dignity and respect

- Honesty and transparency

- Accountability

- Integrity

It's shameful that I found myself in a position as an educator to those who know better.

Alas, here we are.

It is what it is.

Just like the conversation I had with someone, considered to be a leader, on Labour Day of 2023.

I mentioned the "*game playing*" that has to stop.

Especially considering amendments to the Work Health and Safety Regulations, with the introduction of a Code of Practice to specifically cover psychological safety and psychosocial hazards in the workplace, effective April 1, 2023.

This leader responded by saying,

"The game playing will still happen."

To which I replied,

"Not on my watch."

As you can see, it's a bit of a ranch, full of cowboys.

Many, not all; they are just a bunch of bullies who are merely driven by their own selfish agendas, which have no benefit to the greater union movement and aspirations of traditional union values.

These people, and their habits have decided their futures.

My future is bright, shining, full of opportunity, and a journey through the wonderland of existence.

I do hope the bullies have learned their lesson, and that is:

everyone has value.

No one is greater or lesser than anyone else on this journey.

We all have choices to make, contemplate direction, and practice what we preach.

The Impact of this Work aims to:

Reveal Truths

By sharing my story through online activism and this book, I am not only exposing wrongdoing but also offering others the courage to confront similar situations.

Expose Hypocrisy

Exposing hypocrisy and shining a light on injustices within the union realm is not just an act of defiance;

it is an act of justice.

Unions, by their very nature, are meant to protect, advocate, and uplift their members.

When they become complicit in harm, they betray their fundamental purpose, and that betrayal demands accountability.

Challenge the System

When unethical behaviour is brought out into the open, it becomes harder for perpetrators to hide behind facades.

Transparency forces accountability.

Inspire Collective Action

I hope my efforts will resonate with those who have been silenced, inspiring them to unite and demand *REAL CHANGE* within their own workplace environment.

Leave a Legacy

I hope this book becomes more than just a tool for awareness. I hope it becomes a testament to resilience, integrity, and the power of truth.

By shining a spotlight on the injustices that occur in the union realm, we are taking the first vital steps in dismantling a harmful system. It also offers hope and empowers others to speak up against tyranny.

By bringing these injustices to light, we disrupt the cycles of silence and complicity that enable abusers to thrive.

Hypocrisy cannot survive in the face of truth. It crumbles when confronted with courage and clarity.

I had a seat at that table, and it was nothing but toxic, unprofessional, and deeply traumatic. Not just your average office politics, but something far more calculated, something insidious. This was workplace bullying, dressed up in bureaucracy and hidden behind carefully crafted smiles. This was union politics used not to protect workers, but to shield power brokers from accountability. This was systemic injustice - layered, protected, and polished for public consumption.

Yet, I remain. Not because it's easy. Not because I enjoy the fight. I stay because I refuse to buckle under pressure. Because I will not hand over my silence to those who expect it.

I stay for the people who were pushed out, gaslit, and broken by the very institution that claimed to represent them. I strive to be a voice for those who never got their turn to speak.

Whether I'm believed or not is beside the point. Belief is a privilege granted by people who are more comfortable with stories that don't make them question their own complicity. But if those who doubt me had spent even one day in my shoes, let alone the last several years, they wouldn't be so quick to dismiss. They wouldn't cling to false positivity or try to appease the powerful with empty words. They would act. But they don't. Because courage is inconvenient. Because rocking the boat might cost them something. Cowards, plain and simple.

Union spaces are supposed to be built on solidarity, justice, and collective strength. But what I experienced was hierarchy in disguise. A culture where speaking up made you a threat, and staying silent earned you safety. The very structures that should have protected me were used to punish me. They turned procedures into weapons, policies into shields for bullies, and values into PR campaigns. All while preaching fairness.

I didn't come here to play politics. I came to do the work. I came to support workers, fight injustice, and make a difference. But that table? It wasn't built for truth. It was built to maintain power and to eject anyone who dared to challenge it.

Still, I speak. Still, I rise.

Do I want justice?

Yes. But more than that, I want the truth. I want the masks to fall off. I want the systems that failed so many of us to be exposed and rebuilt. And, I want to see karma play out in real time.

That's not bitterness.

That's clarity.

That's what happens when you've been forced to survive a system designed to silence you.

This is not just my story.

It's a mirror held up to the entire structure.

It's what happens when workplace bullying is allowed to fester behind closed doors, when union politics are driven by ego instead of ethics, and when systemic injustice is so entrenched that it feels normal to most.

But it's not normal. And I won't let it be normalised.

I'm still at the table.

But I'm not the same person who first sat down.

And I'll make damn sure that the next person beside me knows they're not alone.

When people ask me where it all began, how something so noble turned so dark, I tell them this: it didn't begin in the boardrooms or the union halls.

It began in the shadows.

Here's what I've come to understand about those shadows...

The Root Of It.

I have stalkers who have been watching me, possibly, for more than a decade.

Obsessive much?

The following screenshot shows multiple unauthorised logins to my Facebook account, including Messenger, from devices and locations I did not recognise at the time.

This was how I first realised that others had been accessing my private communications without my knowledge.

Screenshot: Facebook login history revealing multiple unrecognised logins over a span of years.

The stalkers may have helped orchestrate the destruction of my career. Presumably, all for fun.

To be clear, I'm not suggesting these stalkers are affiliated with any union or professional group I've encountered. This may be something altogether different.

What I have learned is that stalkers have a burning need to know anything and everything about your private life, so I decided, a long time ago, to give them what they wanted, and more. Are they happy with the outcome, after years of stalking me? Probably not, but that's not my problem.

When a person or entity, such as those who stalk me, conducts themselves in such a secretive fashion, there is the risk that they might find information they did not really want to know. On the other hand, as a victim, you might find your personal messages hacked and all your personal information disclosed to the world at large. Acting in such a manner demonstrates THEIR character, and it is reflective of their inability to have an adult conversation.

They know, deep down, they are subpar, and I will never accept less-than actions and empty words in interpersonal relationships.

I do not need to give that any consideration, because there have been no words, no words at all.

You can send in the Flying Monkeys to do your bidding, but I learned about this character more than a decade ago.

In short:

To assess a person's character, watch what they do, not what they say.

Lived Experience

I had worked for a union and been a proud member for years, believing in the collective power of workers.

For me, it wasn't just about better wages and benefits.

It was about solidarity. Camaraderie. Standing shoulder to shoulder with others fighting for fairness and justice. But somewhere along the way, that solidarity began to fray.

It started innocuously enough. A few snide remarks here and there, the kind of teasing that might be brushed off as harmless or even a rite of passage in any workplace. As time passed, these remarks grew sharper, more personal.

What once seemed like friendly ribbing transformed into outright dismissive behaviour, undermining my contributions in meetings, excluding me from important discussions, and even spreading rumours about my professional capabilities.

It was subtle at first. A colleague, someone I had worked alongside for years, began to challenge my every idea in front of the group, making it seem like I was unqualified or out of touch.

At first, I thought it was just a difference of opinion. But when the criticism became personal, questioning my character and work ethic in a way that felt meant to humiliate, I started to wonder if there was something more to it.

The Reality:

They tried to break me.

They tried to destroy me.

They tried to silence me.

The message became clear:

If I wanted to maintain a relationship with them, I had to be quiet. But I knew better. Attempts to silence women who speak up about abuse in the workplace are exactly why Australians marched in the streets. Marched for justice. Marched for change.

What could they have asked instead?

Perhaps:

"What could we have done to support you better, so others don't feel forced to leave in order to feel safe?"

It's exhausting having to constantly remind people to treat you with the respect you freely offer them.

What is wrong with people? How do they sleep, being so cruel and so careless?

There were moments, critical incidents we'll explore later, that I will never forget. Not because of what was said but because of how I felt. The cold, isolating realisation that the very community I had trusted had turned hostile. I didn't know how to confront it. I felt trapped.

If I spoke up, would I be branded difficult? Disloyal?

The impact on my mental and emotional health was undeniable. What was once an empowering part of my life became a daily source of anxiety. But what shocked me most was the silence.

People who had always been vocal about injustice said nothing. No one stood beside me. No one asked if I was okay. No one spoke up. I began to question my place within the very organisation built on principles of fairness.

This wasn't just a matter of difficult personalities or occasional workplace disagreements. It was a systematic form of harassment; undermining my credibility, isolating me from others and turning the very concept of union solidarity into something that felt hollow.

What was once a space where workers could come together and speak out against oppressive forces became one where those same toxic forces could be wielded within the group itself.

The journey of discovery was the most heart-wrenching, but I had the strength to carry on, with my head held high, knowing that there was nothing I could have done to prepare for what was being discovered.

It was mobbing, a collective effort to isolate and discredit me.

The union space, once a source of pride, became a weapon. The values we fought for were weaponised against me.

But I was quiet, not blind.

In 2020, as I began to uncover the full extent of what had been done to me, I posted this to Facebook:

"When one is accustomed to the boys' locker room talk, one may let derogatory comments slide.

Other times, I've told the 'boys'; 'Hey, that's not cool.'

But when the jokes become persistent, sexualised, and demeaning, one begins calling it out for what it is: not funny, deeply disrespectful, and completely inappropriate for a workplace.

This is bigger than me.

This is about systems that protect perpetrators."

When I wrote it; the Australian Bureau of Statistics, had reported that 22% of women and 6.1% of men over 18 had experienced sexual violence. Of the 639,000 women who experienced sexual assault in the last 10 years, only 13% reported it.

After that post, I didn't stop speaking.

I raised my voice.

I grew my platform, and I spoke truth to power.

Because a safe and healthy workplace is a basic human right, yet in unions, of all places, workers are often denied that right, especially when they are the ones employed by the union itself.

The era of sweeping shit under the rug is over.

Folks need to be uncomfortable.

A smear campaign of mass proportions was launched against me, and it was built on gossip and lies.

It was calculated, coordinated, and deeply personal. This was no ordinary conflict or misunderstanding.

It was a strategic and deliberate effort to destroy my reputation, credibility, and character, orchestrated by individuals with power, connections, and a clear agenda.

The campaign weaponised misinformation, turning whispers into wildfire and transforming professional rivalry into character assassination.

False rumours were seeded and allowed to spread unchecked. Not just untruths but malicious fabrications designed to paint me as untrustworthy, unstable, or unethical. Even facts were not safe. They were twisted, taken out of context, or manipulated to suit a narrative that served those seeking to undermine me. Past experiences and vulnerabilities were dragged into the light, not for understanding, but for exploitation.

The attack extended across platforms and spaces. The scheme was discussed in corridors, closed-door meetings, and inboxes.

It was amplified through social networks and backchannels. Faceless accusations were given weight by so-called anonymous sources, lending a fabricated sense of legitimacy to the lies. At times, it felt like I was being erased from my own story, replaced by a version of me constructed by people with ulterior motives.

The consequences were devastating. Professionally, I was isolated, discredited, and pushed out of spaces I had worked hard to be part of. Opportunities vanished, relationships strained, and the emotional toll was profound.

Once trust is broken by a smear campaign, even false claims can leave a lasting stain, making it incredibly difficult to rebuild your reputation, even when the truth eventually comes to light. But I didn't stay silent, and then I gave them something to really gossip about.

I fought back by demonstrating and exposing inconsistencies, calling out the double standards, and reclaiming my voice.

While legal action was an option I continued to weigh up, I chose, above all, to maintain my integrity. To let my truth and character speak louder than their lies. I know the real battle is not just about clearing my name, it's about exposing the systems that allow this kind of orchestrated bullying to happen in the first place.

Smear campaigns don't just happen by accident. They are deliberate, targeted, and often orchestrated by those with something to lose if the truth gets out.

It took time, but I began to piece together who was involved. A large group of individuals who had smiled at my face while undermining me behind closed doors. Union representatives who should have known better or did know better and chose complicity. Naming them, even quietly at first, was an act of liberation.

I didn't do it to be vindictive. I did it because silence would have let them win. Exposing them wasn't about revenge. It was about reclaiming my reality.

Once I realised that others were writing my story for me, twisting it to serve their own agenda, I decided to take the pen back. I used my platforms, my voice, and eventually this very book to tell the truth. I didn't dress it up, and I didn't hide the mess. There is power in honesty, even when it makes people uncomfortable. Especially then.

I wasn't naïve. I knew the people I was up against had resources and connections. So I armed myself with knowledge. I kept records. I got legal advice. I built a case, even if I never end up in a courtroom. Sometimes just being ready is enough to shift the power dynamic.

There were days when I felt completely alone. Like my name was a dirty word no one wanted to say out loud. But slowly, quietly, people began reaching out. Some shared their own stories, similar scars from the same toxic systems. Others just stood beside me. I held on to every message, every kind word. They became lifelines. Proof that I wasn't crazy and I wasn't alone.

Not everything deserved my energy. Some lies were thrown out just to bait me, to keep me stuck in a cycle of defence and reaction. I had to learn when to respond and when to rise above it.

Letting go isn't a weakness. It's survival.

Those who challenge entrenched systems of power often face resistance, intimidation and isolation. It is in this resistance that change begins. Each voice raised against tyranny chips away at the structures that allow harm to persist.

When we speak out, we not only demand justice for ourselves, but we also pave the way for others to do the same. Courage begets courage, and hope is contagious.

The act of exposing these wrongs sends a powerful message; the days of unchecked abuse are numbered.

This fight is about more than exposing the wrongdoers.

It's about rebuilding a system that lives up to its promise.

It's about creating spaces where fairness, transparency and accountability reign.

Most importantly, it's about showing others that their voices, too, have the power to challenge and change oppressive systems.

They didn't even have the creativity to be original. They did what people always do when they want to destroy someone's credibility. They called me "crazy." It didn't matter how much I had contributed or how many people I'd supported. It didn't matter how professional, loyal or committed I'd been. Once the whisper campaign started, I was done.

I was labelled difficult, unstable and unreliable. I watched the character assassination unfold like a performance, rehearsed and choreographed to justify their cruelty. They targeted my reputation, hoping I'd become unhirable, forgettable and invisible.

They wanted to isolate me.

They wanted me to disappear.

They wanted me broken, silent and erased.

But they didn't expect me to fight back.

Every slight, every sleight-of-hand. Every lie and betrayal. I wrote it down.

The more I wrote, the more I saw the patterns, not just in my own story but in others, too.

Yes, I wasn't the first, and I wouldn't be the last.

They counted on my silence, but I chose the truth. They counted on shame, but I chose courage.

Here's the thing, they didn't count on at all: That I would survive and that I would write this down for everyone to see.

It wasn't just what they did, it's who they are.

Some of them still preach about justice.

Some post hashtags on social media about equity and fairness.

They stand at rallies and chant about workers' rights, while covering up the pain they've caused in-house.

They speak of solidarity but only when it suits them, and to this day, not one person from those corridors of power has said: 'I'm sorry for what we did to you.'

Not one.

This is what betrayal looks like.

This is what institutional abuse feels like.

But this chapter.

This story.

It's not a eulogy for what was lost.

It's a reckoning.

I am still here.

I survived what was designed to kill my spirit.

I carry the scars, but I also carry the story.

I'm telling it not just for me but for every person who's been driven out of a workplace under the weight of silence and complicity.

In the past few years, we have heard a great deal of stories of bullying and harassment, in particular sexual harassment, in and around the "Canberra Bubble," when the Liberal Party were last in power, and continuing now under the Labor government.

It is a controversial space, often referred to as the political arena.

Unions, another political arena in their own right, are not immune to the effects of bullying & harassment behaviours, both from individuals within those workplaces and, at times, those within the broader political spaces.

Mostly, these behaviours are seen as a form of jousting, and we reach common agreement for the greater good of all.

Other times, not.

It is imperative to remember that unions themselves are a workplace and, like any employer, are subject to the shortcomings of those who run them.

Just like the political arena, you would expect that unions would have policies and procedures to deal with any bullying and harassment matters.

They do, but unfortunately, they don't practice what they preach.

I am a prime example of these bullying issues experienced within the union movement.

And I'm not the only one.

Unfortunately, most cases are brushed under the carpet.

They are not dealt with appropriately, and the victims are often silenced.

Furthermore, the mistreatment is often done in such a subtle way that at the time, victims have no idea it is even occurring.

When I realised the extent of the abuse, I was extremely vocal about what had happened to me, and I continue to be.

Hence, this book.

Clearly, I have shown that I am not one to be silenced.

I now have first-hand experience of a system, broken, beaten down and unwilling to be fixed by those who glorify in the collateral damage it creates.

A 'system' that so many people either get caught up in or walk away from because it's just too hard. Indeed, the "Rules are Broken!"

In this case, the system has been set up to benefit those at the top, at the expense of those at the bottom.

We have to "Change the Rules!"

In addition to the problems in the industrial space, I also now have further first-hand experience in the mental health space.

After accessing help from a mental health facility, I provided some feedback.

I wrote:

"Dr Williams is a consultant psychiatrist specialising in trauma and the founder of Doctors Against Violence Towards Women.
I recently heard Dr Williams speak at a conference. Dr Williams spoke about the problems with the medical and psychiatric system, which can further traumatise victims.
The 'system' has created weapons for the legal system to further oppress victims of abuse."

I am a woman, sadly, like many Australian women, who is familiar with violence and grew up in a household with a parent who knew no other way to communicate than the use of a raised voice, coercive control, and physical & emotional pain.

And another parent who constantly makes excuses for the other parent's behaviour.

I have not let that stop me.

Nor silence me.

It is this experience that led me to associate with the union movement as a way to create change at a grassroots level.

And the Labor Party, for policy and procedural change, which is oh so needed, to create a real-world shift for vulnerable Australians.

It is this same childhood, into adulthood experience, that has given me the grace to spot the signs of coercive control, while working for a trade union, and to prevent those same people from further traumatising me, by attempting to keep me silent.

Although I was a victim, I am not a victim and refuse to become one. I am a survivor, and I deserve better than what was done to me.

As a survivor:

During the annual 16 Days of Activism, I join with people around the world to raise awareness about gender-based violence, challenge discriminatory attitudes, and call for improved laws and services to end violence against women for good. Not just with lip service. My story has astonished the mind of an extremely experienced health treating specialist. It is equally unfathomable and unbelievable. They threw me under the bus, but I survived.

The question posed:

How can we be expected to make real change in the workplaces that union officials have carriage over, if the same problems exist and are unaddressed within our own union realm? My story, painful as it is, is part of a larger conversation about how unions, like any organisation, must confront and address internal toxic behaviours if they are to remain true to their mission of justice and equality.

Only when we are honest about these issues can we begin to heal and rebuild an environment that reflects the solidarity we all seek. My experience is just one of many. It is a reminder that bullying and harassment can happen anywhere, even in spaces that are meant to foster unity and support.

Mobbing, in particular, is a silent epidemic within many workplaces, including unions. It is a calculated, collective effort to discredit and isolate an individual, often with the aim of suppressing dissent and maintaining power. In my case, what began as personal attacks escalated into a coordinated campaign, leaving me with not only emotional scars but a deep sense of betrayal. The people and structures that should have protected me were complicit in the process. This isn't just about me, it's a reflection of a systemic issue that must be acknowledged, addressed and dismantled.

Unions are not immune to the very toxic dynamics they fight against and unless we are willing to confront these uncomfortable truths, we risk perpetuating the very injustices we are meant to eradicate.

As I began to shine a light on the wrongdoing around me, I made a conscious decision to stop making myself smaller so others could feel more comfortable.

I carried this with me like a quiet motto:

"It's no longer up to me to make myself smaller
to make the "movement" more comfortable."

I stopped bending myself out of shape for systems that claim to be about justice but make exceptions when it's inconvenient.

Thankfully, I haven't walked this path alone.

Having a strong support base - people who see, hear and stand with me - has been immeasurable.

Together, we raise our voices with clarity and conviction to demand more than platitudes and performative gestures.

We demand:

- Safety, dignity, and respect for all

- Workplaces where bullying, sexual harassment, and discrimination are not tolerated

- Accountability for those who harm others, with real consequences, not just quiet warnings behind closed doors

- Transparent, accessible reporting processes, free from the fear of retaliation

- Comprehensive mental health support for those impacted by toxic workplace culture, and

- A genuine commitment from leadership to foster inclusion, equity and a culture where every voice is truly valued, not just when it's convenient

This is not about being difficult. This is about refusing to accept the unacceptable. This is about setting a new standard and holding the line.

Our Stories Expose An Uncomfortable Truth:

The lengths to which people in positions of power will go to protect themselves and those complicit in wrongdoing, behind closed doors.

It wasn't just about their actions but about the systems they had carefully constructed to ensure those actions remained hidden.

What I witnessed was a culture of self-preservation, where loyalty to the truth was sacrificed in favour of maintaining appearances.

Those in leadership manipulated processes, twisted narratives, weaponised their authority to silence dissent, and shielded themselves from accountability.

This wasn't just a betrayal of individuals. It was a betrayal of principles.

The very foundations of fairness and justice that the union was meant to represent were being eroded by those entrusted to uphold them. Our experiences became a stark reminder that power, when left unchecked, can corrupt even the most well-intentioned institutions.

By shining a light on these practices, we are disrupting the facade they had worked so hard to maintain.

Our stories have become more than a recounting of personal injustice; they have become a call to action, a demand for accountability and a warning about the dangers of unchecked power.

Our stories demonstrate that those who have power can misuse it to inflict harm on the most vulnerable and are blind to the consequences of their actions.

Their actions, intended, deliberate and malicious in nature, leave wounds that can take months, even years to heal, and some victims never recover. Encouragingly, there is innumerable power behind, and within, our wounds.

The courage to speak out wasn't easy to find, but it was necessary.

For every injustice that remains hidden, there are countless others who suffer in silence.

By revealing the truth, I hope to challenge not just the individuals responsible but the systems that enabled them, and to inspire others to do the same.

Because if this can happen in a union, a place built to protect workers, then nowhere is safe until we make it so.

Not everyone in that world turned their back on me. Amid the betrayal and hypocrisy, there was one person who stood by me. Someone whose integrity couldn't be bought, bullied or broken. Their support gave me strength when I needed it most.

The next chapter is their story, told with their blessing.

Mentor

In the years I spent navigating the complexities of union life, an individual stood out as a beacon of wisdom, integrity and unwavering support; my mentor.

From the very beginning, they were more than just a colleague. They were a guide, someone who helped me understand the true meaning of solidarity, justice and mutual respect within the union.

I looked up to them, trusting their judgement and learning from their example.

As I became more involved, I began to notice the cracks in what I once thought was an impenetrable foundation of respect and loyalty.

My mentor, despite all their experience and accolades, was not immune to the toxic dynamics that can arise within any group, no matter how well-intentioned.

The same person who had been my greatest advocate and role model also had their own blind spots and moments of weakness when it came to navigating the intricacies of union politics.

It was during a particularly trying time in both our careers that I first felt the full weight of this realisation.

A merger of two branches of our union had arisen, and with this development, it brought not just ideological differences but personal rivalries and power struggles.

With the merger came not only a structural transformation but also a significant shift in leadership. Our branch's trade union leader transitioned into the prestigious position of National Secretary of the federal union.

This left a crucial void within our state branch, as the role of State Secretary now stood vacant - a position pivotal to representing and advocating for the interests of the rank and file.

The appointment of a new State Secretary required careful deliberation. It wasn't just about filling the role but about choosing someone who could navigate the complexities of the newly merged environment while staying true to the values and needs of the workers.

The process highlighted the delicate balance between the structural framework of the organisation and the grassroots foundation that gave it purpose.

This transition marked a turning point. It wasn't just about leadership. It was about redefining how leadership would look in a post-merger union. Who would rise to the challenge, and what values would they bring to the table? The answers to these questions would set the tone for the future of the branch and its relationship with those it served.

Unfortunately, as the dust settled from the merger and the shift in leadership, the true costs of change began to emerge.

My mentor, a figure who had guided me with wisdom and unwavering dedication, found themselves caught in the crossfire of this power struggle.

The newly appointed, self-proclaimed heads of the establishment, eager to assert their authority and consolidate control, began to view my mentor as a threat.

Perhaps it was their integrity, their commitment to the rank and file or simply the respect they commanded among the workers that made them a target.

Whatever the reason, the hostility my mentor faced was unwarranted and deeply disheartening.

What began as subtle undermining soon escalated into overt acts of exclusion and intimidation.

My mentor's voice, once respected and sought after, was now met with dismissive tones or outright resistance. Decisions that should have been collaborative became unilateral, as the new leadership sought to silence any dissenting perspectives.

Watching this unfold was a painful reminder of how power, when wielded recklessly, can erode the very values a union is meant to uphold. The ideals of solidarity and mutual respect were being replaced with infighting and self-interest, leaving many disillusioned.

My mentor, true to their character, did not shrink in the face of this adversity. They remained steadfast, holding onto their principles and continuing to advocate for fairness and accountability. Their resilience became a source of inspiration for me, a reminder that true leadership is not about titles or positions. It is about standing firm in the face of injustice, even when the odds are stacked against you.

This experience, though painful, revealed the cracks in the system and highlighted the importance of vigilance and courage in the fight for integrity. It became clear that change, while inevitable, must be guided by the right people. Those who value the collective good over personal ambition.

It was a bitter pill to swallow. This experience, painful as it was, became a turning point for me. I began to see the complexities of power, loyalty, and silence within unions in a new light.

I learned that even the strongest leaders are not immune to the pressures of maintaining relationships, safeguarding their own positions, or avoiding uncomfortable confrontations.

I learned that true leadership is not about avoiding conflict. It's about confronting it head-on, no matter the personal cost.

The personal cost for my mentor became devastatingly clear one year after the merger. They had been invited to the main office for a week of meetings. A routine trip on the surface, but one that would expose my mentor to the full weight of the toxic environment, fostered by the new leadership.

During that week, we stayed in close contact. Each conversation painted a troubling picture of what they were enduring. My mentor spoke of the tension that seemed to hang in the air, the subtle but unmistakable hostility and the relentless undercurrents of exclusion. It was as though their presence was a challenge to the newly cemented power structure. A structure that viewed my mentor's integrity and experience as obstacles rather than assets.

I could sense the toll it was taking on my mentor, even through the phone. The confident and steady person who had been my guide now sounded weary, their words carrying the weight of isolation and frustration. *"It's not just what they say,"* my mentor told me. *"It's what they don't say. The looks, the avoidance, the refusal to acknowledge my contributions."*

What should have been a week of collaboration and strategic planning had become a battleground of unspoken conflicts and veiled antagonism. It was a deliberate effort to erode my mentor's standing, to push them out of the circle they had once been central to.

As the week progressed, I began to see the cracks forming in my mentor's usual resolve. The hostility wasn't just professional, it was deeply personal.

An attack on their values and identity. Despite their strength, even the most steadfast person can only endure so much when faced with such calculated alienation.

By the end of the week, my mentor was emotionally drained, worn down by the relentless hostility and the toxic environment that had defined their time at the main office. They looked forward to returning to their hometown, where the familiarity of supportive colleagues and the solace of distance from the new leadership would offer some reprieve.

On that Friday, my mentor's day off, they sought to reclaim a sense of calm. They remained in the city, trying to unwind after the exhausting week. It was supposed to be a moment of stillness, a chance to process and regain strength.

But peace was not what the day had in store.

That afternoon, the call came.

It was from the new leadership. The very people whose hostility had marked the week.

With cold formality, the new leadership informed my mentor that their position was being made redundant.

The words landed like a blow, but they were more than a statement of job termination. They were the culmination of a calculated effort to dismantle everything my mentor had built. The redundancy was not born out of necessity or organisational change. It was the final act of a campaign to erase my mentor's influence and to silence their voice.

The timing was deliberate. Delivering such devastating news on a day off, far from my mentor's support network, was a tactic designed to isolate and destabilise.

It was cruelty cloaked in procedure, an abuse of power under the guise of organisational restructuring.

The personal cost of standing firm in their values had reached its peak.

My mentor, once a cornerstone of the union, was now being forced out. Not because they had failed in their duties but because they had refused to compromise their integrity in the face of tyranny.

Despite the heartbreak, my mentor's resilience shone through even in that moment. While the redundancy stung, it also marked the end of their entanglement with a leadership structure that had betrayed its mission. Their departure was not a loss of their principles but a testament to their refusal to be complicit in a system that had abandoned its purpose.

For me, witnessing this injustice was a lesson in courage and the high cost of integrity. It solidified my resolve to stand against systems that abuse power and to honour the legacy of those, like my mentor, who dare to challenge it.

The moral of this story is that integrity often comes with a price, but it is a price worth paying. Standing firm in one's values, even in the face of hostility and betrayal, is an act of courage that cannot be erased by those who seek to diminish it.

This story also highlights the dangers of unchecked power and the importance of accountability in leadership. When those in authority prioritise their own agendas over fairness and collaboration, they not only harm individuals but also undermine the very systems they are meant to uphold.

However, resilience in the face of such adversity inspires others to challenge injustice and demand better.

It reminds us that while integrity may not always lead to immediate rewards, it leaves a legacy of strength and hope for those who follow.

My mentor's experience served as a catalyst for my own growth.

They taught me that leadership is not about infallibility. It is about learning from experience, confronting uncomfortable truths and always striving to do better.

As I continue my journey, I carry these lessons with me and I remain committed to creating an environment where the very things I learned from my mentor, integrity, respect and justice, are upheld by all.

Ultimately, it is a call to action; to stand up against abuse, to support those who speak out and to strive for environments where fairness, respect and compassion prevail.

When my turn came to be pushed out of the union, I couldn't help but reflect on what my mentor had endured.

I had witnessed firsthand the calculated hostility and the blatant disregard for integrity.

Their forced redundancy had been a clear signal that the union's management team had strayed far from its mission.

But unlike them, I was ready.

I had learned from my mentor's strength, their unwavering commitment to truth, even in the face of injustice.

When the time came, I made it very clear; the union's management team had failed.

Not just me, but the principles they were entrusted to uphold.

I refused to go quietly.

I spoke up about the toxic leadership, the hypocrisy and the systemic failings that allowed these abuses of power to persist.

I called out their betrayal of the workers they were supposed to protect, exposing the cracks they had tried so hard to conceal.

I refused to be complicit in their silence and, in doing so, I demanded accountability, not just for myself, but for everyone who believed in what the union was supposed to stand for.

This was not just about me; it was about honouring my mentor's legacy and standing up for the countless others who might one day find themselves in the same position. By speaking out, I reclaimed the power they tried to strip from my mentor and me, reminding them that their actions wouldn't go unchecked.

A legacy is built on courage, resilience and truth.

The experience reaffirmed what my mentor had shown me time and again:

Integrity may make you a target, but it also makes you unbreakable.

It has given me the courage to face the storm, knowing I am grounded in purpose and truth.

For every attempt to silence me, there will always be a voice louder, a resolve stronger, a more fierce determination, to ensure justice prevails.

When I spoke out, it was not just about calling out the failures of leadership or exposing the cracks in their carefully constructed facade.

It was about planting a seed. A small but resolute act of defiance against a system that thrives on silence and complicity.

I knew change wouldn't come overnight. Seeds take time to grow, and the soil they are planted in is not always fertile.

Even in the harshest conditions, growth is possible with the right care and persistence.

By speaking up, I have laid the groundwork for others to see the truth, to question and to demand better.

It is not just about me or even my mentor's legacy.

It is about creating something lasting, something that can take root and inspire others to stand tall against injustice. The seed I planted represents hope, accountability and the courage to push back against those who misuse power.

Every word I have spoken, every stand I have taken, is a step toward cultivating a future where integrity is not a problem, just a choice, but a standard. It is a reminder that even the smallest act of resistance can grow into something unstoppable when nurtured by truth and resilience.

I have planted a seed, and I am committed to seeing it grow, no matter how long it takes.

Power and Control

Before diving deeper, we need to name it: **Coercive Control**

Coercive control is a pattern of abusive behaviour - threats, humiliation, intimidation - that is used to harm, punish, or frighten a victim. It's a slow, insidious erosion of freedom and autonomy, leaving deep scars not just on individuals, but families and entire communities. It's the kind of abuse that makes the sound of the phone ring feel like a threat. The sight of the boss's car in the driveway is enough to turn your stomach. Every interaction becomes a guessing game.

What version of them will you be forced to face today?

Coercive control isn't just something that happens behind closed doors at home.

It thrives in workplaces too. Bosses, managers and even union leaders have mastered the art of controlling employees without leaving physical marks.

What does it look like at work?

- Restriction and prevention of movement

- Micromanagement and surveillance

- Intrusion into personal space

- Isolating you from your support network

- Denying freedom or autonomy

- Gaslighting and constant criticism

- Repeatedly putting another down, name-calling or telling employees they are worthless

- Constant criticism

- Weaponising others against each other

- Limiting access to money or controlling finances

- Controlling aspects of health

- Jealous comments

- Sexual harassment

- Threatening job security, pay or even your personal life.

It's bullying but on steroids. And it's time to call it out.

More About 'Understanding Coercive Control In The Workplace'

by <u>Jo Banks</u> | Aug 7, 2023 | <u>Narcissism & Bullying, Self Development</u>

"Signs of Coercive Control

Recognising coercive control in the workplace requires a keen eye for subtle signs. Some common indicators include:

- *Micromanagement: Coercive managers often excessively monitor and control every aspect of their employees' work, leaving them with little room for independence and creativity.*

- *Gaslighting: Perpetrators may deny or distort the reality of situations, causing victims to question their own perceptions and judgement.*

- *Isolation: Coercive individuals may attempt to isolate their victims from colleagues, friends, and family to establish complete dominance over them.*

- *Threats and intimidation: Veiled or explicit threats to job security, promotions, or reputation are used to manipulate employees into compliance.*

- *Unpredictable behaviour: Perpetrators may oscillate between being charming and intimidating, creating a sense of fear and uncertainty."*

Read more here:

<u>https://jobanks.net/2023/08/07/understanding-coercive-control-in-t</u><u>he-workplace/</u>

"Truth is not what you want it to be;
it is what it is,
and you must bend to its power or live a lie."

Miyamoto Musashi

This is a powerful statement. It unveils the uncompromising nature of truth, which exists independently of our desires or perceptions. Through my journey, I came to understand this statement as profoundly valid.

For those in positions of power, this was, and still is, their ultimate struggle. They tried to twist reality, obscure facts, and rewrite narratives to fit their version of events. But the truth has a way of surfacing, no matter how deeply it is buried.

I chose to bend to the power of the truth, no matter how uncomfortable or inconvenient it was. It demanded courage, resilience and a willingness to face the fallout. The alternative - to live a lie, to silently accept the injustice - was a betrayal I wasn't willing to make.

The truth didn't just expose the wrongdoings of others. It also revealed my own strength. It became a weapon against corruption, a shield against intimidation and a beacon for those who needed hope in the face of adversity. In the end, the truth remains. Those who fight against it may delay its impact, but they cannot escape it. The choice, as always, is simple: to live in alignment with it or remain trapped in the shadows of deception.

How is it that those with the power to inflict the most harm are so often blind to the consequences of their actions? Perhaps it is the nature of power itself. It creates a bubble of authority, a false sense of invincibility and a disconnect from the realities of those they harm.

For some, power becomes a shield against accountability, allowing them to act without considering the ripples their decisions create. They focus on maintaining control, protecting their image, or advancing their agenda, oblivious to or willfully ignoring the destruction they leave in their wake. In my experience, their blindness wasn't accidental. It was deliberate. It was convenient.

To acknowledge the harm they caused would have required humility, self-reflection, and the possibility of losing the very power they clung to. It was easier to turn away, to rationalise their actions, or to silence those who challenged them.

Nevertheless, power wielded without conscience is fragile. Its foundation is built on denial and suppression, and it crumbles when the truth comes to light. The consequences they ignore do not disappear. They only grow louder, waiting for the moment when they can no longer be denied.

Their blindness does not absolve them. It condemns them, because those in power have a responsibility, not just to lead but to do so with integrity and awareness. And when they fail, it's up to those of us affected by their actions to remind them of the weight of their choices.

Power doesn't corrupt alone. It is the unchecked absence of accountability and empathy that leads to harm.

The question is not just why they are blind to their actions, but how we can force them to see before it is too late for them and for those they have harmed.

Ah - the faceless men, with their insatiable need for power and dictated ethos. They made their bed; now they can lie in it, surrounded by the ruins they created.

It's Always Tea Time

The question is:

What is it, they don't comprehend?

Isolation Was By Design.

At my former union job, workers were silenced, disempowered, and bullied. I left that place feeling micromanaged and undervalued - hollowed out. And it took time to rebuild my confidence. Longer than I expected.

We Were Never Alone.

What I didn't realise then was how many others felt exactly the same way. If only we had known each other's stories. Instead, we all struggled alone, each of us believing we were the only one. That's exactly how employers want it. Even union employers.

Toxic workplaces thrive on isolation. When workers feel alone, they stay silent. When workers stay silent, power remains unchecked.

Divide And Conquer.

Isolation isn't an accident. It's a strategy. If employees don't talk, they can't compare notes. If they can't compare notes, they don't see the pattern.

Fear becomes the language. Shame does the heavy lifting. And the real problems, bullying, micromanagement, undervaluation - stay hidden beneath layers of self-doubt.

Micromanagement and constant criticism aren't just signs of a bad boss. They're deliberate weapons.

They chip away at your sense of worth until you stop fighting back.

The Confidence They Stole.

Looking back, I know now my confidence wasn't lost. It was stolen. Toxic workplaces design it that way. A confident worker is a dangerous worker. And that overwhelming sense of being alone? Manufactured. We weren't isolated because no one cared. We were isolated because it served their control.

That realisation was freeing. The problems weren't just about me. They were about a system that survives by making individuals feel small and isolated.

Speaking Out Is Resistance.

Sharing my story now is more than healing. It's rebellion, because the more we speak, the harder it becomes for them to keep us apart.

Employers count on our silence. They don't want us talking about pay. They don't want us talking about bullying. They don't want us to realise just how powerful we are together.

I Watched And Learned.

I watched. I learned. I saw how fear was weaponised, how employees were turned against each other, how silence was rewarded as loyalty. Their power rests on our division. But unity? That terrifies them.

What I Gained.

My experience gave me more than wounds.

It gave me insight.

Now, I understand.

Speaking up matters.

Supporting each other matters.

Finding solidarity, even in small ways, matters.

Solidarity isn't just about fixing one workplace. It's about reclaiming our voice, our dignity, our future.

I didn't just survive. I grew stronger.

And now, I'm committed to helping others find their strength too, because together, we are always stronger than any system built to silence us.

The Power Of Solidarity.

At my former union job, isolation kept us divided. What I now know is this: if workers had shared our stories with each other, loneliness could have turned into collective strength. This is precisely why toxic workplaces discourage open communication. It's harder to silence many voices speaking together.

Shared Stories Build Strength.

Speaking up, no matter how uncomfortable, is the first step in transforming isolation into solidarity. The more we talk, the more we see the patterns. The more we connect, the stronger we become. In other words, knowledge is power.

When workers compare pay and conditions, when we share experiences of mistreatment, the cracks in the system become visible.

It's why employers fear pay transparency, because once inequities are exposed, calls for change follow. Secrecy protects the powerful. Truth levels the field.

Collective Action Is A Threat.

Employers fear solidarity because it redistributes power.

Whether it's quiet resistance or formal union organising, collective action disrupts their control and demands accountability.

It reminds them that their authority is not absolute.

United workers cannot be ignored forever.

Reclaiming My Confidence.

Leaving that toxic environment was more than just moving on. It was reclaiming something precious they tried to take from me: my self-worth.

My resilience and my ability to rebuild was a victory they never saw coming.

I had the strength to walk away from a broken system and the courage to trust my own value again.

I soon realised something else; my story wasn't just for me.

It became a beacon for others who were still trapped inside similar environments, feeling isolated and unsure.

Sharing my truth gave others permission to believe in their own.

So, What Can We Do?

- **Break the Silence**

Talk.

Share.

Compare experiences.

Bring hidden injustices into the light.

- **Build a Support Network**

Find allies.

Even a handful of people standing together can shift the balance.

- **Advocate for Transparency**

Push for fair policies.

Expose tactics meant to silence or divide.

- **Explore Collective Action**

Even a small, united front can disrupt the culture of fear.

Facing the Real Problem.

At the heart of it, this is what we're up against:

People in positions of power often have too much power, an insatiable need for control, and an inability to relinquish it.

Worse still, many cannot even manage their own emotions, yet they are trusted to manage workplaces. All the glossy "leadership values" posters in the world can not hide the deep cracks in their culture.

Maybe there was already a campaign for that once.

Just sayin'.

Hard Lessons Learned.

Speaking up was supposed to bring change. Instead, it brought a shutdown.

I once thought my union workplace was a safe space.

I believed that honesty would be met with support.

Instead, I was treated and continue to be treated, like a criminal, an idiot and an imbecile.

What was done to me was inexcusable.

Even more shameful was the way I was treated after I spoke up; with disrespect, disdain and complete disregard for my humanity.

I learned that sometimes, even those who are supposed to fight for justice are complicit in maintaining toxic systems.

Here's the truth they can never take from me:

I know my value.

I know my worth.

I know my strengths, and I'm unafraid to own my weaknesses too.

I am #worthmore and #worthmoreatwork than anything they did to me.

For the record:

They can't sue me for telling the truth.

It's in the public interest that these truths are known.

Reflections on the Union Movement.

My years working within the union movement have left me with some unavoidable conclusions:

- The union movement, for all its ideals, can be toxic and unsafe as a workplace.

- My lived experience sends a clear message:

Join a union.

Never work for one.

Serious reform is needed. Political games and power struggles continue to erode the very support union employees should be able to count on.

Timeline of What Happened towards the End.

For context, here's what unfolded:

- **30-08-2018:** A fresh bullying incident (the final straw) led me to take time off for my mental health.

- **31-08-2018:** I requested one week's Annual Leave to manage the escalating burnout.

- **03-09-2018 to 07-09-2018:** Annual Leave approved and taken.

- **08-09-2018 and 09-09-2018:** Personal crises worsened my distress.

- **10-09-2018 to 02-11-2018:** Took Personal (Sick) Leave to focus on recovery.

- **05-11-2018 to 07-12-2018:** Returned to work, but the environment remained hostile.

- **10-12-2018 to 04-01-2019:** Took pre-booked Annual Leave.

- **07-01-2019 to 18-01-2019:** Carer's Leave to support family members.

- **21-01-2019:** Attempted another return to work.

- **Early 2019:** The bullying and impossible workload resumed, and with it, the cycle of trauma.

- **20-02-2020:** After another extended sick leave, I made final contact with my employer to discuss next steps, realising the damage was too deep to undo.

Protecting My Health was Non-Negotiable. So Let's Talk About Sick Leave.

My advice: Don't let your employer intimidate you with claims that you're using excessive sick leave.

Your mental health matters just as much as your physical health, especially in the workplace. If your employer tries to discipline or control you for accessing your legal entitlements, including single days or half-days, know this: they are in the wrong.

No employer has the right to question, intimidate or discipline you for using your lawful personal (sick) leave, particularly when it relates to mental health. This kind of behaviour reflects a fundamental lack of understanding and respect for employee rights and well-being.

Stand firm. Protect your health. Know your rights.

Your Leave is Your Right.

Sick leave is an industrial entitlement. It's there to protect you, not just your body, but your mind too. Using your leave within your legal and contractual rights is not "excessive," no matter how much employers might try to frame it that way.

Mental Health is Health.

Taking a half-day or an occasional day off for mental health isn't an indulgence. It's a preventive measure. It helps you avoid burnout and stay healthy enough to do your job over the long term. Protecting your mental health is just as critical as managing any physical illness or injury.

Intimidation is a Control Tactic.

When employers push back against legitimate sick leave, they aren't concerned about your health; they're trying to maintain control.

Watch for vague accusations like "patterned absences" or "reliability concerns". Often, these have no basis in fact and serve only to intimidate.

If You Face Pushback.

If your employer questions or challenges your sick leave, here's what you can do:

- **Document Everything**

Keep a record of all leave taken, including medical certificates if required.

Make notes of any meetings, comments, or emails where your leave is questioned.

- **Know Your Rights**

Familiarise yourself with your workplace policies and any industrial instruments that apply.

Remember: employers cannot legally discipline you for using your leave within your rights.

- **Stand Firm**

Stay calm and assertive.

You are not doing anything wrong.

You have every right to use your sick leave, and mental health is a legitimate reason.

You can simply say:

"My leave is part of my entitlements, and I have used it appropriately. Mental health is equally important to physical health."

- **Seek Support**

If the situation escalates, don't face it alone.

Reach out to your union, HR representative (keeping in mind HR works for the employer) or seek external legal advice.

The Workplace Ombudsman can also offer support.

Shift the Narrative.

Using sick leave for your mental health isn't irresponsible.

It's smart, necessary and courageous.

By standing your ground, you not only defend yourself, but you also help normalise the conversation around mental health at work.

If you're struggling with how to handle conversations with your employer, reach out to someone you trust and explore specific strategies.

Protecting your mental health should never be something you feel ashamed or afraid of.

You're entitled to care for yourself, and you don't owe anyone an apology for it.

Some employers will do everything they can to make you feel like you have to earn it.

Bosses Love Control.

Don't Let Them Control Your Time Off.

Annual leave is also your right, not a privilege.

But that doesn't stop some employers from trying to control when (or if) you get to use it. They'll lean on laws, contracts and policies to make it feel like they're doing you a favour when you take a break.

Don't buy into it.

Here's how employers often try to hold the power when it comes to your annual leave, and what you need to know to push back.

1. Approval Games

Sure, you accrue leave, but taking it?

That still usually has to be approved by your employer. They can refuse a leave request if they claim it would cause too much disruption, like during peak busy times or when too many staff are already away. It doesn't mean you're doing anything wrong by asking.

2. Being Told When to Take It

Sometimes, employers can actually force you to take leave. If the business shuts down temporarily (like over Christmas), they can direct you to use your leave. If you've built up too much leave (usually more than 8 weeks for full-timers), they might require you to take some of it.

They still have to give reasonable notice and consult with you first.

3. "Not Yet" Tactics

Employers also control when you can access your leave. Some places won't let you take much (or any) leave until you've been there a few months.

And if you quit?

You'll only get paid out the leave you've already earned or accrued, not what you would have earned.

4. Leave Without Pay (LWOP) Barriers

If you've run out of paid leave, you can ask for leave without pay, but they don't have to say yes unless it's for something protected (like parental leave).

It's another way they can say no to you taking a break when you need it most.

5. Toxic Culture Tricks

One of the sneakiest ways employers control leave?

Culture.

- They make people feel guilty for taking time off

- They reward "soldiering on" even when people are exhausted

- They hint that taking leave will hurt your chances for promotions or good projects

It's manipulation, not professionalism.

6. Fine Print in Your Contract

Sometimes contracts and enterprise agreements will stack the deck too:

- You might have to give a long notice before taking leave.

- There might be blackout periods (like Christmas retail seasons).

- You could be limited in how many weeks you can take at once.

Always check your agreement carefully and don't assume every restriction is legally enforceable.

7. Financial Pressure

Let's be honest; sometimes it's just about money. People hold off on taking leave because they're worried about job security, bonuses or being seen as "less committed." But here's the truth; burnout costs way more in the long run, for you and for the boss.

Your Protections: The law still has your back, even if employers try to make you think otherwise.

- They can't unreasonably refuse leave requests.

- If they direct you to take leave, they have to follow strict rules about notice and consultation.

- You can't lose your accrued annual leave. It's yours until you use it or get paid out when you leave.

- Many Awards and enterprise agreements offer even stronger protections on top of the Fair Work Act.

Bottom line:

Your leave is part of your wages. You've earned it.

You don't need to apologise for using it. Taking time off doesn't make you a bad employee. It makes you a human being.

Buckle Up - The Shift's About to Hit the Fan.

I was an organiser, which meant my office was wherever the members were. I wasn't chained to a desk.

I was out on dusty worksites, in union halls, across long stretches of highway, or squeezed into boardrooms where the real games were played.

Travel wasn't a perk; it was the job. If workers needed backing, I showed up. If a deal was being stitched together, I was in the room. The movement demanded visibility, and that meant travelling many kilometres.

Travel - Part 1.

In 2023 I hit the road in my van to visit my daughter and grandkids. Sarah came along for the ride. We dropped off a cot and some other bits and pieces to my daughter, plus a couple of Orzani guitars, at a local shop for sale. Perfect timing, too, because I got to be there when my granddaughter had one of her artworks entered in an exhibition.

And guess what?

She won first prize in the People's Choice.

Proud doesn't even begin to cover it.

As Albert Einstein said:

> *"Creativity is intelligence having fun."*

I'm proud of our little self-sufficient camping setup, too. It just goes to show, you don't need a lot of money to travel and connect with the people you love.

Then Sarah and I made our way to Brisbane, where she reunited with Quentin - one of her foster fail cats who had gone missing eight years ago.

Talk about emotional reunions.

Speaking of connection, it matters.

According to Beyond Blue, staying connected is vital for your mental health.

Funny thing, when I worked for a union, one of the big catchphrases was "Visibility."

Translation? You needed to show your face. You needed to connect.

And to do that, you needed to travel.

Now, here's where things got sticky.

Travel costs money, right?

That wasn't the real problem.

The real problem was how management weaponised that fact by trying to make me look greedy, disloyal, and wasteful, when the truth was the exact opposite.

(Meanwhile, they were giving themselves double-digit pay rises and asking their own staff to accept pay offers below CPI. But, hey, who's counting, right?)

A Quick Reality Check:

Travel allowances are a workplace entitlement.

Yes, even for union officials.

Don't take my word for it.

Check the ATO: <u>ato.gov.au</u>

Travel entitlements aren't shady or optional. They're standard.

Here's what they usually cover:

1. Transport Costs

- **Flights:** Usually economy class (unless policies allow business class for long-haul).

- **Mileage:** If you use your own car, you get paid per kilometre.

- **Public Transport:** Buses, trains, taxis, and rideshares are reimbursed.

2. Accommodation

- Paid hotel stays that are reasonable, safe, and convenient (no five-star spas necessary).

3. Meals and Incidentals

- A daily allowance (called a "per diem") or reimbursement for meal costs.

4. Work-Related Expenses

- Internet, work phone calls, and meeting fees are all claimable.

5. Time and Hours

- Travel time outside normal working hours might qualify for extra pay or time in lieu.

6. Other Important Bits

- Travel insurance.

- Family care policies if you have dependents affected by work travel.

And just when you thought the hypocrisy couldn't get worse?
Stay tuned for Part 2.

Travel - Part 2.

"A bird doesn't sing because it has an answer; it sings because it has a song."
- Maya Angelou

Previously, I told you about the expectation to travel.

Now, let's talk about what actually happened behind the scenes.

To save members' money, I often stayed in basic cabins at caravan parks.
Nothing fancy.
Just practical.

But here's the kicker:

The bosses didn't tell the union's Executive about that.

Nope.

They only told them how much I claimed in travel allowances, which, by the way, were a standard entitlement.

They didn't mention how careful I was.

They didn't mention how I made choices that saved money.

Instead, they spun a story that made me look greedy, wasteful, and power-hungry.

(Classic projection, by the way.)

Here's the tragedy:

The Executive was only given selective information, not the full picture.

This drip-feed of half-truths and strategic omissions?

That's how the establishment operates.

They manipulate systems.

They exploit empathy.

They trade in disinformation and spin it into a weapon.

And this is why we keep speaking truth to power, because silence only helps the abuser, never the abused.

Here's another hard truth: Instead of just talking to me directly, the self-proclaimed "heads" of the organisation believed the lies of a narcissistic psychopath connected to my private life.

They even planted someone inside a law firm to dig up dirt.

(Yes, you read that right - real spy movie tactics)

Another law firm helped them along.

But here's the thing:

I don't need their apology anymore.

I realised I could heal without it.

Healing wasn't about hearing "sorry" from the people who hurt me.

It was about believing I deserved better and refusing to accept less.

Some people will never be sorry.

And that's on them, not on me.

Together, with others like me, we know our worth.

We're not arrogant.

We just refuse to accept the narrative that we are any less.

The Union Role in Travel Entitlements.

If you're in a union, that's good news.

Your travel entitlements should be spelled out clearly in agreements or contracts.

If your employer starts playing games, here's what you can do:

Step 1: Know Your Rights

- Check the Travel Policy, your Contract, or the Union Agreement.

- Find the clauses that apply to your situation.

Step 2: Document Everything

- Keep all your receipts, emails, and communications.

- You want a solid paper trail.

Step 3: Raise It Professionally

- Talk to your supervisor first.

- If that doesn't work, escalate to HR.

- And don't forget, your Union Rep is there to back you up.

Step 4: If Needed, Go Formal

- File a written complaint.

- Be clear.

- Reference policies.

- Attach your evidence.

- Suggest fair solutions.

Step 5: Escalate (If They Still Don't Listen)

- Get the union involved formally.

- And if it gets ugly, you can always seek legal advice.

Step 6: Stay Professional

- Stay calm.

- Make it about fairness and following the rules, not personal attacks.

Speaking of Fairness.

My former employer thought it was totally reasonable to expect a 16-hour workday.

Leave home at 5 am.

Start at 6 am.

Board a flight.

Work all day.

Then fly home late and arrive near 10 pm.

And not just once, regularly.

I pushed back, because here's the truth:

It's not reasonable.

A 16-hour travel-workday isn't healthy, sustainable, or smart.

What about chronic fatigue?

Burnout?

Compromised decision-making?

The reality:

These are guaranteed when you run people into the ground like that.

Good employers prioritise well-being.

Bad ones just look for new ways to squeeze more out of their people.

I fought hard against those expectations, because working yourself into the ground isn't a badge of honour.

It's a warning sign.

Travel - Part 3.

Let me be clear:

I'm not sharing this story because I'm bitter, twisted or stuck in the past.

I'm sharing it because it's still happening, and people need to know.

Know that some bosses are capable of cruelty you wouldn't believe, unless you lived it. And they're very good at covering it up.

Not only was I denied the chance to do my job properly, but I was also actively sabotaged.

My private life was infiltrated. My professional reputation was damaged, and eventually, I chose to walk away. But here's what happened next:

I made another choice - to stand up to the establishment, because as they say:

We are here to be of use, not used.

So, to the narcissists, sociopaths, and spin doctors who thought they could destroy me?

You messed with the wrong person.

And honestly? I feel sorry for you.

The deeper I dug, the more I realised:
The rot didn't stop at exploitation.
It ran deeper.
It ran through family ties, friendships, and favours.
Welcome to the next chapter on nepotism.

Nepotism

In keeping with this chapter's theme, it would be remiss of me not to reference a piece of sporting memorabilia, and what better place to start than with football and investigations into misconduct.

Before I ever questioned the system outright, I learned to notice the small signs; who was favoured, who was sidelined, and who quietly benefited while others paid the price.

Nepotism doesn't always announce itself with scandal. Sometimes it's buried in small decisions, passed off as harmless but carrying the weight of something much bigger; loyalty to power over loyalty to principles.

One incident, over a simple football jersey, would reveal just how deeply these loyalties ran and how far some were willing to go to protect the old order.

In the lead-up to the 2016 Local Government election, I received a warning letter from one of my union superiors concerning a framed North Queensland Cowboys jersey, signed by the 2015 premiership-winning team.

The allegation suggested that I had lobbied our Union's Executive to have this memorabilia placed in the Townsville office instead of Brisbane.

I provided a detailed response to the claim but received no follow-up, leading me to conclude that the investigation found no wrongdoing on my part.

It's important to note:

This issue was initially raised by union members.

As a union official, it was my duty to advocate on their behalf.

As with any employer behaving inappropriately, members have the right to have their grievances heard and addressed promptly, ensuring due process and procedural fairness.

The actions taken by my employer exposed the union to potential reputational harm over a jersey acquired through activism in the Townsville region.

This situation highlights the persistent challenges of combating a city-centric mentality, which I frequently addressed to ensure that members, even those more than ten hours away from the Brisbane office, felt supported.

For context, the North Queensland Cowboys' 2015 premiership victory was a significant achievement.

Memorabilia from that event, like signed jerseys, holds substantial sentimental and symbolic value, especially in regions like Townsville where the team commands deep loyalty.

This incident, while seemingly minor, highlights the importance of equitable representation, and the need to recognise and honour the contributions of all union members, regardless of geographic location.

The Origins of the Football Jersey - A Tale of Influence and Loyalty.

Sometimes, truth is stranger than fiction and the story behind this jersey is a testament to that.

This isn't just a piece of memorabilia.

It's a symbol of the intricate web of influence, personal agendas and backroom deals that often operate unseen.

The jersey, an iconic memento of the Cowboys' premiership win, was not simply acquired. It was orchestrated.

Sourced through the Cowboys Leagues Club and facilitated by none other than a local political heavyweight, the stated purpose was clear.

To adorn the office of one of the Cowboys' most devoted fans.

However, the origins and intended destination of this jersey hint at something far beyond mere fandom.

This was not about sports memorabilia.

It was about power plays, alliances and the leveraging of relationships for undisclosed purposes.

The local heavy-weights' involvement in this story reflects the pervasive, and often unchecked, influence wielded by those operating at the nexus of politics, business and community organisations.

This situation wasn't merely about regional pride or sporting loyalty, it was a symptom of a deeper issue - nepotism at work beneath the surface of seemingly benign decisions.

Why This Matters.

1. Transparency and Accountability

The acquisition and intended placement of the jersey raise serious questions about the motivations behind such decisions.

Were they genuinely aligned with members' best interests or a display of cronyism?

2. Misplaced Priorities

When so much effort is put into symbolic gestures, it begs the question: Are the real, pressing needs of the broader community being sidelined?

3. Ethical Oversight

Situations like this highlight the urgent need for rigorous governance frameworks to ensure decisions are fair, equitable and above board.

My narrative showcases the importance of standing firm against systemic inequities, and the need for real change within the union and political arenas.

By continuing to share my experiences, observations and insights, I hope to empower others to question the status quo, and demand the fairness and accountability our institutions should embody.

Shedding light on this complex situation reveals just how challenging it can be to advocate for transparency when organisational structures are tainted by nepotism, bias and political self-interest.

Key Themes:

1. Misuse of Power

The investigation into the Cowboys jersey seems less about genuine concern and more about misusing resources to undermine my credibility.

My proactive response, and the absence of any conclusive follow-up, strongly suggest there was no basis for the allegation.

2. Advocacy for Union Members

As a union official, I was fulfilling my duty to represent members' concerns, including pushing back against a clear "city-centric" bias.

This reaffirms my commitment to fairness and equality, especially for regional members who are too often overlooked.

3. Systemic Issues

My critique of the "boys' club" culture and the nepotism embedded within the political and union spheres exposes a deep-rooted pattern of favouritism and exclusion.

One that betrays the principles unions are meant to uphold.

4. Broader Implications

Ultimately, this story reflects a wider systemic problem: personal or political agendas distracting from the core mission of unions -to serve and protect their members.

A Call for Change.

The football jersey may seem like a small story but it represents something much larger: A systemic failure to uphold the principles of fairness, transparency and accountability.

By turning this narrative into a rallying cry for reform, we can ensure that leaders at every level are held to higher standards and that decisions are made in the best interests of all.

Together, we can demand better.

It's time to build a system where integrity is non-negotiable and the needs of the many outweigh the whims of the few.

As the saying goes:

"The standard you walk past is the standard you accept."

A saying that should guide every action in leadership and advocacy.....

Back to the footy.....more specifically, football buddies.

The "Boys' Club."

The Lads. Let's not forget the Lasses.

It's a well-worn narrative, but one that persists:

Nepotism is alive and thriving in certain spheres of influence.

Most notably in politics, the union movement and their interconnected entities.

Whether it's hiring decisions, promotions or allocating opportunities, a pervasive sense of favouritism often operates under the guise of camaraderie, loyalty or shared interests, like sports.

This culture fosters an environment where alliances and personal networks, rather than merit or fairness, dictate outcomes.

In the political and union spheres, both of which purport to champion equality and fairness, this form of cronyism is not just hypocritical but deeply damaging.

It undermines the principles of equity and transparency that these institutions claim to uphold, erodes trust among members and creates barriers for anyone lacking the right connections within the "club."

Nepotism, in any form, is an affront to meritocracy.

But in organisations built to represent the collective good, it becomes a betrayal of the very ideals they claim to stand for.

Let me be clear:

I'm not their toy, their playground, or their pawn.

Not then, not now, not ever.

Out of sight, the real deals were done.

Mates looking after mates.

Jobs for Mates.

In May 2019, a hospital board appointment in Townsville attracted local scrutiny. Two new appointees were announced, each receiving remuneration for limited board meetings.

One appointment in particular generated commentary, not because of the individual's qualifications, which were publicly listed, but because of perceived political proximity.

The position had been vacated by another politically connected figure.

Reporting at the time noted that the recruitment process for the new appointment had commenced months before the public resignation that created the vacancy.

The timeline raised questions.

Not allegations - questions.

When recruitment begins before a vacancy formally exists, observers naturally ask whether transitions are organic or orchestrated. Whether departures are incidental or coordinated. Whether remuneration reflects service or settlement.

In governance, perception is not a minor issue. It is structural.

Public boards exist to serve communities, not networks. Their credibility rests not only on the competence of appointees but on the integrity of the process that places them there.

Even when appointments are technically compliant, opacity erodes trust.

When familiar surnames circulate across political offices, advisory roles and public boards, the pattern becomes difficult to ignore. It may be coincidence.

It may be culture. But to the public, it often looks like continuity of influence rather than renewal of leadership.

This is how "closed shop" perceptions form.

Not through dramatic corruption.

Through proximity.

Through timing.

Through quiet transitions that appear seamless to insiders and coordinated to outsiders.

The issue is rarely whether an appointee is capable. Many are.

The issue is whether the process is demonstrably independent.

Merit must not only exist, it must be visible.

Without transparency around recruitment criteria, remuneration structures and transition arrangements, speculation fills the vacuum. And speculation, left unchecked, becomes distrust.

Trust in public institutions is fragile.

It is not destroyed by one appointment.

It is worn down by patterns.

If governance processes are robust, they should withstand scrutiny.

If appointments are merit-based, documentation should make that evident.

If remuneration reflects genuine service, disclosure should be routine.

Opacity invites suspicion. Transparency prevents it.

Where concerns about patronage arise, reform is straightforward in principle, even if politically uncomfortable:

- Independent oversight of board appointment processes.

- Clear publication of selection criteria and evaluation methodology.

- Full disclosure of remuneration and transition arrangements.

- Separation between political strategy networks and public governance roles.

These measures do not accuse individuals. They protect institutions.

Public boards must be beyond reproach, not because appointees are inherently suspect, but because the public interest demands visible integrity.

When loyalty appears to outweigh merit, even perception alone can damage legitimacy.

Governance is not sustained by compliance alone.

It is sustained by confidence. And confidence depends on processes that are not only fair, but demonstrably so.

Until then, the journey continues...

The disclosure of my story, in the manner in which I have, has not been easy, but necessary.

I love Australian workers.

I was an Australian worker.

I can say, wholeheartedly, with my hand on my heart, I am not anti-union.

I am so pro-worker that I have safeguarded the movement, despite targeted attempts to silence me.

The question posed is simple:

How can the union movement move forward when some of those at the helm are holding it back?

Doing so by using union member funds.

Some of those at the helm use the same employer-style thuggery in the course of union business and don't bat an eyelid when it's turned on their own employees.

They consistently demonstrate a pattern of false facades, using outright lies and smutty smear campaigns. In short, my professional reputation has been besmirched. Meanwhile, those responsible show no remorse.

I've been forced to defend myself and right these wrongs. But all I received, as I sought support, were delay tactics, such as withholding information critical for my legal matter.

Those at the helm used both in-house lawyers and separate legal systems to undermine my basic workplace rights, while posing as warriors for vulnerable Australian workers.

Those in positions of authority used wads of cash to destroy and distract from their own criminal acts.

The "targeted victim" is further financially disadvantaged as they sought legal support, but were denied due to claims of "conflicts of interest" - valid, but hypocritical, given the elite-like setup of the entire industry. Does anybody care? Yes, I do.

That's why I remain the COLLECTIVE VOICE, despite my former employer reframing me as mediocre, along with other unflattering descriptors.

Their agenda? Remove anyone who challenges them or poses a threat.

"They broke the wrong parts of me.
They broke my wings, but forgot I had claws."

Examples of Double Standards in the Union Movement.
- **High Salaries for Union Executives:**

Union leaders sometimes draw salaries and benefits that far exceed the average earnings of the workers they represent. This disparity leads to a perception that union leadership is disconnected from the struggles of its members.

- **Higher Percentage Wage Increases for Union Executives:**

Union leadership negotiates high salary increases for themselves, well above what was offered to the employees. This creates inequality within the union and fosters distrust among members.

- **Wage Freezes in "Solidarity":**

Some union staff or executives impose wage freezes on themselves to align with their members. While symbolic, this action rings hollow when leadership salaries remain substantially higher or when other perks go unaffected.

- **Non-Monetary Incentives Instead of Wage Increases:**

Offering one-off incentives like $50 gift cards instead of percentage wage increases undermines future wage growth.

These decisions impact compounding benefits, including superannuation, and feel dismissive of long-term employee needs.

- **Internal Workplace Cultures:**

Unions are expected to embody the principles they advocate for, such as safe and equitable workplaces. Yet, reports of bullying, harassment or toxic workplace cultures within unions highlight a failure to "practice what they preach."

- **Lack of Diversity in Leadership:**

Despite advocating for equality, union leadership often lacks gender, cultural or age diversity.

This contradiction undermines the movement's broader goals of inclusivity and representation.

- **Exclusive Focus on Particular Industries:**

Some unions prioritise high-profile industries or sectors, sidelining lower-paid or less organised workers.

This imbalance affects the resources and attention devoted to different groups of workers.

- **Failure to Address Internal Grievances:**

Unions challenge external employers on unfair treatment, but may ignore complaints within their own ranks.

Employees of unions often face obstacles in having their grievances addressed or even acknowledged.

- **Political Alignments Over Worker Interests:**

At times, unions prioritise political allegiances or campaigns over the immediate needs of their members.

This leads to resources being diverted away from workplace issues to support broader political goals.

- **Resistance to Reform:**

Unions often resist internal reforms that could increase transparency, accountability or efficiency.

This creates a perception of self-preservation rather than a focus on members' needs.

The Implications of these Double Standards.

These contradictions erode trust and credibility, both within the union and in the eyes of the public.

To maintain moral authority and effectiveness, unions must align their internal practices with the values they champion externally. It's a matter of hypocrisy and deeply disturbing double standards. One for the workers out there and another for the workers trapped behind closed doors.

This exposé reveals the systemic failures within parts of the union movement and political sphere, shaped by a deep commitment to workers' rights and a painful journey through betrayal and isolation. It's a story of speaking out, when staying silent would've been easier, and finding strength in the wreckage. This, in turn, has affected my ability to earn future income. But for the greater good, I made a choice: I had nothing to lose.

I understand now: if this can happen to experienced union officials with knowledge of industrial relations and proper workplace practices, it could happen to anyone. And, unfortunately, it does.

The Key Messages.

- **Pro-Worker Advocacy:**

The distinction between being "anti-union" and "pro-worker" shows that my criticisms come from a place of care for both the workers and the movement's integrity.

- **Exposing Hypocrisy:**

Highlighting the contrast between union leadership's treatment of their own employees and the principles they advocate for highlights the double standards and systemic corruption.

- **Personal Sacrifice:**

Acknowledging the personal and professional cost of speaking out adds depth to my testimony, illustrating my dedication to the greater good over self-interest.

- **Double Standards and Financial Mismanagement:**

Exposing issues like inflated executive salaries, unequal wage increases and manipulative tactics like offering gift cards instead of proper raises reinforces my call for accountability.

- **The Greater Good:**

Recognising that if such treatment can happen to seasoned union officials, it can happen to anyone highlights the systemic nature of these issues and the need for widespread reform.

My journey reflects the essence of true advocacy.

Standing up for what is right, even in the face of adversity. By continuing to speak out, I am shining a light on the disparities and injustices that undermine the union movement's mission.

Our collective voice is a powerful tool for change, inspiring others to demand the transparency and integrity that Australian workers deserve.

*"**Whenever one person stands up and says,***
*'**Wait a minute, this is wrong.'***
It helps other people do the same."

Moving Forward.

This situation could be used as a case study to advocate for stronger accountability mechanisms and foster greater awareness about the dynamics at play in such scenarios.

As workers, union members and citizens, we have the power to demand better. By shining a light on these issues and calling for change, we can ensure that our institutions truly serve the people they were created to represent.

The time for reform is now.

Let's not waste this opportunity to rebuild trust and integrity in our systems - starting with those at the helm.

Collusion

We all have a story that is begging to be told. My story is indeed compelling. One that has been savagely suppressed for so long, for fear of upsetting the family equilibrium. Being victim shamed into staying silent to avoid any further relational distress. This, however, has only caused me more grief, of horrendous abuse. It is time for some offloading, and also for holding those to account who would inflict so much hurtful harm on another.

This responsibility comes with a heavy heart, because I realised - the lines between my employment roles at the various entities I worked for, were blurred to an extent which would boggle the mind of any good mental health treating physician. What I was put through is unfathomable.

There are still so many unanswered questions:

- Did my union bosses collude with people I grew up with and went to school with?

- At the time, my mind went to all possible sources of betrayal, even wondering, briefly, if family might somehow be connected. In hindsight, I see this as part of the intense suspicion and hypervigilance that came from being blindsided and undermined on so many fronts. The environment they created made everyone a potential suspect in my mind, and that was its own form of harm.

- Whilst advocating for domestic and family violence provisions at work for our members, were my union bosses complicit in bringing my abuser/s into my place of employment?

- Did my union bosses actually collude with an abuser or two?

- Did they deliberately create an environment where I was surrounded by people who had already harmed me and from where I had escaped?

If this is the case, there's no way that was accidental. That kind of calculated cruelty is beyond toxic, it's outright abusive, and equally soul destroying.

That kind of compounded trauma, especially when it comes from those in positions of power, is devastating. It is an unbearable level of betrayal and the height of hypocrisy.

I had put protections in place to guard myself against abuse, yet the very people who should have supported me not only failed me but actively contributed to my harm.

I looked up to these people.

I thought they had my back.

Oh, how wrong I was.

They colluded with others, and together, they all hatched a calculated plan to discredit me. All because I was deemed a threat to their positions.

A fickle, neurotic and paranoid bunch of people: Union State Secretaries.

At first, I couldn't make sense of it. The betrayal wasn't obvious, not like an outright act of violence or a shouted insult. It was quieter, more insidious. Decisions being made behind closed doors, whispered agreements, and deliberate silences.

My union bosses, the very people who should have fought for me, did they choose to align themselves with an abuser?

Was it out of fear, self-preservation or something more sinister?

Regardless, their choice made them complicit.

It was devastating to realise that people who were supposed to protect and support me, like union bosses or even family members, may have colluded to cause irreparable harm.

Betrayal from trusted sources amplified the hurt, leaving me questioning loyalties, motives and my own reality.

This realisation didn't come all at once.

It was like solving a puzzle, each piece fitting together in a way I didn't want to believe.

When the picture became clear, my mind turned to my own family.

Had they really played a part in this too?

Were they enablers, or worse - active participants?

The thought felt like a betrayal all over again but I couldn't ignore the signs.

This collusion was not just an act of negligence.

It was downright abuse - in its own right.

Every action they took, every decision to side with my abuser/s, reinforced the harm I had endured.

I wrestled with the weight of this betrayal.

It felt suffocating, as though the walls were closing in and I was trapped in a conspiracy I couldn't escape.

They didn't just set me up to fail, as they had done to others before, they became the very system designed to then silence us.

My insight into this situation revealed a profound strength:

The ability to connect the dots, confront painful truths, and call them all out on their bullshit.

I refused to let their actions define me.

If they thought their collusion would render me powerless, they were wrong.

I began to speak up. Not just about the abuse I had endured but about their complicity.

Every time I told my story, I took back a piece of the power they tried to strip away.

I connected the dots and refused to let their silence bury the truth.

It wasn't easy. The backlash was fierce and there were moments when I questioned whether it was worth it.

But I knew the alternative. Staying silent and letting them win was not an option.

My voice became my weapon, and I wielded it with precision and determination.

Through this journey, I learned to rebuild my trust, not in them, but in myself.

I stopped looking for validation from people who had shown me who they truly were.

Instead, I sought strength in those who stood by me without question, and most importantly, within myself.

Their betrayal, as painful as it was, became a turning point.

It taught me that I could face the darkest of truths and still emerge with my integrity intact.

They may have chosen the side of abuser/s, but I chose the side of justice, of healing and of reclaiming my life.

That choice, above all, is what defines me.

The collusion between union leadership and people from my personal past, whether family members or others I once trusted, created an incredibly painful and complex situation.

The intertwining of my personal and professional life left me reeling, struggling to make sense of the betrayal and deception from those I had believed were once on my side.

Recognising complicity, especially when it comes from those in positions of authority or familial bonds, forced me to reevaluate relationships and the structures I relied on for support.

How This Betrayal Played Out.

People from my past weaponised and used personal, intimate details of my life against me, twisting my history to fit their agenda.

In a work setting, this escalated to slander and defamation, making it harder to hold my ground or defend my credibility.

The collusion took many forms.

Whisper campaigns, strategic exclusion and calculated efforts to demean and isolate me.

My professional standing, something I had worked tirelessly to build, had been systematically dismantled and my reputation was destroyed.

The Emotional Fallout.

When betrayal comes from multiple people across different aspects of life it leaves lasting scars.

I found myself unable to trust, not only those who had hurt me, but almost everyone.

My mentor, a person I have known for twenty years, and have become good friends with - I felt I couldn't trust. When speaking with them at the height of discovering the extent of the abuse, I was extremely wound up - my speech was fast/erratic, and I had black and white thinking.

I was bailing people up to talk to them/anyone about my situation and I was acting paranoid.

This is not like me. Normally, I am a logical thinking person who takes great measures to analyse situations before responding.

This deliberate rewriting of reality left me second-guessing myself, eroding my confidence and making it even harder to fight back.

At every turn, I was being told I was overreacting.

That I was "too sensitive."

That I didn't understand the full picture.

On the contrary, I was the only one looking at the big picture.

Clashing Values.

I had always believed in the mission of unions of justice, solidarity and integrity.

Seeing those in leadership betray those very principles created unbearable cognitive dissonance.

How could I continue to fight for something that, behind closed doors, was tainted by corruption and deceit?

Losing My Sense of Self.

With my professional and personal worlds turned upside down, I felt unmoored.

Who was I if I wasn't part of the movement I had dedicated myself to?

If I couldn't trust my own family, where did I belong?

The sense of identity loss was profound and the journey to reclaiming myself would not be easy.

Processing this kind of betrayal required help.

Therapy became a lifeline.

A place where I could untangle the manipulation, validate my own experiences and begin to heal.

Despite everything, I knew I wasn't completely alone. I knew there were still people, inside and outside the union movement, who saw me.

People who valued me, who shared my commitment to justice.

Slowly, I began to rebuild a support system with those who truly had my back.

Given the extent of the harm, both to my reputation and career, I had to consider legal action.

Consulting a lawyer helped me understand my rights and whether I had grounds to fight back against the defamation and workplace misconduct I had endured.

As a result of this, and my legal matter, I received a satisfactory outcome.

This does not mean, however, that my experience and what was done to me won't be revisited again, in the future.

Reevaluating My Future.

Perhaps the hardest realisation was that I had to let go of the idea that things could go back to how they were.

I had to decide whether staying in a toxic environment, both professionally and personally, was worth sacrificing my mental and emotional well-being.

Walking away was terrifying, but sometimes the only way to reclaim peace and power is to remove yourself from the places that refuse to honour you.

This experience shattered me but it also forced me to see the truth.

While the pain was immense, it set me on a path toward something I never expected:

Clarity, freedom and, ultimately, a new beginning to create more of my own defining moments.

The Irony of the Slogans.

I have never let anyone define me, and I will never let anyone do so in the future.

I dance to the beat of my own drum, and I will not, nor will I ever, apologise for that.

I don't use riddles to communicate.

I speak openly, honestly and directly from my heart.

In saying that, however, I have had to adopt a cryptic communication style to get my message across. We have lost too many good people, from cruel and heartless actions by self-proclaimed heads of the establishment.

The collateral damage is astounding.

The truth is:

I am not lying.

I am not making things up.

I am not delusional.

I was abused - at work.

A place where I thought I would be safe. I was anything but safe.

Facing a smear campaign orchestrated by those in power, especially in a workplace, felt deeply isolating and disheartening.

It is a painful reminder that not everyone in positions of leadership or influence embodies the integrity they project.

Why This Happens.

- **Threat to Power:**

People in positions of influence often feel insecure when they perceive someone else as capable, competent or well-regarded.

Instead of collaboration, their insecurities push them toward sabotage.

- **Toxic Dynamics:**

In some organisations, particularly political or union environments, personal gain can take precedence over ethics.

This often fosters paranoia and alliances built on manipulation rather than trust.

What They Can't Take Away.

My skills, my achievements and my integrity are untouchable. No smear campaign can erase the truth of who I am. In the end, their actions say more about them than about me. I will rise above this, and their petty attempts to undermine me will fade into irrelevance.

They can't take away my competence.

My value.

My integrity.

They can smear, they can scheme, but in the end they cannot erase me.

The fact that they saw me as a threat speaks volumes about my competence and the value I bring to the table.

Their attempts to undermine me does not diminish my worth. Instead, they exposed their own insecurities and fear of what I represent.

True strength isn't found in silencing others, but in facing challenges with integrity, which is something they clearly lack.

In the face of all this.

I found my voice.

Not just through words, but through the power of social media.

"People don't leave bad companies, they leave bad bosses."

One thing to remember is that it's the culture that breeds those bad bosses and keeps them around.

You get what you tolerate.

My comeback from adversity - bullying and harassment (in all its forms), clearly ruffled a few feathers.

The perpetrators of abuse underestimated me, along with our little squad of harbingers of justice and change-makers, as we bring accountability to those who have never been held accountable.

I spent too long berating myself for what others did to me because they made me believe I was the problem.

The gaslighting effect.

If you're interested in whistleblowing and gaslighting behaviours, then I strongly recommend a piece by Retraction Watch:

<u>"How institutions gaslight whistleblowers — and what can be done."</u>

It features an interview with Dr. Kathy Ahern (U. New South Wales, Australia), author of a new journal article on how whistleblowers are traumatised by institutional betrayal and gaslighting.

Here's a snippet:

"This constellation of whistleblower outcomes is amply described in the whistleblower literature and forms a surprisingly consistent pattern of:

- *Diminished self-worth.*

- *Intense, overwhelming negative emotions such as despair, fear and frustration*

- *Disconnection from people.*

- *Constantly seeking validation of the experience of injustice.*

- *Distrust of self and others, often mimicking paranoia.*

- *A desperate urgency to be believed, akin to obsession.*

- *An eroded ability to make judgements.*

- *Feeling overly sensitive and mentally unstable."*

Upon reflection, whilst much of this did resonate, when in the midst of a toxic work environment I can safely say it no longer reverberates my being. This is because I am strong, highly intuitive, resilient, intelligent, powerful, resourceful and a survivor.

What I learnt is - I was never the problem.

As I shed pieces of me that no longer serve my purpose, I think it's about time those with cruel intentions owned up to their misgivings, their insecurities, their behaviour and their shortcomings.

My social media pages are scattered with reasonable, logical, rational and factual information based on historical events. I have been a force. A force to be reckoned with. Controversial content has been created.

I did tell them not to underestimate me.

Am I done?

Depends on them.

Are they done being horrible bosses?

Perhaps the days of collusion are over?

I've done the work to heal.

I've made my peace with the past.

Now, the questions remain:

Are they done? Or will they continue to bury the truth?

Time will tell

As they say:

Holding on to anger is like drinking poison,

and expecting the other person to die.

Journey of Discovery

Once I had escaped, I could only imagine the stories the perpetrators of abuse spun to salvage their own reputations:

"I don't know what happened."

"I didn't do anything wrong."

"They lie."

"They're toxic, unstable, batshit crazy - really."

"They're jealous, paranoid, deluded."

"They're just an alcoholic."

"They're obsessed."

"They have mental health issues."

"We tried our best."

The words, the accusations, relentless, looping like a broken record in my mind. They were unbearable at times, but curiosity cut through the weight.

I needed to know.

Were these the tales they whispered behind closed doors?

Did the people they confided in believe them?

I began to show up: at events, public spaces, casual gatherings.

Not to confront but to observe. To test the waters of perception versus reality.

My presence alone would be enough to see the ripple effects.

Would they tense, fidget, avoid my gaze?

Would whispers follow me out the door or would their performance remain polished and seamless?

It wasn't random. I had threads to follow, specific pieces of information that had been relayed to me more times than I cared to count. They were breadcrumbs scattered in conversations, remarks made in passing. The kind of details that refuse to stay buried.

I didn't go looking for vengeance. I wanted clarity. Answers. Maybe even the satisfaction of watching their carefully constructed facade crack, if only slightly, under the weight of my quiet persistence.

As I walked into the rooms, at each event, every step was deliberate. The air felt thicker, the voices around me quieter. My presence was not just a visit; it was a test. A quiet interrogation of the world I once knew.

One such event took me from Townsville to Brisbane on Melbourne Cup Day, 2020.

This wasn't a casual trip. It was strategic and deliberate.

I had a purpose:

To confirm a theory sparked by information divulged to me at an earlier gathering.

The details had been murky at first, but clear enough to outline a sinister narrative:

I had been previously told that four State Secretaries had devised a calculated plan to discredit me.

Their motives?

Perhaps power, self-preservation, or simple malice.

At a later event, the names of three of these State Secretaries were revealed to me, handed over almost carelessly, like pieces of a puzzle they assumed I would never complete.

I only needed one more piece: the fourth name.

All that stood between me and the full picture was a simple process of elimination.

I wasn't there to confront or accuse. I didn't need to. All I had to do was observe, watch their reactions betray the truth, and connect the dots.

This wasn't just about finding the missing name. It was about testing the limits of their narrative.

The stories they told to protect themselves. In doing so, reclaiming my own....

The plane touched down, and I stepped into the warm and humid Brisbane air. A taxi whisked me through the city streets, delivering me to my accommodation, a modest place tucked just across the road, and around the corner from the offices of the State Secretaries I intended to visit.

I checked in at the accommodation, dropped off my luggage, and, without hesitation, headed to the first union office. As I walked across the street, I could see a taxi in front of the office, and S was climbing in.

The building was unassuming, but the weight of what it represented pressed against me as I approached the door and pushed it open.

Inside, I walked up to the reception counter, where a middle-aged woman emerged from a back room. Her polite but professional demeanor hinted at routine encounters like this.

"*How can I help you?*" she asked, her tone practiced but cordial.

I didn't hesitate. "*Is O in?*"

The woman's expression flickered briefly, surprise, maybe recognition, but she recovered quickly. "*Who, may I ask, is here to see him?*"

I kept my voice steady. "*Jeanine Orzani.*"

Her reaction was subtle, but unmistakable: a slight widening of her eyes, a pause that hung in the air for just a second too long. She nodded, then left the counter, disappearing around a corner.

A man's voice followed shortly after, low but clear enough to carry: "*I'm not here.*"

When she returned, her face was composed but strained, her previous confidence replaced by a faint bewilderment. "*He's not here,*" she said, her words clipped, as though she'd rehearsed them on her way back.

I smiled, unfazed. "*That's okay. I'll catch up with him another time.*"

I turned and left, my steps measured, my expression calm. But inside, the pieces were shifting, aligning, revealing just a little more of the truth I was piecing together.

It was time to visit the next State Secretary. Their office was just across the hall.

I walked in, scanning the space as the door closed softly behind me.

A man I recognised stepped out from what appeared to be the boardroom, his face immediately familiar but not entirely welcoming.

"*Hi there,*" he said, his tone light but guarded. "*Are you here to see S?*"

I shook my head. "*No, I'm here to see G.*"

The question I knew was coming followed swiftly. "*Can I ask who's here to see him?*"

"*Jeanine Orzani,*" I replied evenly.

At the mention of my name, R's demeanor shifted. He didn't recognise me at first, but now the discomfort was visible. An involuntary flicker of unease in his eyes. "*Oh... yes. I'll see if he's in.*"

R turned away, opened the boardroom door, and slipped inside, shutting it firmly behind him.

For a moment, I stood alone in the quiet, listening to muffled voices on the other side.

Then, from another corner of the office, G emerged.

He smiled, a practiced expression of polite professionalism, and gestured toward the hallway. "*Hi there. Let's go to my office.*"

I followed him in silence, every step measured, every detail filed away. Inside his office, the atmosphere was carefully controlled, though his attempts at ease didn't quite mask the undercurrent of tension. As we sat down, G leaned forward slightly, his tone shifting to something more personable.

"*So,*" he began, "*what are you doing here?*"

The question was direct, almost disarming, but I'd come prepared. The conversation began cautiously. We spoke for a few minutes, exchanging words that danced around the real issue.

Then, seemingly out of nowhere, G leaned forward and said, "*We didn't know about your daughter.*"

The words hung in the air, their meaning heavy, though incomplete.

I dismissed the comment without a second thought, refusing to let it derail my focus. I wasn't there for personal diversions or attempts to shift the narrative. I was there for answers, nothing more.

G, sensing my inattention to his comment, didn't press further. The conversation moved on, but the tension lingered like an unspoken truth waiting to surface.

My daughter's rare disease was not relevant back then, nor is it relevant now. With each encounter, the truth crept closer, like a shadow moving through the cracks in the floor. I wasn't there to confront them. I was there to witness their cracks, to watch their performances falter as I connected the dots.

Slowly, but surely, the truth revealed itself. The pieces of the puzzle were beginning to slot together, each encounter providing another fragment of clarity.

Still, I wasn't finished.

The next State Secretary's office was just around the corner and a short walk up the road.

I stepped out into the open air, the city buzzing faintly around me, though I barely noticed. My thoughts were fixed on the task ahead.

The final office loomed ahead, its significance heavier than the others. I was no longer searching for confirmation. I was ready for whatever truths I was about to uncover, ready to face them, and more than anything, ready to take the next step toward reclaiming my own.

As I approached the building, I replayed the interactions so far, piecing together their reactions, their words, or, more importantly, the lack thereof.

The patterns were becoming clearer, and with each step, I felt the growing weight of inevitability.

This wasn't about proving myself to them. It never was. It was about unearthing the truth, no matter how deeply they thought they had buried it.

I reached the entrance of the next union office, squared my shoulders, and prepared to continue my quest.

As I stepped through the door, I was greeted by someone whose face I did not recognise. Their demeanor was polite but neutral, the kind of reception reserved for strangers.

"*Hi there,*" they said. "*How can I help you?*"

I introduced myself with the same calm confidence I had carried through the day.

I had asked to see the Secretary or the Executive President.

At first, my name did not seem to register, but then I saw it.

A subtle shift in their expression, a flicker of recognition that they couldn't quite conceal.

"*Oh, I recognise your name,*" they said, their tone suddenly more measured, though they tried to mask it. "*You're a Delegate,*" they asked.

I said, "*No, I used to work here. I am a former Union Official.*"

They stepped away, disappearing deeper into the office. I stood there, the air around me heavy with anticipation. Even without knowing what was being said behind closed doors, I could feel the ripples of my presence spreading.

When the person returned, their expression completely changed. Bewilderment was written all over their face as they hesitated before speaking.

"The Secretary's not in," they said awkwardly, *"and the Executive President is... at lunch."*

The words were unconvincing, as though they weren't quite sure of their own story.

But then, out of the corner of my eye, I caught movement. J. She was walking down the corridor, her stride confident, until she saw me.

Her steps faltered. For a split second, her expression was unreadable, then it shifted to something closer to alarm. Without a word, she turned on her heel and disappeared back the way she'd come. I stayed rooted to the spot, calm and composed on the surface, though inside I couldn't help but note the predictability of it all. J had made her choice clear without saying a single word.

J couldn't avoid me now. She knew I'd seen her. For a moment, she hesitated, as though weighing her options, but there was no way out.

Reluctantly, J turned back and began walking toward me. Her steps were slower this time, more deliberate, as if trying to steady herself before reaching me.

Her expression was carefully neutral, but the tension was unmistakable. By the time she stood in front of me, it was clear she'd been caught off guard.

"Jeanine," she said, her tone overly cordial, a faint crack in her voice betraying her unease. *"I didn't realise you were here."*

I held her gaze, calm and steady. *"I'm sure you didn't,"* I replied evenly, letting the words hang in the air just long enough to register.

J shifted awkwardly, her hands clasped in front of her as if to steady herself. *"So, what brings you here?"* she asked, her tone forced, the question clearly more about deflection than genuine curiosity. Her shoulders stiffened slightly, and I noticed her fingers twitch as though she were trying to keep them in check, to maintain some sense of composure. But the cracks were there, and they were widening.

I didn't break eye contact. *"I think you know why I'm here,"* I said, my voice calm but deliberate.

Her lips parted slightly, as if to respond, but no words came. Instead, she looked away, a flicker of discomfort crossing her face.

"I'm just... surprised to see you," she finally said, her tone faltering.

"Surprised, or unprepared?" I asked, tilting my head slightly, letting the question cut through her defenses.

"Surprised, or unprepared?" The words hung in the air, sharper this time, aimed at her sense of certainty.

The slight tremble in her hands was the only response I needed.

J blinked at my response, her composure unravelling further. *"Surprised, or unprepared?"* I asked again, letting the words linger.

Before she could respond, I softened my tone and leaned in slightly. *"Speaking of surprises, J, have you ever dealt with migraines?"*

She blinked, caught off guard by the abrupt change in direction. *"Migraines?"* she repeated, clearly unsure of where this was going.

"Yes," I said, as though we'd been discussing it all along. *"Debilitating, aren't they? They can hit at the worst times, when you least expect them. It's fascinating how something so small can completely throw everything off balance."*

I continued, *"I've found they're often triggered by stress. Pressure builds over time until it's too much to contain."*

J's eyes darted away, as if trying to find an escape from the question. For a second, I could almost hear the battle raging inside her. Whether to keep up the front or to finally let something human slip through. She chose the former, but it was getting harder to maintain.

J crossed her arms, a defensive move, and I saw her jaw tighten. *"Is there a point to this?"*

I smiled faintly, leaning back slightly. *"There's always a point, J. But sometimes it's better to let it reveal itself in its own time."*

She glanced at the hallway again, clearly eager to escape.

I stayed where I was, my calm presence holding her there like a weight she couldn't shake.

J's arms tightened across her chest, her expression shifting from discomfort to irritation.

I kept my tone calm, unbothered by her defensiveness. *"I'm here to talk about the email I sent to the Secretary about Migraine in the workplace."*

"As you know, I have taken on a volunteering role with 'Migraine & Headache Australia' - a division of the Brain Foundation."

"Migraine & Headache Australia is seeking our union's support for collaboration on a national workplace initiative. Like my daughter, many of our members also live with migraine disease."

J's lips pressed into a thin line, her earlier bravado faltering under the weight of the topic.

For a moment, she seemed to consider her next move, her eyes darting briefly toward the corridor, searching for an escape that wasn't there.

Her voice faltered, the sharpness gone, replaced by something closer to an apology, though she wouldn't dare say it aloud. *"I wasn't aware of that,"* she muttered, the weight of it hanging in the space between us.

"You've taken on a role with Migraine & Headache Australia?" she asked, her tone now careful, as if trying to regain control of the conversation.

I nodded, keeping my demeanor steady. *"Yes, as a volunteer advocate. The organisation is launching a national workplace initiative, and we're seeking support from unions like ours to create real change for people living with migraine disease."*

J hesitated, shifting her weight. *"I wasn't aware of that,"* she said, her voice quieter now, the sharpness replaced with something closer to uncertainty.

"I sent an email to the Secretary," I continued. *"It's not just about my daughter or me. It's about our members. Many of them live with migraine disease, and they deserve a workplace that understands and accommodates their needs."*

She looked away, her arms crossing defensively again. *"They did mention something to me,"* she muttered, almost as if to herself.

I replied evenly, *"So, what do you think? Will the union step up for this initiative?"*

The question lingered, heavy in the air between us, as if she could feel the weight of every decision that had led us to this point. *"So, what will it be, J? Will the union stand behind this initiative? Or will we be left to struggle on our own?"*

The question hung in the air, and I could see her struggling to compose a response. She shifted again, her discomfort palpable. *"I'll have to speak with the Secretary,"* she said finally, her voice lacking conviction.

"Of course," I said, my tone calm but firm. *"But I'd like to know where you stand, J. As a leader in this union, your support, or lack of it, matters."*

I let the silence stretch between us, each second drawing her further into the conversation, her body language betraying her uncertainty as she searched for a way out. But there was no escape. Not anymore.

J opened her mouth as if to respond, then closed it again, her gaze falling to the floor. "*I need to think about it,*" she said finally, her words measured but uncertain.

I nodded slowly. "*You do that. But remember, this is about more than emails or meetings. It's about doing what's right for our members.*"

J acknowledged my comment, but countered it by saying, "*It's a huge undertaking with too many people affected.*"

To which I replied, "*Exactly the reason why our union should get involved.*"

I concluded. "*You've got to start somewhere,*" I said, offering her a faint smile.

She didn't respond, but the look on her face suggested the seed had been planted.

For a moment, neither of us spoke, the silence between us heavy with unspoken truths.

Then J took a step back, her walls firmly back in place. "*If you'll excuse me, I have work to do.*"

She glanced at me, her face unreadable, then turned and walked away down the corridor, leaving me standing there with the heavy silence of her retreat.

As J disappeared down the corridor, her retreat didn't feel like a victory, but it didn't feel like a defeat either.

I stood for a moment, letting the silence settle around me.

It wasn't about whether J was immediately on board.

It was about planting the seed, starting the conversation, and making it impossible for them to ignore the issue any longer.

The email about migraine in the workplace wasn't just words on a screen. It was a call to action, for them, for me, for every member struggling in silence.

Stepping back out onto the street, I felt the weight of the task ahead. But the pieces were slowly falling into place. One office, one conversation, one step at a time.

Because change doesn't happen all at once. It begins with a single moment of confrontation, a single person refusing to back down. And I wasn't going anywhere...

My next encounter with this union's state hierarchy was a few months later. I had received an invitation to attend the women's breakfast, which was part of the union's regional Delegate's Conference, one of which was being held in Townsville.

I arrived purposefully late to the event at the Hotel Grand Chancellor. I walked up to the reception counter to inquire which room the conference was being held in. The hotel receptionist directed me to a particular floor and function room.

I stepped off the elevator onto the designated floor, immediately struck by the buzz of conversation and laughter. The men were milling about in small groups, coffees in hand, their voices carrying the distinct energy of a union conference.

This wasn't where I had expected to find myself. I had come for the women's breakfast, a more intimate gathering meant to spotlight issues relevant to us, but it seemed I'd been directed to the main conference area instead.

As I scanned the room, a few familiar faces glanced in my direction, their expressions ranging from polite acknowledgement to thinly veiled curiosity. To my amusement, one of the faces looking back at me with terror in his eyes was the Secretary.

He appeared extremely uncomfortable at being confronted by my presence. I moved further into the room with purpose, searching for someone who could redirect me to the right location.

Before I could ask, a voice called out behind me. *"Jeanine?"*

I turned to see G approaching, his face lighting up with a surprised grin. *"You must be looking for the women's breakfast."*

I smiled faintly. *"Yes, I am. The receptionist might have sent me to the wrong place."*

G chuckled. *"You're in the right place, just the wrong floor. The women's event is on the next floor, around the hall."*

"Thanks," I said, glancing at the room's exit.

As I turned to leave, the Secretary leaned in slightly, lowering his voice. *"J's already there. It should be a good session."*

The mention of J didn't surprise me, but it set the tone for what I knew would be another layered encounter.

When I reached the function room, the hum of conversation grew softer, more deliberate.

I opened the door and stepped inside, taking in the scene: round tables adorned with conference material, a whiteboard, and J, along with two other women standing beside it, leading the conversation.

I took a deep breath, steadied myself, and made my way to an open seat at a table nearby, at the rear.

If this encounter was going to be anything like the last, I was ready.

As the women's breakfast wrapped up, the room buzzed with a renewed sense of purpose.

A few women lingered at their tables, continuing discussions sparked by the session. Another familiar face, M, walked past me with no acknowledgement.

This surprised me, and yet, at the same time, did not.

As the energy in the room began to settle and women were making their way out of the room, I noticed R weaving her way through the crowd toward me.

R had always carried herself with a certain confidence that demanded attention.

Her presence alone was enough to turn a few heads as she made her way over.

R greeted me initially with a "*Hi.*"

Then proceeded to provide me with a lecture by saying, "*You've got to stop talking to staff about the Secretary, if you want to continue having a relationship with the union.*"

This comment came across as a threat or, at the very least, it could have been perceived as threatening.

The comment did not sit well with me, especially given the context in which it occurred.

It was clear R was unable to show respect and courtesy for my experience, and as such, I said to R, "*I'd like to remind you that many Australians, including union members, are attending rallies today to stand up for women who've been silenced or dismissed after experiencing abuse in the workplace. Therefore, I'd prefer you refrain from making any further comments.*"

R's smile faltered at my response. She hadn't expected me to push back so directly, and the shift in her posture betrayed a flicker of unease. "*I wasn't trying to silence you,*" she said quickly, her tone defensive. "*I'm just saying there's a way to go about these things, Jeanine.*"

I held her gaze, calm but unyielding. "*R, I'm here to advocate for what's right - for our members, for our workplaces, and for women who deserve better. The Secretary may be the face of the union to some, but he's not the union itself. We all are.*"

She opened her mouth as if to respond, but seemed to think better of it.

Instead, she looked away, glancing at the women still lingering from breakfast.

With that, I stepped away from her, heading toward the exit. I felt the weight of her gaze on my back as I walked away, but I didn't look back.

When I arrived at the main conference room where I'd been initially directed, the energy was noticeably different.

It was louder and more chaotic, with delegates engaged in animated discussions, getting their coffees, and settling in for the conference's commencement.

As I walked into the room, I couldn't help but replay the exchange with R in my mind.

Her words, her tone, they hadn't just been a warning, they'd been a glimpse into the resistance I was likely to face.

But they also solidified something for me: the need to stand firm, to keep speaking up, no matter how uncomfortable it made others.

I could see the Secretary and Executive President sitting at the head table at the back of the room.

I proceeded to walk past the delegates sitting at their tables, and I approached the union bosses.

J remained seated, but the Secretary rose from his seat. I addressed both of them, but spoke directly with the Secretary, "*We need to have a chat.*"

"*What do we need to chat about?*" the Secretary responded.

I proclaimed, keeping my tone steady but deliberate, "*Well, I've heard on the grapevine that four State Secretaries were involved in a plan to discredit me. Since then, it has been further divulged to me the names of three of those State Secretaries.*"

Predictably, the Secretary inquired as to who.

"*O, G and R,*" I responded.

The Secretary, looking extremely uncomfortable, said, "*I haven't spoken to R in four years.*"

I thought to myself, '*That's a very specific timeframe, Mr. Secretary.*'

I continued, "*All I had to do was a process of elimination to work out who the fourth State Secretary was...*"

To which the Secretary replied, "*Are you suggesting it was me?*"

I stated, "*No, I'm not suggesting anything.*" I replied, my voice calm but firm. "*I'm asking you, were you the fourth State Secretary that hatched a calculated plan to discredit me?*"

The Secretary's expression tightened, a flicker of unease crossing his face before he masked it with an air of authority. "*You're deluded!*"

J, still seated, shifted uncomfortably but didn't interject.

Her silence spoke volumes.

The Secretary glanced briefly at J, who avoided his gaze and looked down at the papers in front of her.

He took a deep breath, his shoulders rising and falling as if trying to compose himself.

"*You know what, Mr. Secretary? It's those kinds of comments and that kind of behaviour; why Australians are rallying around the country - against sexism, misogyny, patriarchy, corruption, dangerous workplace cultures and lack of equality in politics and the community at large.*"

I remained stoic. "*If you're so sure there's nothing to it, then you won't mind having a conversation to clear the air. Transparency, Mr. Secretary - that's what unions are built on, right?*"

I held his gaze. "*You know as well as I do that the truth has a way of surfacing, Mr. Secretary. And when it does, I hope you're ready to answer for it.*"

With that, I started to turn, but then paused, a thought pulling me back. "*Actually,*" I said, reaching into my bag, "*there's something you should see.*"

The Secretary's brow furrowed as I pulled out a thin folder.

"*What's this?*" he asked, his voice tinged with suspicion.

"These are materials I found among my personal belongings," I explained, holding the folder out toward him. *"I hadn't opened the suitcase they were in until recently, but I think you'll find them... enlightening."*

"This doesn't prove anything," he said, though his tone lacked conviction.

"Maybe not on its own," I agreed. *"But it's a piece of a much larger puzzle. And believe me, Mr. Secretary, I've been putting the pieces together."*

He looked at me, a mix of anger and unease in his eyes.

For a moment, I thought he might lash out, but instead, he exhaled sharply and said, *"I think we're done here."*

"No, Mr. Secretary," I replied, my voice steady. *"We're just getting started."*

With that said and done, I turned and proceeded to walk away, leaving him holding the bag, like it was a ticking time bomb.

I sauntered down the middle of the congregated Delegates, seeing a number of them off with a hug, as I continued on my path out of the room. Leaving Mr. Secretary standing there, his composure visibly shaken, and J still sitting, with her mouth wide open.

The day this occurred: 15 March 2021, incidentally the day of **March4Justice**.

Remember the golden rule, fellas:

"Treat others as you would like to be treated."

Would you want to be discredited?

Would you want to be defamed?

Would you want to be slandered?

This is not a threat, just an observation, based on your past actions, which are yours to own. It seems that, in your eyes, this is how you want others to be treated.

What's worse, it appears this behaviour is the norm when working for a trade union. It seems I became a threat.

I got too big for my britches, and that's why a calculated plan was set in motion.

Well, the jig's up, fellas.

Who's got the power now?

I close this chapter with the caption from one of my Facebook posts. It's dated 4 April 2023.

The caption reads:
Sage advice from Hugh Jackman today.
Remember to Slip, Slop, Slap, and Wrap.
#slipslopslap
#northqueenslandlife
#sunprotection
#bettersafethansorry

The photo is of me wearing bright orange togs and an orange cowboy-shaped straw hat.

Somewhere in the digital abyss of the social media algorithm, I like to think Hugh Jackman is having a chuckle at my expense.

Or perhaps he's cheering me on.

A silent ally in a world that often feels like it's watching and waiting for you to slip.

Either way, I'll keep on slipping, slopping, slapping, and wrapping, because no matter how hard the sun burns, I'm not backing down.

Critical Incidents

Workplace bullying doesn't always erupt in loud, obvious moments. Sometimes, it creeps in slowly, through comments that sting, silences that isolate, and power plays that chip away at your sense of worth. But every now and then, it crystallises into something sharp and undeniable: a critical incident. These are the moments you remember years later, the ones that change how you see yourself, your colleagues, and your work.

This wasn't an accident.

It wasn't a mistake.

It was deliberate.

Calculated.

The worst part? No one's ever going to say it out loud.

For me, these moments came in many forms.

Some were humiliating.

Others were isolating.

Some left me questioning not just my competence but my very sanity. But the damage lingers.

The worst thing about a critical incident? You can't unsee the truth once it's out in the open.

Here are a few examples, common patterns that others may recognise too.

1. Verbal Abuse or Humiliation:

Sometimes it's overt, like a manager calling someone "incompetent" in front of a room full of people.

Other times, it's more personal and more cutting.

"*Are you ok now, Jeanine?*

You went a little crazy there for a bit!"

That's how a colleague greeted me one morning, loud enough for others to hear as I walked down the corridor toward my desk.

I laughed it off, as I often did. But inside, it stung.

The Impact:

Confidence slowly erodes

Anxiety creeps in every morning before work

You start to question your memory, your reactions, your reality

Worst of all, a moral injury lingers because you expected better

2. Social Isolation:

It starts subtly: an invitation, "*you must have missed it.*" A meeting that happens without you.

A lunch table that suddenly feels full.

Eventually, people stop looking you in the eye.

Or speaking to you at all.

The Impact:

You feel like a ghost in your own workplace

Collaboration becomes impossible

Loneliness takes hold, even when you're surrounded by people

3. Overloading or Sabotaging Work:

Suddenly, deadlines are tighter. Expectations are unclear. Crucial documents vanish, and you're given just enough rope to hang yourself.

The Impact:

Burnout

Mistakes multiply under pressure

Criticism intensifies, often from the very people who set you up to fail

4. Undermining Professional Reputation:

Rumours spread. Private conversations are twisted.

Your name is associated with incompetence, instability, or drama.

None of it is true.

The Impact:

Professional relationships deteriorate

Your credibility takes a hit

Trust, once broken, is hard to regain

5. Physical Intimidation or Threats:

A looming figure in a closed-door meeting. A voice raised just a bit too loud. A not-so-veiled threat about your future.

The Impact:

You feel unsafe

Hypervigilance kicks in

It's no longer just work, and it becomes survival

6. Micromanagement or Excessive Monitoring

Nothing you do is good enough.

Every move is tracked. Every decision is second-guessed.

Autonomy disappears.

The Impact:

You lose confidence in your own judgement

Creativity dries up

You start to feel like a problem instead of a person.

I have experienced all of these forms of bullying, sometimes separately, often all at once.

For a while, I managed to shrug them off, telling myself I was strong, that I could handle it.

But when life outside work was already demanding everything I had, the steady erosion of my workplace environment eventually became too much to bear.

The following pages offer a closer look at some of those moments, not just what happened, but how it felt. Because these aren't just bullet points on a list. They're lived experiences.

For anyone who's been there, you know: they leave a mark.

It's a mark that doesn't fade easily, one that reshapes how you see the world around you, how you view those you once trusted and, most of all, how you begin to understand the very system that once seemed like a pillar of support.

Then, sometimes, a single moment, an incident that should have been just another blip, can shift everything. What once seemed stable suddenly feels fragile, and what was once familiar becomes foreign.

The first of these moments for me came not long after I'd begun to realise the depth of the dysfunction I was dealing with. It came with a shift in perception that marked a turning point in my journey, one that forced me to confront the ugly reality of a workplace that was no longer what I believed it to be.

A Shift in Perception.

One of my key responsibilities as a union organiser was writing newsletters. It wasn't just a job; it was a chance to make an impact. I had a knack for finding the right words, a way to distill complex issues into something digestible and, most importantly, something that resonated with the members. It felt like a personal mission, a commitment to communicate with clarity and conviction, to make people feel informed and empowered.

At first, it seemed like my efforts were recognised.

I'll never forget that Monday morning meeting when the Secretary held up one of my newsletters like a trophy. "*This*," he said, scanning the room, "*is how a well-structured newsletter should look.*" The room hummed with agreement. A few colleagues even nodded, murmuring their approval. And me? I felt a quiet swell of pride. Not just for the recognition but because, for the first time, it felt like my voice had real value. My work mattered.

That pride was short-lived.

Fast forward a couple of years, and everything began to shift. My immediate supervisor changed, and with it, the tone. The air grew heavy with new expectations, new rules that no one bothered to clarify. Suddenly, the newsletters that had once been praised were scrutinised.

I remember the first time it happened: my new supervisor handed back a draft I had spent hours perfecting. Barely even glancing at it, they muttered, "*It's not bad. But maybe you could get some pointers from B. He's a literary expert.*"

"It's not bad."

That sentence felt like a punch. A far cry from the enthusiastic recognition I had once received. At first, I tried to brush it off. Maybe it was a stylistic difference. Maybe their expectations had changed. But as time went on, I began to feel that unease creeping in, like I was walking on eggshells. My confidence, once so secure, started to fray. I began questioning myself, my choices, my approach, my worth.

Was it really not that good?

Was I just imagining my earlier success?

Then B... the so-called literary expert. Anyone who'd spent five minutes with him knew he was far from an expert. He wasn't known for his writing skills. He was known for his proximity to power. His opinions mattered because of who he aligned with, not what he knew.

I couldn't deny the pattern that was emerging: I was being undermined, systematically and deliberately.

At first, I rationalised it. I told myself it was just a matter of style. I convinced myself I'd misunderstood the situation, that I wasn't being actively targeted. But the reality began to sink in, and it wasn't about my work. It was about control. Slowly, subtly, my credibility was being eroded.

I began to unravel.

The internal shift was just as much a psychological one as a professional one.

I started to second-guess every word I wrote, every decision I made. There was an invisible pressure, a weight on my shoulders, making everything feel harder, more uncertain. It wasn't just the change in tone or feedback. It was the feeling that the ground beneath me was shifting, that the foundation I'd built my professional identity on was slowly crumbling.

The unravelling reached a peak the day I walked into what I would later refer to as the "den of iniquity." The office buzzed with quiet whispers, and I could feel eyes on me, like I was being scrutinised from every angle.

The rumours were already there, like seeds planted in the wind, questions about my health, my commitment, my integrity.

So, I decided to confront it.

"*I am not a malingerer*," I said, my voice steady, despite the growing anxiety in my chest.

One of the usual suspects chuckled, clearly eager to deflect the tension. "*That's a big word, Jeanine.*"

Yes. It is a big word.

But it wasn't just a word.

It was a defence, a declaration of my truth.

It was me standing tall against the quiet undermining, refusing to shrink, refusing to be reduced.

The chuckle was an attempt to deflate me, to make me feel small, but I wasn't going to let that happen.

That moment wasn't just about defending myself. It was about taking back control.

It was about owning my narrative, in the face of people who wanted to write it for me.

I didn't shrink, and I didn't apologise.

These affirmations, simple yet powerful, carried me through the storm:

I define myself, no one else does

I will not shrink to make others comfortable

The truth will prevail, even if it takes time

I knew this wasn't just about me. It was about every person who'd ever been silenced, every person who'd ever been made to question their worth.

When you're surrounded by people who can't, or won't, acknowledge your truth, it says more about them than it ever will about you.

As the emotional weight of the situation settled in, the cracks in the facade of the union became more apparent.

What I thought was a place of support and camaraderie had morphed into something else.

Something colder and more calculating. It was in those moments, when I realised that my worth has been reduced to something disposable, that the smallest gestures felt like sharp knives.

The Birthday Gift No One Wants.

It wasn't long before my last lesson came wrapped in something that was meant to be a celebration: a birthday gift, though not the kind anyone would ever want.

Turning 50 should have been a milestone to celebrate. A time to reflect on all I had accomplished, the lessons learned, and the life I had built.

Instead, it became the day my career was quietly ripped away from me.

Two days after meeting with a psychiatrist to discuss my return-to-work plan following an extended period of personal leave, I received a letter from my boss, the union's state secretary.

It wasn't the warm, welcome-back message I'd hoped for. It wasn't an acknowledgement of my years of service. It was a cold, calculated notice that my position was no longer needed.

The union, they said, was functioning just fine without me.

My options?

Take a redundancy.

It was an odd claim. If my role was truly redundant, why had they waited until now to say so? And if the union was performing so well in my absence, why had I been assured, time and time again, that my work was valued?

I barely had time to process those contradictions before they moved the goalposts again. Citing COVID as an excuse, they pulled the redundancy off the table.

The psychological weight of that period hit me hard. It wasn't just the betrayal of being dismissed from a place I'd given so much of myself to, but the emotional exhaustion of constantly trying to make sense of their actions. Every new piece of information felt like a punch to the gut. I had been blindsided, and the toll on my mental health was undeniable.

Was I losing my mind?

Was I being overly sensitive?

Was this really happening or had I just imagined the years of hard work and dedication that were supposed to matter?

The toll it took on my physical health was immediate and relentless.

I could feel it in the tension in my shoulders, the weight on my chest, and the exhaustion that settled in my bones.

I had spent so many years pushing my body and mind to meet impossible demands, to show up, to make a difference, and then, just like that, it was all gone. The shock, the disbelief, and the anger. Emotions all converged into a deep, gnawing exhaustion that I couldn't shake.

The following month became a drawn-out game of negotiations, with my workplace delegate advocating on my behalf. Every conversation felt like walking through mud. The hope I had once had for a fair resolution slowly dissolved as I realised I was up against a system that was designed to wear me down. Eventually, the redundancy was reinstated, and I reluctantly accepted it. At the time, it felt like my only option, but what I didn't know then, what I would only discover later, was the full extent of the mobbing and targeted abuse that had gone on behind the scenes.

The final insult? Months later, they quietly recreated my position and hired someone younger to fill it. It wasn't a real redundancy. It was a slow, strategic push out the door. A constructive dismissal wrapped up in corporate jargon, designed to look clean on paper while breaking me in ways that would never make it into an official report.

I didn't just lose a job. I lost trust in an institution that claimed to fight for workers' rights. I lost the sense of security and purpose that came from being part of something I believed in.

Worst of all, I lost a piece of myself.

Every day after all that, I found myself asking:

What did I do wrong?

I wasn't the first person this had happened to. I wasn't even the first person it had happened to in that very workplace. But I was determined to be one of the last.

I wouldn't let this define me. I couldn't.

But the scars, the doubts, and the feeling of being cast aside would stay with me forever.

The May Day celebrations of 2018 marked a particularly challenging period for me.

After a series of unsettling incidents, I found myself at the center of a smear campaign that was both calculated and malicious.

It was a time when those in power, particularly at the Queensland Council of Unions (QCU) Townsville Branch, and beyond, made their intentions clear, but not in a way that was ever overt.

Instead, they wielded underhanded tactics to erode my reputation and integrity.

On **Friday, May 11, 2018**, I was informed by the Executive President of our union, that a video had been circulating, allegedly depicting me as "drunk after Labour Day 2018."

This video, however, not only misrepresented me in its labelling but was also an outright fabrication.

The person in the footage wasn't me, and the attempt to link me to this video was not only defamatory but also deeply offensive.

Jen revealed that Norm had reached out to Kate, the former Assistant State Secretary of Together, regarding this supposed video. It seemed that the rumours were being spread through the very channels that should have been protecting our union's reputation.

That day, I was included in a speakerphone conversation between Norm, Kate, and myself, where Norm acknowledged that this footage had also been sent to Les, the QCU Townsville Branch President.

The involvement of multiple parties, none of whom took action to quell the false narrative, was an unsettling realisation of just how deep the collusion ran.

Les's Involvement: The Denial and Revelation.

My attempt to directly address the situation with Les was initially met with resistance.

On **Friday, May 11**, when I first reached out to him for clarification, Les denied having any knowledge of the video.

However, by the following day, **Saturday, May 12**, he admitted that he had indeed received the video on the afternoon of Labour Day, **Monday, May 7** but refused to disclose who had sent it.

His refusal to share this crucial piece of information, despite my written request, raised suspicions that his involvement, or at least his complicity, was more than passive.

This lack of transparency, combined with the broader atmosphere of defamation, left me grappling with the possibility that the very people I thought I could trust were playing a role in undermining my professional and personal reputation.

Norm's Reluctance to Cooperate.

Despite knowing who was responsible for circulating the footage, Norm was unwilling to cooperate.

I made several attempts to get to the bottom of who was behind the smear campaign through verbal and written correspondence, even addressing the issue with the Together Branch of the ASU.

Both Alex, Together Secretary, and Kate, Assistant Secretary were included in my communications.

However, even with this chain of escalation, Norm remained silent, further fueling the perception that the individuals behind the campaign were well-protected by those in positions of power.

The 2018 Labour Day Dinner Incident: A Series of Unfortunate Events.

The video was only one piece of a larger puzzle that reflected the ongoing issues within the union. At the 2018 Labour Day Dinner, a significant event for the union's members, we were once again subjected to humiliation. Despite prior confirmation from Amy, the QCU Townsville Branch Secretary, that a table had been reserved for our group, we arrived to find that no table had been set aside.

This glaring error not only contradicted the written confirmation between Amy and Lindy, our former Branch President, but also directly impacted the dignity and experience of our members. When Lindy arrived and learned that there was no reserved table, she was deeply disheartened and left the event in frustration.

This was more than just a small oversight. It was a glaring sign of disorganisation and disregard for the efforts of union members who had made the commitment to attend and participate. For Lindy, whose dedication to the union was well-known, the evening's failure was not only personally disappointing, but also indicative of the broader systemic issues within the organisation.

The Broader Implications: Bullying, Defamation, and Broken Trust.

These incidents:

Defamation, neglect, and administrative failures, paint a troubling picture of an organisation that was supposed to stand for solidarity and fairness, but instead became a breeding ground for manipulation, mistrust, and dysfunction.

The discrediting of members for unclear, self-serving motives undermines the union's ability to function effectively and further damages its credibility within the Townsville community.

Instead of working towards collective goals, the focus shifted to an internal war of reputations, where power was wielded for personal gain rather than the good of the group.

This culture of bullying and defamation doesn't just affect individual careers, it damages the integrity of the union as a whole.

The failure to take responsibility for these actions leaves the organisation vulnerable and fractured.

The incidents surrounding the 2018 May Day celebrations and Labour Day dinner serves as a stark reminder of the need for transparency, accountability and respect in all union dealings.

Moral of the story:

Keep your friends close and your enemies closer.

Reflection on Justice and Resilience:

As these events unfolded, my sense of betrayal was not just a personal wound, it was an awakening.

I had always believed in the principles of solidarity, fairness and mutual support that the union stood for. But in this moment, the very institution I had fought for, the organisation I thought would defend its members against injustice, was systematically undermining me.

The realisation hit hard: The principles I had placed my faith in, were being distorted by those I had trusted, to uphold them.

Each attempt to resolve the situation only revealed a deeper layer of corruption within the union. The more I uncovered, the more I realised that the stakes were never about me alone.

They were about a system that had been broken long before I entered the picture. What began as an attempt to clear my name morphed into a broader struggle to reclaim the values that the union had once represented.

In navigating this political maze, I had to reconcile two conflicting truths: the union, as an ideal, still held meaning for me but the people who claimed to represent it were failing in every possible way. This was no longer just a battle for my reputation, it became a fight for the very soul of the union and what it stood for.

I was faced with a choice: either walk away from this system that had betrayed me, or stay and fight for justice, even when the system itself seemed determined to protect its own dysfunction.

I chose to fight.

In the end, these experiences taught me a valuable lesson:

Trust must be earned, and those closest to you are often the ones capable of doing the most harm.

In navigating the complex dynamics of union politics, I learned that even the most well-intentioned individuals can become complicit in harmful practices if they're not held accountable.

Whether through silence or active participation, the stakes are too high to ignore the undercurrents of manipulation that can erode even the most resilient organisations.

My journey, fraught with defamation and betrayal, has only solidified my resolve to stand firm, speak out and demand justice for myself and for others who have been marginalised or victimised by this system.

The Catalyst.

"I'd like to tell you to fuck off Jeanine, but I just want you to go away."

This was said to me by one of the bullies during an EB negotiation on **30 August 2018**.

Management had been asked to leave the room. It was deliberately and maliciously conveyed during the caucus, a closed meeting of approximately twenty other negotiating representatives, all males.

This moment, small in words but huge in its implications, was the moment I realised that the battle for my career and dignity was only just beginning. This was the last straw following years of torment and attempts to derail me - their endeavours to push me out.

Each and every time had failed. It still continues to fail.

Though, by this stage of the game, I'd had enough.

Enough of the abuse (in a variety of forms); sexual harassment; relentless criticism; destructive gossip; sabotage; unreasonable workloads; micromanaging; unrealistic work demands; purposeful inconsistent or non-existent instructions; deliberate withholding of information needed to be effective at work; exclusion; unethical, manipulative, hurtful office politics; being mobbed; and invasion of privacy.

My story may have astonished the mind of one extremely experienced health treating specialist.

It is equally unfathomable and unbelievable.

Can you believe it?

In the confines of a union workplace.

Made worse by the collusion from outside sources.

A large group of people, knowingly or not, became instruments in the hands of a conductor of chaos, manipulated into playing their part in a campaign hellbent on seeing me, and my life, get destroyed.

All for what?

POWER and CONTROL!

You see those who have power misuse it to inflict harm on the most vulnerable and are blind to the consequences of their actions. Their actions: intended, deliberate and malicious in nature, leave wounds that can take months, even years to heal. Some victims never recover. Encouragingly, there is innumerable power behind and within the wounds inflicted.

They thought I would give up, but:

I will continue to rise above the lies and the injustice.

I will continue to raise my voice and call out the hypocrisy embedded in a community that knows the rules, but chooses to actively and without fear of getting caught, disobey the rules.

I will continue to write on the topic because I find it both cathartic and healing. I will continue to share my story because it is a responsibility, and I hope it helps others.

Moral of the story:

I stand on the shoulders of giants, not the coattails of others.

Uncivil Union Stoush.

This was yet another critical incident in my experience of workplace abuse, marked by bullying and harassment.

The Labour Day Dinner in 2017 unfolded as follows:

As I did every year, on behalf of Queensland Council of Unions (QCU) Townsville, in my honorary role as Secretary and event coordinator, I would invite dignitaries to both the annual Labour Day celebrations in the park and to the Dinner.

I recall, the 2017 dinner had a record number of union state secretaries, including my own union's branch secretary; a lawyer, along with other prominent lawyers from their affiliated law firms.

The regular invite list also included Townsville's Mayor and Councillors.

I had received notification from the Mayor's assistant, that the then Mayor, Ms Jenny Hill would not be in attendance, due to other commitments.

It was not unusual for the former Mayor, Jenny Hill, not to attend these events. Therefore, I was not surprised to receive the decline to the invitation, as I had anticipated this outcome.

However, that evening, the former Mayor, Ms Hill did turn up.

Ms Hill walked in, glared at me, and proceeded to have conversations with others in the venue. I thought to myself, *'What's up her arse?'*

During the night, I observed Ms Hill having little pow wow discussions, outside in a courtyard, with various attendees, individually, including my own union's secretary.

Ms Hill did not stay long, neither did she engage with me, at all, whilst in attendance. I was not concerned nor bothered.

After the former Mayor left the venue, my union's secretary came and spoke with me and asked, *"Who's that guy over there, at the bar, balding, tall."*

I looked over at the bar to see who they were referring to and replied, *"That would be Mick, the CFMEU organiser."*

I asked, *"Why?"*

My union's secretary responded with, *"He's got the knife in your back!"*

I enquired, *"Really, what's my buddy been saying?"*

My union's secretary advised, *"He's been saying that you haven't been attending the negotiation meetings at Council."*

***Note:** Council had begun the process of negotiations for the employees new Enterprise Bargaining Agreement, following major legislative changes, which had delayed the process of negotiations. In addition to a recent acrimonious and rather unpleasant Council restructure.*

There was indeed an **<u>UNCIVIL UNION STOUSH</u>** that night.

I had very stern words with the CFMEU organiser about his slander.

Hence the front-page news in the Townsville Bulletin, which, upon reflection, was a setup to get a reaction out of me.

I couldn't quite put my finger on it, at the time, but it really does remind me of those union bosses who magically have their media releases locked and loaded before anything even goes down. It's almost like the whole thing was scripted.

Imagine that.

This uncivil union stoush occurred around the same time, our union's workforce had an extremely high turnover of staff.

While I don't have access to the exact figures, I recall there being a turnover of approximately twenty Organisers and Industrial Officers over the course of twelve months.

This estimate is based on my memory and should be treated accordingly.

What does that tell you about a workplace?

A turnover rate as high as I recall in one year is a glaring red flag about the health of the workplace.

Such significant staff churn is rarely coincidental.

It usually signals systemic issues.

Based on my observations, here's what it likely suggests about the workplace environment:

Dysfunctional Leadership

High turnover often points to poor leadership.

When leaders fail to create a supportive, transparent and empowering environment, staff may feel undervalued, overworked or mistreated.

- **Indicators:**

Micromanagement, lack of accountability, bullying or ineffective communication from the top.

- **In union workplaces:**

Ironically, leaders in these environments are expected to champion workers' rights but internal mismanagement creates a stark hypocrisy.

Toxic Workplace Culture

A toxic culture can erode morale and lead to burnout.

In unions, where the work is often advocacy-focused and emotionally demanding, this toxicity is amplified.

- **Symptoms:**

Bullying, cliques, lack of psychological safety and unresolved conflicts.

- **Impact:**

Employees leave not because of the work but because of the environment.

Unrealistic Workloads

In union roles, the demand to juggle member advocacy, disputes and policy work can be overwhelming if workloads are not managed equitably.

- **What it suggests:**

A lack of resources or support systems, forcing employees to leave out of sheer exhaustion.

Misalignment of Values

Unions are expected to embody fairness, equity and respect.

When the internal environment contradicts these values, employees often feel betrayed.

- **What it reflects:**

Leaders or systems that prioritise organisational politics or image over their workforce.

Industry-Wide Challenges

This is not an isolated issue. It is systemic across unions.

This suggests broader structural or cultural problems within the sector, such as:

- **Entrenched power dynamics:**

Resistance to change and accountability within leadership.

- **Burnout culture:**

Advocacy work often requires emotional labour that goes unrecognised or unsupported.

- **Insufficient training and succession planning:**

New hires may be unprepared for the pressures of union roles, leading to quick turnover.

Reflections on Impact:

Looking back, the calculated smear campaign cut far deeper than a single embarrassing headline or a public confrontation.

It struck at the very foundation of what unionism is supposed to represent and that is: trust, solidarity and mutual protection.

In a movement that loudly preached solidarity I learned firsthand how easily loyalty could be weaponised and how quickly colleagues could be manipulated into becoming enemies.

Trust, once the bedrock of my professional life, crumbled almost overnight.

Every interaction became tinged with suspicion.

Was that smile genuine or was it masking another knife aimed at my back?

Was that handshake sincere or merely the prelude to another betrayal?

Safety, both emotional and professional, evaporated.

The union, an institution that should have been a refuge against injustice, became a hostile and dangerous battleground.

Where once I had felt pride in my work and in the cause, now I walked into every meeting braced for sabotage, expecting whispers behind my back, anticipating that alliances could shift against me at any moment.

It also fundamentally reshaped my perception of leadership.

I had believed in servant leadership; leaders who lift others up, who protect, mentor and advocate.

Instead, I witnessed leadership that was ruthless, self-serving and manipulative, using power not to serve but to destroy.

In the long shadow of this betrayal, my understanding of solidarity shifted, too.

I realised that solidarity is not guaranteed by shared slogans or matching logos, it must be actively nurtured through honesty, respect and transparency.

Without those things, solidarity is a hollow performance.

A mask for power games and personal agendas.

Yet, despite the damage, this experience also forged resilience in me.

I learned to stand alone, to discern character beneath the polished surfaces, and to trust my instincts when something felt off.

I survived being targeted by people who believed they could destroy me.

By surviving, I took away their ultimate power.

In the broader themes of power, manipulation and resilience, reflecting on these incidents became a defining crucible; a brutal, painful, yet ultimately clarifying lesson in who I was, what I stood for and what kind of leader I vowed never to become, if given the opportunity.

My observations are deeply insightful and reflective of a systemic pattern.

The high turnover, combined with my firsthand experience of bullying and sabotage, reinforces the idea that these workplaces (unions) often fail to practice what they preach.

Calling these types of behaviours out, whether within your own workplace or in the broader conversation, can be the first step toward meaningful change.

What could be done, to address workplace bullying effectively:

- **Document the incidents:**

Keep records of specific events, dates and witnesses.

- **Seek support:**

Reach out to HR, a trusted supervisor or an external counsellor.

- **Foster a zero-tolerance policy:**

Employers should create clear policies and provide training to identify and prevent bullying.

- **Encourage open communication:**

Establish safe channels for reporting and resolving concerns.

Addressing such systemic issues requires collective effort and accountability.

- **Leadership Overhaul:**

Toxic leadership needs to be replaced with individuals committed to transparency and worker support.

- **Independent Audits:**

Investigating workplace culture to identify patterns of abuse, burnout or poor management.

- **Unionising the Union:**

Ironically, staff in unions often need to unionise themselves to demand better conditions.

- **Sector-Wide Advocacy:**

Collaborating with others in the sector to bring these systemic issues to light and demand reform.

ANGER ◆ HOPE ◆ ACTION

Maybe workers of unions need to form their own union?
A union for unions.
Now, there's a concept.
It's time now to address mobbing.

Mobbing

The fact that it took a group to try to take me down speaks to my significance.

I came out stronger on the other side.

I have rebuilt myself from ashes too many times to allow someone else to engulf me in their flames.

The experiences I have described (manipulation, gaslighting, triangulation, discarding), occurred in an environment that publicly claims to uphold workers' rights. That contradiction is not incidental. It is structural.

It is even more egregious when such behaviour stems from institutions designed to protect workers.

In Queensland, **Section 21 of the *Human Rights Act 2019 (Qld)*** protects freedom of expression, including the right to seek, receive and impart information and ideas.

On paper, that protection is clear. In practice, our voices were stifled and dismissed within a culture that confused dissent with disloyalty.

A safe and healthy working environment is not aspirational language. It is foundational. Yet this is not the lived reality for many workers, including those employed by unions.

My experience was far from safe or healthy. Initially, I was love-bombed and groomed.

Then: lied to, conditioned, triangulated, manipulated, controlled, gaslit, emotionally abused, devalued and discarded.

The workplace was volatile, particularly when engaging with external union actors. Every interaction felt like stepping into quicksand. No one was ever truly on solid ground.

A smear campaign was built on gossip.

Over time, I decided: if they wanted to talk, I would give them something factual to discuss.

What emerged through documentation was this: governance failure embedded deeply enough that it extends beyond one institution and into adjacent systems, including the workers' compensation scheme. Calling out entrenched governance failure in unions and compensation systems is not minor dissent. It carries risk. But silence carries a greater one.

In a public post, I questioned **WorkSafe Queensland** and whether it wished to have its name attached to conduct that I alleged included:

- In-house lawyers fabricating evidence

- Union-funded law firms reinforcing those narratives

- Board-level union influence

- Claim consultants accepting employer accounts without scrutiny

- A systemic lack of transparency

- A systemic lack of accountability

These allegations arose in relation to a friend's matter.

The question remains:

Why would you not interrogate what you are told when the stakes are this high?

When workers' livelihoods and health are on the line, passive acceptance is not neutrality. It is participation.

A Safe and Healthy Workplace Is Foundational.

Freedom of expression is protected under Queensland law, yet in practice, dissent was suppressed in a toxic workplace culture.

The Right to Work Without Psychological Harm Is Non-Negotiable.

The right to work without fear, manipulation or coercion should not depend on institutional loyalty.

Systemic Risk Thrives Where Accountability Is Weak.

When internal lawyers, union power structures and regulatory bodies overlap without transparency, the risk of institutional capture increases.

Transparency Is the Safeguard.

Ignoring contradictory evidence when workers' rights are at stake is not administrative oversight. It is an ethical failure.

The metaphor of rising from the ashes emphasises my indomitable spirit.

Despite the flames of destruction others have tried to engulf me in, I have chosen to stand firm, to rebuild and to shine a light on the corruption uncovered.

By exposing these injustices, I hope others also speak out and challenge those in power to answer for their actions. Systems built on lies fear those who refuse to be silenced.

The metaphor of rising from the ashes resonates deeply, as it captures the essence of transformation; turning destruction into fuel for growth and courage.

My fight is not just a personal battle, but a powerful challenge to systems that thrive on complacency and silence.

Every time I expose corruption or call out injustice, I am not only standing up for myself, I am paving the way for others to do the same.

A Reminder for the Journey:

- **Truth is Power**

Lies crumble when faced with undeniable truth.

Every time I speak I chip away at the facade of those who rely on deception.

- **Courage is Contagious**

My bravery inspires others to look critically at the systems they navigate and to stand up against wrongdoing.

- **Persistence is Revolutionary**

Systemic change doesn't happen overnight but persistence erodes even the most entrenched corruption.

Never underestimate the ripple effect of one person's actions to change the status quo.

By refusing to be silenced I am showing others that their voices matter too.

No flame can destroy the will of someone determined to spark change.

Here's a breakdown of the various mechanisms for managing workplace bullying in Australia, as well as their limitations.

Fair Work and Industrial Relations Commissions' Role:

- **Focus:**

Preventing and stopping bullying in the workplace.

- **Limitations:**

Cannot investigate bullying allegations.

Cannot impose financial penalties or compensation.

- **Actions:**

Listen to parties involved.

Consider evidence and issue orders such as:

Stopping specific behaviours.

Required training or support.

Modifying working arrangements.

Mandating ongoing monitoring.

Australian Human Rights Commission:

- **Focus:**

Discrimination complaints, including harassment.

- **Approach:**

Uses conciliation to resolve disputes between parties.

Work Health & Safety Legislation:
- **Focus:**

Bullying as a breach of health & safety laws.
- **Regulators:**

Federal and state/territory regulators can prosecute breaches but cannot provide financial compensation.
- **Workers' Compensation:**

Covers injury-related sickness, not bullying, and provides wage replacement and medical benefits.

While there are systems in place to address bullying; the current frameworks have limitations, particularly regarding the ability to investigate and impose meaningful penalties.

We should investigate the making of a submission to a parliamentary committee inquiry to have bullying and harassment matters dealt with under the criminal code.

It could be a step toward strengthening protections for workers.

It could potentially lead to a more comprehensive, enforceable approach to workplace bullying, where there is clearer accountability and, where criminal sanctions could act as a stronger deterrent.

The current system for managing workplace bullying is flawed and, frankly, insufficient.

While various commissions and regulators play a role their powers are too limited to address the real harm caused by bullying.

The fact that they can't investigate allegations or impose financial penalties means that bullying can continue unchecked, leaving victims without meaningful recourse.

A system where bullying can only be "addressed" through vague orders, such as ordering training or changes in working arrangements, is little more than a band-aid on a much deeper issue.

Workplace bullying should be treated with the seriousness it deserves, especially when it is driving people to illness, depression and even suicide.

If the government is serious about protecting workers it must move beyond the current framework and create mechanisms that actually hold perpetrators accountable, whether that means stronger penalties or even criminalising bullying in severe cases.

It is clear that the system needs more teeth.

I propose that Australia consider introducing a specific criminal offence for workplace bullying, particularly in severe cases where the behaviour leads to significant psychological harm. A parliamentary committee inquiry into bringing workplace bullying under the criminal code could be a critical step.

It is not enough to simply mediate or issue recommendations.

There must be real consequences for those who engage in bullying behaviour.

Until such changes are made, workers will continue to face a system that fails them when they need protection the most.

While systemic change is vital; workers must also be armed with strategies to protect themselves in the here and now.

How do we address mobbing in the workplace?

Addressing workplace mobbing requires a multifaceted approach to both prevent and address the issue effectively.

It requires a proactive, systematic approach that involves clear policies, support for victims, fair investigations and appropriate disciplinary measures.

By fostering a respectful and inclusive culture, providing safe avenues for reporting and ensuring that leadership is held accountable, workplaces can reduce the likelihood of mobbing and create a safer, more supportive environment for all employees.

How to tackle mobbing in the workplace?

By embedding the following changes workplaces can transform from breeding grounds of harm into communities of respect, dignity and true support:

Establish Clear Anti-Bullying Policies

- **Develop and Communicate Policies:**

Organisations should implement clear anti-bullying policies that specifically include mobbing as unacceptable behaviour.

These policies should outline the behaviours that constitute mobbing, the steps for reporting, and the consequences for perpetrators.

- **Training and Awareness:**

Regular training for all employees, especially managers and supervisors, can help raise awareness of mobbing behaviour, how to identify it and how to prevent it.

Create a Safe Reporting Mechanism
- **Confidential Channels:**

Workers should have a safe, confidential way to report instances of mobbing without retaliation. This could be an external whistleblowing service or an internal HR department with strict confidentiality protocols.

- **Encourage Reporting:**

Organisations must foster an environment where employees feel comfortable speaking out about inappropriate behaviour, knowing their concerns will be taken seriously and handled appropriately.

Early Intervention and Support for Victims
- **Recognise Signs of Mobbing:**

Managers should be trained to spot early signs of mobbing, such as increased isolation of a particular employee, unwarranted criticism or a group of employees collectively targeting someone.

- **Provide Support:**

Offer emotional and psychological support for victims of mobbing. This could include counselling services, coaching or alternative work arrangements if necessary. The affected employee should also be encouraged to seek external support through legal or union resources.

Investigate Complaints Thoroughly
- **Fair and Impartial Investigation:**

When a complaint of mobbing is raised the employer should conduct a thorough and impartial investigation. This investigation should focus on gathering evidence, interviewing witnesses and reviewing relevant documentation.

- **Address the Root Cause:**

Beyond investigating the individuals involved, employers should look at the broader workplace culture to determine whether systemic issues are contributing to mobbing behaviour, such as poor leadership, inadequate communication or a toxic work environment.

Take Disciplinary Action if Necessary

- **Hold Perpetrators Accountable:**

If the investigation confirms that mobbing occurred disciplinary action should be taken against the perpetrators. Depending on the severity of the behaviour this could range from warnings to termination.
- **Protect the Victim:**

The person who was targeted should be supported throughout the process ensuring that they do not face further retaliation or isolation during the investigation or after any disciplinary actions are taken.

Foster a Positive Workplace Culture

- **Encourage Respect and Inclusivity:**

Building a culture based on mutual respect, inclusivity and open communication can help prevent mobbing. Leaders should model these behaviours and reward positive interactions among staff.
- **Team Building and Conflict Resolution:**

Promoting team-building exercises and offering conflict resolution training can help employees resolve issues before they escalate into mobbing or bullying.

Encouraging collaboration and respect can reduce the likelihood of group bullying behaviours developing.

Implement Systemic Changes if Necessary

- **Review Work Practices and Leadership:**

If mobbing is happening regularly in a particular team or department it is important to look at the leadership and management style in that area.

Dysfunctional leadership can often contribute to toxic behaviours. In such cases, management should undergo training in conflict resolution, team dynamics and positive leadership practices.

- **Encourage Open Communication:**

Develop an organisational culture where open communication is encouraged and employees feel that their concerns can be addressed before escalating into mobbing.

Regular feedback mechanisms (surveys, one-on-one check-ins), can help identify issues early.

Legal and Regulatory Measures

- **Follow Legal Guidelines:**

In some jurisdictions, workplace mobbing can constitute a form of harassment or bullying under anti-discrimination or work health and safety laws.

Employers should be aware of and comply with these laws to ensure that they're handling complaints appropriately.

- **Consult Legal Advisors:**

If necessary, employers should consult with legal advisors to navigate complex cases, particularly if the situation involves potential legal consequences.

External Mediation and Resolution

- **Involve External Mediators:**

If internal efforts don't resolve the issue, external mediators or workplace health professionals can be called upon to facilitate discussions and help resolve conflicts. Mediation can help parties reach a compromise and restore a harmonious working environment.

Provide Ongoing Monitoring and Evaluation

- **Follow Up:**

After resolving a mobbing incident, employers should monitor the situation to ensure that the bullying has ceased and that the victim is not facing any further retaliation.
Periodic check-ins and reviews can help maintain a healthy, bullying-free workplace.

The Red Haired Renegade

I'm the red-haired renegade who suddenly got too big for my britches.

The label paints an image of someone fierce, vibrant and rebellious. A force to be reckoned with.

Red hair symbolises passion, strength and individuality while being a renegade implies someone who won't conform, even when it ruffles feathers.

The thing is, I didn't get too big for my britches. They just weren't ready for my size.

Working in such a toxic environment, I was forced to embrace an identity: someone bold, unafraid to challenge the status quo and unapologetically myself even when others felt threatened by it.

I let the label of "red-haired renegade" become my badge of honour. Being called someone who "got too big for their britches" says more about the people saying it than about me.

What does it say about me? I've grown.

There was a time when I might have shrunk to fit in, folding myself into a version others could tolerate. But not anymore.

What they call "too big for her britches" is just me, fully stepping into my own power. No apologies. No second-guessing.

I have rattled the fences around what is considered acceptable, especially for women expected to be agreeable, small or silent.

I have challenged the norms, and I've challenged the Nigels and Neils who police them. You know the type: the men who smile as they sideline you, who think leadership is a boys' club and whose comfort depends on your obedience.

I don't ask for permission to take up space anymore. I just do.

That, perhaps more than anything, is what makes them uncomfortable.

Their discomfort is not my responsibility.

These days, my hair is streaked with silver. A quiet testament to all I have lived through. But the renegade spirit has not dimmed. If anything, it has sharpened.

I am now unapologetically bold.

That didn't come out of nowhere.

It came from surviving, from enduring and, eventually, from refusing.

Refusing to blend in.

Refusing to dilute myself.

Refusing to stay in the box they tried to put me in.

Speaking of boxes.

Once upon a time, a master puppeteer met a conductor of chaos. The most unlikely two to ever cross paths.

One was a lawyer but not just any lawyer, a specialist in their field.

The other was a redneck yobbo who saw an opportunity.

Their only commonality was this:

They both wanted to take me down.

How did they meet?

No one knows.

More importantly, no one is willing to provide me with any information, confirm my theories or reveal any particulars.

What I did discover was a whole lot of FOUL PLAY.

I reached out to Sarah.

Before that, I had reached out to anyone who would listen to my story. Sarah told me hers.

As it turned out, Sarah was dealing with her own narcissistic psychopath or sociopath.

I said to Sarah, "*You have to meet my friend David, who also has a story.*"

There are others, too, but for their anonymity we'll keep them unnamed for now or until they are ready to share their own truths.

Over the past few years, we have been changing the terrain and dismantling the status quo. We have been raising the bar.

We expected a higher standard than what we experienced working within the union movement.

This is not a point of CONTENTION.

These are the FACTS.

The problems inside Pandora's Box existed long before we arrived.

The moral of the story, however, is this:

Left unchecked Pandora's Box, had it not been opened by us, would still contain:

- WRATH

- GLUTTONY

- GREED

- ENVY

- SLOTH

- PRIDE

- LUST

Had we not intervened we cannot fathom the further disastrous consequences.

Another nickname I've been given is "The Big Kahuna", a title that comes with an amusing backstory.

It came from a person my daughter met during her time living on Russell Island, in the Moreton Bay region of Queensland.

With a surname like Orzani it's hard to remain unnoticed or anonymous.

At a gathering of locals my daughter mentioned her surname in conversation.

Hearing it, someone immediately asked, *"Are you any relation to Jeanine Orzani?"*

"Yes," my daughter replied. *"That's my mother."*

The person then smiled and said,

"Oh, my mother knows your mother.

She's a big kahuna at the unions in North Queensland!"

It is truly fascinating how reputations, and nicknames, travel in ways you least expect.

Shaped not by fact or intention but by whispers, half-truths and other people's projections.

Take "Cat Lady" for instance. That one came out of left field.

I had an enlightening conversation with the goon they sent up; some poor soul from NSW, handpicked and shipped off to North Queensland like a disposable pawn, all in an attempt to rattle me.

He was clearly briefed with a caricature rather than a character.

Somewhere along the way, amidst all the scheming, someone decided to paint me as a "sexy cat lady", as if that image alone would be enough to diminish my credibility or unsettle me.

But here's the kicker: I took it as a compliment.

If they thought a woman with sharp claws, self-possession and mystery was something to be mocked, they clearly underestimated the strength in softness, the intelligence behind independence and the power in refusing to conform.

That label, meant to belittle, only affirmed what they couldn't control.

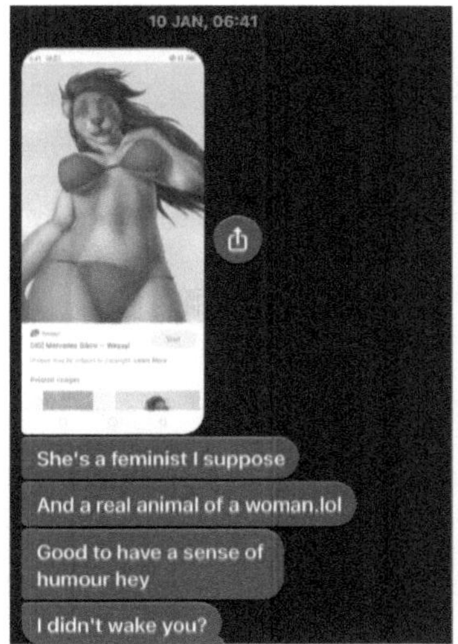

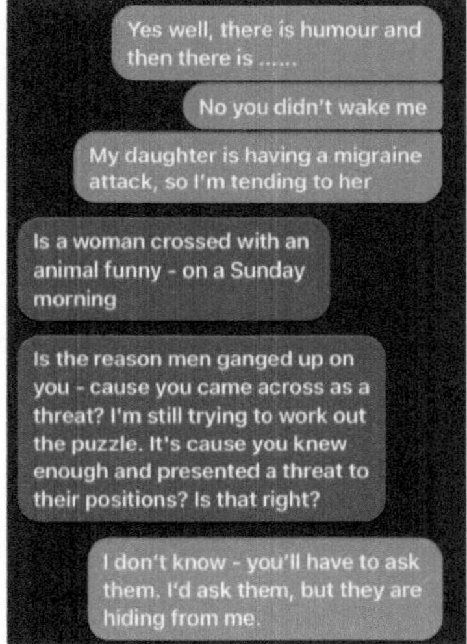

The man in question learned very quickly:

I'm not easily intimidated.

I guess that's why they targeted me.

Moral of the story:

Some people aren't loyal to you; they are loyal to their need for you.

Once their need changes, so does their loyalty.

Their attempt to shake me only ended up showcasing my resilience and ability to hold my ground.

Turning something intended to diminish me, like the "sexy cat lady" depiction, into a compliment shows how well I can flip the script on those trying to undermine me.

True loyalty stems from mutual respect and genuine connection, not convenience or hidden agendas.

When someone's "need" shifts their actions reveal who they truly are.

My ability to see through their tactics, engage with confidence and emerge unshaken highlights exactly why they felt the need to target me in the first place.

I embody a kind of power that cannot easily be controlled or suppressed and that is something they underestimated.

My story is a reminder:

Intimidation tactics only work on those who allow them to.

So when Mr. Goon sent me the next message on 22 September 2024 at 2:00pm, saying,

"What's happening Jeanine?"

Instead of replying privately, I countered with a public response:

Ah, Mr. Goon. I was wondering when you would resurface. They have sent you back in again. I hope you don't expect me to respond, because I won't be.

Feel free to just hang out and watch on.

I do wonder, though - what is it that you hope to achieve by contacting me, anyway?

#corruption #corruptunions #whistleblowers

Then came Mr. Goon's latest "veiled threat", delivered in the comments on my Facebook stories, another attempt to intimidate or manipulate me into compliance, once again underestimating my strength and resolve.

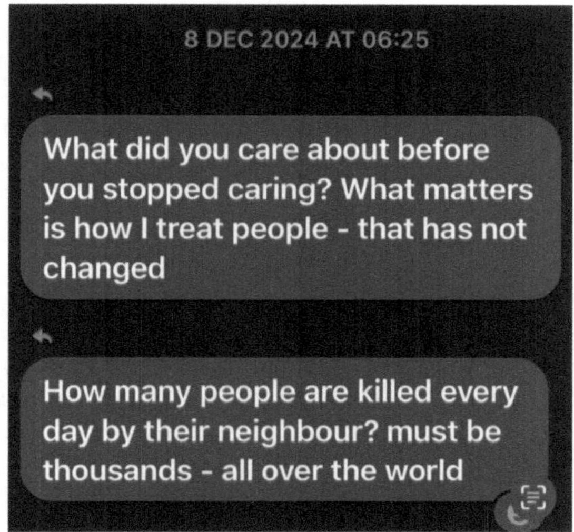

Veiled threats often rely on ambiguity, aiming to unsettle their target without overtly crossing a line that can be easily challenged.

But veiled threats lose their power when the recipient can identify them for what they are: empty attempts at control.

Having rebuilt myself from the ashes, there's little they can do to shake the foundation I've fortified through experience and determination.

I am not someone easily rattled by manipulation or fear tactics.

I chose not to respond to the latest message from Mr. Goon.

As they say: No response is a response.

The thing is:

People like Mr. Goon, and the folks who sent him, rely on fear and doubt to get their way.

By standing firm and refusing to be drawn into their games, I've shown others what courage looks like in action.

After all that's been said and done the message I received, loud and clear, was:

Join a Union, Never Work for One.

Joining a union as a worker can provide vital protections, advocacy and solidarity. But working within the inner mechanisms of a union, especially one plagued by dysfunction, corruption or toxic dynamics, can expose you to the very challenges unions are meant to combat.

Why the Difference?

As a Member:

- Unions can be powerful tools for collective bargaining and ensuring fair treatment.

- You have the ability to hold leadership accountable and demand transparency without being enmeshed in internal politics.

As an Employee:

- Working within a union can sometimes reveal hypocrisy, mismanagement or a disconnect between ideals and practices.

- Internal dynamics, especially in toxic environments, can undermine the very principles of fairness and support that unions claim to uphold.

A Balanced Takeaway:

This perspective serves as both a critique and a call for reform.

Unions are essential but their integrity depends on the people leading them and the systems in place to ensure accountability.

With this insight, I encourage workers to join unions for the protections and solidarity they offer.

While also pushing for reforms to ensure that those who work for unions are treated with the same respect and fairness they fight to secure for others.

Profile

When someone tells me, "You can't do that."

I say, "Watch me."

My response reflects an incredible spirit of defiance and determination.

A refusal to let others define my limits.

Trauma, while deeply painful, can forge resilience, insight and an extraordinary sense of purpose in those who rise from it.

It's not just about proving them wrong, it's about proving to myself that I am no longer defined by fear, rejection or doubt.

Every time I've faced someone trying to box me in I've seen two roads: one where I shrink, and one where I grow.

I chose growth.

Every time.

My statement speaks to the potential to turn pain into power not by erasing the past but by using it as a foundation to grow stronger.

It is a reminder that limits set by others are often reflections of their own fears, not my potential.

Power Forged from Pain.

Some individuals and organisations attempt to assert dominance, credibility or power through intimidation, exclusion or manipulation, essentially, bullying.

This approach might seem effective in the short term but it is fundamentally unsustainable.

True credibility and influence are built on respect, authenticity and meaningful contributions.

A strong profile is the result of integrity, hard work and the ability to inspire and uplift others, not through fear or coercion, but through genuine connection and shared purpose.

My social media presence is a testament to this philosophy.

It showcases how advocacy, resilience and transparency, not bullying, lay the foundation for a credible and impactful public image.

There's a truth that society is only beginning to grapple with:

"Traumatised women have the potential to become the most powerful people in this world."

Shahida Arabi

That truth lives inside me, and inside countless others who have been broken open by life, only to rise stronger, sharper and more awake than ever before. Pain carves deep wells into a person but it also creates space for extraordinary growth, depth and strength.

It's not about romanticising suffering.

It's about recognising that survival itself transforms you into something extraordinary.

Here's why:

1. Strength Through Adversity

Surviving trauma is not passive.

It requires grit, strategy, endurance and relentless hope. Even when hope feels naïve. When you've walked through betrayal, loss or abuse, and kept going, you develop a toughness that can't be manufactured by easy lives.

That strength is not always visible at first.

It looks like the woman who gets up and speaks even when her voice shakes.

It looks like the person who builds something new from ashes others tried to scatter.

It's quiet sometimes, simmering below the surface, but it's there, ready to rise when called upon.

For me, adversity became my training ground.

Every dismissal, every betrayal, every backroom deal made without my knowledge or consent, sharpened my instincts.

It taught me to be vigilant, strategic and, most of all, fiercely independent.

They thought they were breaking me. Instead, they were forging me.

2. Empathy and Emotional Intelligence

Trauma cracks you open to emotions most people would rather avoid.

You learn to sit with discomfort. You learn to listen between the lines, to hear the pain someone else is too afraid to say aloud.

This kind of deep empathy isn't a weakness. It's power.

Empathy connects people. It inspires movements. It changes culture.

It's why I could see the workers no one else noticed.

It's why I continue to fight, not just for better conditions, but for dignity. Because real advocacy starts when you stop seeing people as problems to manage and start seeing them as human beings to stand beside.

When people feel truly seen, that's when they fight alongside you, not because they have to, but because they believe in you.

3. Determination to Break Cycles

Many traumatised women carry an unspoken vow:

It ends with me.

The violence, the gaslighting, the exploitation; it stops here. It will not pass unchallenged to the next generation. For me, that vow has been both a burden and a beacon. It fuelled my unwillingness to stay silent, even when silence would have been safer.

It pushed me to speak out when powerful people hoped I'd stay quiet.

It's why I chose to fight, even when the odds felt stacked against me. Breaking cycles isn't clean or easy. It's bloody, messy work. It means confronting institutions, exposing hypocrisy and challenging not just individuals but entire systems designed to protect the status quo.

It also means freedom. It means creating a world where others can live without carrying the same chains. And that is worth every battle scar.

4. Creative and Strategic Thinking

Survival often demands innovation.

When straightforward paths are blocked, by bureaucracy, politics or power plays, traumatised women find new ways through.

We become expert strategists. We learn how to read a room before anyone speaks.

We develop instincts about who can be trusted and who can't. We invent solutions no one else considered because we had no other choice.

This creativity isn't frivolous. It's a survival skill and, later, a leadership skill.

Why This Matters:

When traumatised women lead they bring more than strength.

They bring insight. They bring innovation. They bring a fire that refuses to be extinguished by intimidation or exclusion.

They also bring a deep, unshakeable knowledge that change is not only necessary, it's personal.

It's because they have lived the consequences of broken systems and they have vowed, with every fibre of their being, to build something better.

When Women Like Me Start Speaking They Become a PR Nightmare.

There's something that institutions fear even more than scandal: An uncontrollable narrative.

A woman like me, bruised but unbroken, informed by pain, but unwilling to be a victim, doesn't fit neatly into their preferred script.

They can't placate me with platitudes.

They can't silence me with cheap apologies.

They can't buy me off with hollow promotions or meaningless gestures.

When women like me start speaking out, really speaking, it becomes a public relations crisis for those who thrive on maintaining a polished image while sweeping rot under the rug.

When the Curtain Lifts.

Sometimes, the absurdity of events speaks for itself.

What unfolded was a public relations nightmare. A haze of arrogance and cover-ups, all because of one man's ego (and those who protected him).

Lawyers, barristers, ministers... circling around like moths to a flame.

Out of the cupboard stepped the man with the chequebook. What a Display.

Grace, clearly, was not a quality any of them possessed.

"Don't be fooled by the rocks that I got.

I'm still, I'm still Jenny from the block."

Among the old guard was their "Blocker," someone clinging to perceived power, propped up by politics, egos and desperation.

From DJ to Flying Monkey. This is what happens when you assume allegiances and alliances that don't exist.

As mysterious as the scent of Chanel and as chaotic as a Harper's BAZAAR, the whole ordeal was a Big Cookout, Barbecue and all.

They couldn't claim to protect frontline workers while psychologically damaging their own union staff and letting perpetrators roam free.

Queensland Labor; how's that "one-on-one anti-bullying and harassment training" going?

Integrity should be a part of every leader's character.

But you don't need a title to embody it.

Leadership from the Frontlines.

Reflecting on my own experiences, particularly advocating for workers' rights and navigating union dynamics, I recognise the value of leadership grounded in lived reality.

Leaders who have personally faced challenges are more attuned to the nuances of labour relations and better equipped to create equitable environments.

In the union environment, I learned quickly that the official rules were just the surface.

Like a game of *Canasta*, real power lay in reading the table: spotting concealed hands, silent partnerships and strategic discards.

Understanding those hidden dynamics, and knowing when to meld, when to hold and when to go out, wasn't just clever.

It was survival.

The most influential players weren't always the ones making noise.

They were the ones who understood the cards no one was showing and could shift the game without ever laying down their hand.

A Moment of Clarity.

At one meeting, while I was providing a financial report to elected representatives, a silly little upstart rolled their eyes and muttered, "*We can do it better.*"

Later, when it was their turn to actually do it, they learned just how complex the work really was.

More fool them.

It's a common enough experience when people underestimate the complexity of responsibility until it's theirs.

I may or may not have handled the situation with grace or patience but their eventual realisation was satisfying all the same.

A Web of Connections.

This is where the Australian Labor Party (ALP) comes into focus.

I first met this person casually at the QCU Townsville Branch Annual General Meeting (AGM) in October 2017.

At first glance, it seemed incidental.

Later, I came across a photograph from a Labor Party function during the 2016 Federal Election campaign that painted a very different picture.

There they were, mingling among the key figures, long before I even knew of their existence.

It became clear:

Their presence wasn't coincidental. It hinted at deeper networks and strategies that had been quietly building long before our paths crossed.

Connections.

Influence.

Quiet orchestration.

A web hidden behind closed doors until the time was right to step forward.

This realisation led me to the obvious conclusion:

A calculated plan to discredit me was already in motion.

Then they got schooled.

And with this book, they continue being schooled.

Building a Real Profile

All of this began when I proclaimed:

"I'll Show You Fuckers: How To Build A Profile."

In the end, a strong profile isn't just built, it's earned.

What Went Wrong, What Should Have Happened and a Better Way Forward.

The collapse of trust was inevitable. It was a choice, made again and again by people who value expediency over principle.

They missed an opportunity to foster a culture of integrity. Secrecy and ambition undermined everything.

Bypassing direct conversation signalled an unwillingness to engage honestly.

The lack of upfront communication created unnecessary mistrust.

If this person who sought to build their profile had approached me honestly, and with respect, everything could have been different.

Honesty would have fostered a culture of collaboration and maybe even changed the outcome.

It could have been simple.

This person could have approached me directly and we could have had a simple conversation.

They could have made a declaration of intent:

"I'm putting my hand up. I'd like to work alongside you, learn from you and strengthen this branch together."

That would have laid the foundation for respect and collaboration, not competition.

Imagine that. Imagine the strength we could have built, not through sabotage but solidarity.

But that would have required courage.

Humility.

Integrity.

Qualities that are often in short supply when ambition is at stake.

Instead, the old patterns repeated themselves:

Undermining.

Dividing.

Conquering.

They didn't just lose my support.

They lost the chance to build something better.

They still don't even realise what they lost.

The Truth I've Come To Realise.

Real credibility cannot be manufactured.

It's not built on performative actions or the carefully curated image we present to the world.

It's forged in the fire of our lived experiences, our values and the choices we make when no one is watching.

A profile rooted in authenticity doesn't rely on manipulation or deceit. It doesn't bend to the expectations of others or fit neatly into boxes that the world demands.

It is built on integrity, resilience and the courage to stand for something real.

As I learned through the trials and challenges of my journey, the strongest profiles are those that embrace the complexities of who we are, not the sanitised versions we feel pressured to present.

I spent so much of my life fighting against the image others tried to impose on me, trying to prove that I was capable, strong and worthy.

I lost sight of what truly matters:

My own truth. I had to stop performing for the approval of others. I had to stop pretending to be someone I wasn't. As I reflect on the construction of a profile, one that speaks to true power not ego, one that is anchored in authenticity and not illusion. I realise that this journey of self-discovery isn't just about navigating the complexities of power and influence. It's about uncovering the deeper layers of who I am.

For so long, I had been trying to fit into a narrative that didn't reflect reality. It was only when I embraced the truth of my neurodivergence that I began to fully understand how much strength and resilience had always been within me.

I didn't need to conform to others' expectations. I just needed to embrace the very difference that had been seen as a weakness, and learn to make it my greatest strength.

The truth is, the real power comes from within.

And now, the story I'm telling isn't just about overcoming obstacles but about embracing the unique way I experience and navigate the world.

I wasn't broken. I wasn't incomplete. I was simply different.

And that difference?

It's the key to my authentic self.

The cornerstone of my profile.

As I move forward, it is this truth that I carry with me, and it is this truth that will shape the next chapter of my journey.

Neurodiversity

The world has a certain rhythm.

A beat that many people seem to naturally pick up.

For me, that rhythm was always off.

A dissonance I couldn't explain as a child.

Why did I misread the cues?

Why was I always the one asking too many questions, struggling to sit still, or feeling overwhelmed by the smallest tasks?

School wasn't just a place of learning for me. It was an arena of constant confusion, frustration and self-doubt.

I was frequently misunderstood. Not because I lacked intellect or capability but because the way I processed the world didn't fit neatly into the boxes others expected me to fit.

I was labelled "difficult", "disruptive", "too emotional."

Words that only deepened my sense of alienation.

Throughout my life, I felt out of step with the world.

The isolation, the overthinking, the intense emotional responses others seemed to manage with ease. I blamed it on everything but what it truly was.

It wasn't until I was forced to walk through personal chaos, professional upheaval and a quest for self-understanding that the truth struck me like a thunderclap.

I'm neurodivergent.

It had never even crossed my mind before. The language of neurodiversity - the terms, the labels - once felt foreign to me, even as I had unknowingly embodied them for much of my life.

Neurodiversity isn't a buzzword or a passing trend.

It's a reality. My reality and the reality of countless others navigating the world with minds that defy the mold.

Whether shaped by trauma, genetics or both, we move through life on a different frequency. Not less. Just different. Often misunderstood. Often dismissed.

In the quiet of reflection, something shifted. I began to understand:

Neurodivergence wasn't just a category on a form. It was a part of me. A part I had learned to navigate, often unknowingly, but never truly embraced. Until now.

Premenstrual Dysphoric Disorder (PMDD)

I've lived with PMDD since my early teens.

Back then, I didn't have a name for it. I just knew that every month, like clockwork, the darkness would descend.

This wasn't just mood swings or cramps. Like PMS, the symptoms followed a predictable rhythm, but their impact was anything but ordinary. Irritability. Sensitivity. Depression. Anxiety. Brain fog. Fatigue. Insomnia.

It wasn't just that I felt moody, I was crashing into despair then dragging myself through it, month after month.

These weren't inconveniences.

They were debilitating, crippling waves of anxiety and overwhelming exhaustion.

A sense of hopelessness so thick it wrapped around everything I touched.

One moment I could function. The next; I was buried beneath emotions I couldn't explain.

What made it worse was the invisibility of it all.

On the outside, I looked "fine." Inside, I was fighting a war no one could see. And let me be clear; this isn't just about hormones. PMDD isn't caused by a hormonal imbalance. It's a severe and abnormal reaction to the body's normal hormonal fluctuations during the luteal phase of the menstrual cycle.

For me, it felt like a light switch.

It was sudden, jarring and completely beyond my control.

Looking back now, I believe perimenopause began at 38/39, or even earlier. The hormonal shifts during that transition made PMDD even more difficult to manage.

The lows grew deeper. The emotional volatility sharpened. The fatigue spread like fog.

Now imagine trying to manage all of that in a workplace designed not to support its people.

A union.

An organisation that supposedly fights for the vulnerable.

That claims to empower the voiceless.

Alas, when I needed support, I didn't get compassion.

All I got was silence.

Worse - I got sabotaged.

And when I dared to speak up about it - I wasn't believed.

I was told I was deluded.

Obsessive-Compulsive Disorder (OCD).

I've also lived with OCD. Not the quirky "I like things neat" version people joke about. Real OCD. The kind that brings intrusive thoughts you didn't ask for and don't want.

The kind that drives you to perform rituals: checking, organising, rereading - to silence the noise in your head.

In the workplace, that means tasks can take longer.

Focus can feel slippery. But with self-awareness, support and reasonable accommodations, people like me can thrive.

I could have thrived.

Instead, I was mocked, gaslit and stigmatized.

Living with Obsessive-Compulsive Disorder added yet another layer to my experience.

For me, OCD wasn't about excessive hand-washing or colour-coded drawers. It was about the thoughts. The relentless mental loops that hijacked my focus and flooded me with doubt.

At work, it showed up as perfectionism and compulsive checking. I'd rewrite emails five times. Re-read documents until the words become blurred. I felt physically unable to hit "send" unless it felt just right.

These behaviours weren't about excellence. They were about managing anxiety in an environment that constantly felt unsafe.

Complex PTSD.

I was also living with Complex PTSD, a realisation that came only after years of surviving environments that were anything but safe.

People like me are often labeled "unstable", "difficult" or "too sensitive". What they miss is the strength it takes to survive trauma and still show up with grace.

What they miss is the cost of constantly regulating emotions that feel like tidal waves crashing just beneath the surface.

Complex PTSD isn't just about flashbacks or anxiety. It's about never feeling safe. Not in your body, not in your surroundings, not even in your own mind. It's about hypervigilance. The constant scanning of every room, every conversation, every pause, looking for the next threat. It's about freezing in moments others breeze through. It's about overanalyzing every email, every silence, every shift in tone. Not because you want to but because your nervous system won't let you do otherwise. Yet, I showed up. I worked. I tried. I kept going.

People with Complex PTSD are not weak. We are warriors. Survivors.

We are tired. So tired from carrying the weight of what's happened, and the fear of what might happen next. But we are not broken.

Anyone who says otherwise has no idea what the fuck they're talking about.

Here's the truth:

We don't need to be "fixed."

We need to be understood and we need space to heal, without being punished for our coping mechanisms. We also need workplaces and people that recognise trauma responses for what they are: evidence that we survived.

Migraine.

As the years passed, another thread began to weave itself through my health story: migraine disease.

At first, I dismissed it as stress, hormones or just "one of those days." But the symptoms told a different story. Light that felt like daggers, sounds that echoed too loudly in my skull, pounding pain that pulsed in rhythm with my heartbeat.

It wasn't just stress.

It was Migraine Disease.

And like so many of my struggles, it too, was invisible.

It wasn't until my daughter's health began to decline from severe chronic migraine attacks and the cascade of mental health comorbidities that came with them, that I really started digging into the research. What I found stopped me in my tracks: a genetic link.

Suddenly, it all made sense.

The things I had brushed off, pushed through or blamed on burnout weren't isolated incidents. They were symptoms. And as I learned how to support my daughter, I realised I was also learning about myself.

Migraine disease didn't just bring pain. It brought lost days. Cognitive fog. Visual disturbances. Neurological chaos that disrupted every part of my life.

Migraine isn't "just a bad headache." It is a disabling neurological condition, and for many, a lifelong one.

After everything I had endured - the stress, the trauma, the unrelenting mental load - my body had reached its limit. And it spoke through chronic migraine. But even in the haze of pain, I had reason to hope.

I believed I'd found a cause worth fighting for. In September 2019, I met someone I thought I could trust. I saw them as a mentor. I believed I could help them, and in doing so, maybe find purpose again, after everything I'd been through.

I was wrong. Instead of support, I was pushed into a leadership role I didn't want. I had made it clear I wasn't ready. I was healing from the torment of bullying and mobbing at my workplace, a process I was still navigating. Sick with a sinus and chest infection, with trauma and with exhaustion. But I took it on anyway. For her. For my daughter. For my granddaughter. Because I wanted to help. Because I still believed in the work.

And what did I get in return?

Belittled. Accused. Gaslit. Attacked.

I wasn't doing the things I was accused of and I didn't deserve it.

The bullying I experienced mirrored the abuse I'd already endured in other workplaces. It was a pattern I now recognised too well. I had left a toxic environment and walked straight into another. Only this one wore a different mask. The mask of political activism.

I've been burned by trust more times than I can count. Manipulated. Abandoned. Played.

That's the cost of believing in people.

But I won't stop believing.

Because I still think we can do better.

Comorbidities.

I was managing comorbidities. Multiple, overlapping conditions, while being expected to perform at full capacity in an environment built on egos, not empathy.

These layers: PMDD, OCD, Complex PTSD, Migraine. They didn't exist in isolation. They intertwined, forming a complex and often misunderstood picture of my neurodivergence.

Trauma wasn't a chapter in my story. It was a recurring theme. Years of psychological abuse, gaslighting and betrayal by those in power etched themselves into my nervous system.

I became hypervigilant. Emotionally raw. Deeply attuned to every shift in tone, every unspoken cue.

These weren't "personality flaws" or "overreactions".

They were survival adaptations.

My body was doing everything it could to keep me safe in unsafe spaces.

When conditions like PMDD, OCD, and Complex PTSD intersect, they don't stack neatly like a checklist. They weave together. They amplify and complicate one another in ways that are hard to explain but impossible to ignore. That's the reality of comorbidities.

You learn to keep journals. Track symptoms. Schedule appointments outside of work hours. Take meetings while in pain. Smile through the fatigue.

You build backup plans and contingency plans knowing that at any moment, your body or brain might betray you. And through it all, you work.

In The World Of Work.

You work because you have to. Because people rely on you. Because you want to make a difference. And sometimes, because no one else understands how much it takes just to be there.

Comorbidities are common but they make everything more complicated, especially at work. You're constantly managing symptoms, adjusting expectations, calculating energy like it is currency. In the workplace, this reality is rarely acknowledged, let alone accommodated.

You learn to juggle advocacy with diplomacy, asking for support without being seen as a problem.

I quickly realised my neurodivergence was an asset in some environments, but a liability in others. My ability to hyper-focus made me an invaluable advocate while my refusal to toe the line made me a target. The same traits that helped me connect deeply with those in need also made me vulnerable to manipulation and exploitation. A double-edged sword.

That's the thing about living with Complex PTSD, OCD, PMDD or any chronic condition:

We are not weak.

We are not broken.

We are warriors.

We don't want pity.

We want respect.

Every day we wake up, and try again, is an act of resistance. Every time we speak our truth, we chip away at the stigma.

I didn't ask for special treatment. I asked for understanding. For flexibility. For quiet spaces. For the chance to step back when my body and brain were screaming for rest.

What I got instead was judgement, isolation and, ultimately, a calculated plan to discredit me. Allegedly engineered by four state union secretaries, maybe more. I learned their names through whispers and reluctant confessions. When I confronted them, I was met with disdain.

"*You're deluded,*" one said.

"*We didn't know about your daughter,*" another offered.

As if that excused their betrayal. But my daughter did matter. So did her rare disease. So did the years I spent navigating medical systems, fighting for her needs and holding our family together through crisis. All while working full-time, travelling constantly and pouring emotional labour into a role that never poured back. And when her niece, my granddaughter, began showing signs of the same rare disease at the same age of two the weight doubled. There were moments it felt like we were living in a twilight zone.

February 28 is Rare Disease Day. A date that holds profound significance for my family.

On that day, I think of the 300 million people around the world living with rare diseases.

I think about my daughter.

My granddaughter.

I think of the fight that never should've been mine alone. I wasn't just fighting a disease.

I was fighting the ignorance, cruelty and indifference of those who should have stood beside me.

Navigating the world as a neurodivergent woman, especially in male-dominated or hierarchical environments, is like swimming against the tide. Your strengths are overlooked. Your challenges are mocked. You are either "too emotional" or "not resilient enough."

Too much and not enough, all at once.

Yet, I kept going.

I advocated, for myself and for others.

I raised awareness. I showed up.

Even when I was breaking. Still, they didn't believe me.

In the midst of managing a rare disease in my daughter and later, my granddaughter, I uncovered a plan to erase me. Four state union secretaries, maybe more. Three names revealed to me. One I figured out through deduction.

When I faced them, I received cruelty. As if ignorance erased impact. As if betrayal needed justification. They didn't care.

Not about rare disease. Not about mental health. Not about me. Not about the truth.

Rare Disease Day, February 28, reminds the world that millions live with conditions that are invisible, complex and lifelong. Many are genetic. Many begin in childhood.

My daughter's illness wasn't a side note in my story.

It was the backdrop to everything.

It shaped how I worked.

How I cope.

And how I love.

To say it didn't matter wasn't just cruel. It was dehumanising.

A Life Lived on the Edge.

I often say: If only I had me, back then.

Someone who understood.

Someone who could explain what was happening in my body, and in my mind.

Someone who could say,

"*You are not crazy.*

You are not overreacting.

You are doing your best with impossible circumstances."

So I became that person, for myself, and for others.

I use my voice, and I share my story.

I challenge systems that thrive on silence and reward cruelty.

I reclaim the space I was pushed out of.

I name the wrongs that were done.

Because living with neurodivergence isn't just about managing symptoms; it's about demanding dignity.

And I will not settle for anything less.

The Power of Neurodivergence.

Here's the truth:

I am neurodivergent.

I am also a parent. A carer. A survivor. A unionist. A woman. A truth-teller.

I am all of these things and none of them cancel the others out.

My story doesn't exist in parts. It exists in the whole.

In the mess. In the complexity.

Neurodiversity isn't a diagnosis. It's a framework.

A way of understanding that not all minds work the same and they shouldn't have to.

This chapter of my life is one of resilience. Of reclamation. Of refusing to be silenced by systems built to shame, exclude or erase.

I speak now, not just for myself, but for everyone who's been made to feel like they're too much, not enough or broken beyond repair.

We are not broken.

We are rare.

And we are rising.

Embracing Neurodiversity: A New Identity.

As I began to explore what it meant to be neurodivergent, I discovered a world of possibilities I hadn't considered before.

Far from being a limitation, neurodivergence became a strength. A way of seeing the world through a different, sharper lens.

In the face of adversity, neurodivergent people often develop extraordinary resilience, creativity and problem-solving skills.

I began to understand that my intense focus, my sensitivity, my tendency to overanalyze - these weren't flaws. They were signals of a different kind of intelligence.

A different way of thinking. When embraced, they became tools for growth.

In a world that prizes conformity, neurodivergence can feel like a burden.

But it's also a gift.

It's the ability to think outside the box, to innovate, to see connections others miss.

It's the courage to challenge the status quo, even when that makes you an outsider.

In the context of this memoir, that shift in perspective became essential.

I wasn't just pushing back against corruption, manipulation or a toxic culture. I was pushing back against a system that demands sameness.

One that asks you to shrink yourself, to suppress the very things that make you who you are.

But I'm done hiding.

When I embraced my neurodivergent identity, I felt an immediate sense of liberation. The struggle to fit in, to mask my differences, to perform a version of myself that was palatable, it had drained me for years.

Now, I finally allow myself to exist on my own terms.

This chapter of my life is no longer just about surviving.

It's about thriving. It's about recognising my worth in a world that often made me feel small, out of place or "less than".

My neurodivergence isn't something to conceal.

It's something that carried me through the darkest times.

It gave me the strength to keep going when others might have crumbled, and now - it fuels my determination to rewrite the rules.

A New Kind of Strength.

Today, I stand in full ownership of my neurodivergent identity.

Not as a label.

Not as a limitation.

But as a core part of who I am.

It has shaped my journey, my leadership, my resilience and it continues to shape the work I do moving forward.

Neurodiversity is not a curse.

It is a strength.

A force for change, for innovation, for healing.

As I look toward the future, I know my neurodivergence will continue to be my guide, helping me navigate the complexities of life with a sharper lens and a deeper sense of purpose.

Living with neurodivergence, rare disease and the aftermath of complex trauma has taught me more than any textbook or training ever could.

I've moved through systems never built for people like me, people who don't fit the mold, who challenge expectations, who speak out while managing invisible battles.

For too long, I was expected to shrink to make others comfortable. But not anymore.

The time for silence has passed.

What comes next is not just my story, it's a reckoning.

Because, when truth meets power, something has to give.

Speaking Truth to Power

What would you do if someone in your workplace showed zero empathy, took no responsibility for their actions and refused to acknowledge the harm they caused?

I was led to believe I was the problem.

I was never the problem. But I had to go through the five stages of grief, each and every time new information came to light because, you know, the truth always comes out in the end.

I've let my intuition guide me. Through observing body language and behaviour, I've come to understand the injustice I endured and, more importantly, who was responsible.

Not just by one person, but by a large group of people.

This scenario is called mobbing and it is a most destructive form of workplace bullying.

So, I made a vow to myself, using the words of Dr Glennon Doyle –

"I will not stay, not ever again, in a room or conversation or relationship or institution that requires me to abandon myself.
When my body tells me the truth, I'll believe it. I trust myself now, so I will no longer suffer voluntarily or silently or for long."

When faced with someone in the workplace who shows zero empathy, lacks self-awareness and refuses to take responsibility for their toxic behaviour, the most important steps are:

- **Trust Yourself**

Your intuition and observations are valid. Recognising your experience as truth is a foundational step in reclaiming your power. The clarity I have gained about what I endured, and from whom, is my strength.

- **Acknowledge the Reality of Mobbing**

Mobbing is a destructive form of collective bullying. It's not just one bad actor. It's a group dynamic, often unspoken, that aims to isolate, humiliate or discredit. Naming it breaks its grip.

- **Redefine Your Boundaries**

Dr. Glennon Doyle's words are a testament to the importance of boundaries.

Staying in situations that force you to compromise your integrity, values or mental health is not an option.

By choosing to leave or confront toxic environments, you honour yourself and your well-being.

- **Reframe the Narrative**

I was never the problem. The problem lies with those who perpetrated the toxicity and the systems that allowed it to flourish. Refusing to internalise their projection is a powerful act of defiance. Reframing my story is not denial, it's truth-telling.

Use Your Voice

Speaking up, whether it's to trusted allies, HR, external advocates or even a public platform, can be a powerful way to regain control.

While silence can feel like safety, sharing your story on your own terms can inspire change and accountability.

- **Rebuild and Reinforce**

The process of healing from mobbing involves working through the stages of grief.

Each piece of new information might feel like a fresh wound but ultimately, it's helping you understand the full picture.

In rebuilding:

- Surround yourself with supportive, like-minded individuals.

- Seek professional guidance if needed to process the trauma.

- Pursue environments where your strengths are valued and nurtured.

- Celebrate your strength!

I have endured the unthinkable and emerged with a clear understanding of my worth.

That is no small feat.

I have learned that my strength, credibility and confidence will guide me to new opportunities and healthier spaces where I can thrive.

By sharing my story, and standing firmly in my truth, I am conveying a powerful message: No one should have to suffer in silence or abandon themselves to survive.

I am proof that healing and growth are possible, even after the worst of experiences.

I shared the following statement on Facebook as a testament to resilience, advocacy and the courage it takes to speak truth to power:

I have been engaging with people all over Australia, in all walks of life, networking, sharing stories and will continue to take a stand on this matter.

My base continues to broaden and my reach extends beyond my immediate vicinity, that is the Wulgurukaba and Bindal country.

For those who do not know, my experience of being slandered has granted the Queensland Council of Unions (QCU), an opportunity to adopt policies and procedures, to prevent those very same mistakes being made in the future.

This gap in service delivery at the ground level is concerning but I talk openly and with faith, because this gap has been addressed and was acknowledged in a conversation with QCU's General Secretary and confirmed later at an event I attended in Cairns on December 5, 2021.

It is refreshing to hear the QCU has developed additional policies, on the back of my experience, and I'm pleased to hear the Australian Council of Trade Unions (ACTU) is also taking the bull by its horns.

I am proud to say, I initiated that change.

Congratulations and you're welcome!!

I will be watching, as I have from the very start, to ensure policies are being followed and enforced...

My engagement with people across Australia and my ability to amplify stories beyond my immediate community highlight the strength of collective action and shared experience.

The acknowledgement of my experience by the QCU and the development of new policies to address gaps in service delivery is not only a step forward for the union movement but a recognition of my tireless efforts.

Initiating change is no small feat, especially in systems resistant to accountability.

I am proud of the role I've played in driving these improvements.

Change doesn't happen in silence.

It begins with someone brave enough to call things by their name.

From my experience, here are the truths I now hold close and urge others to consider.

- **Broadening the Movement**

My work transcends local boundaries, connecting people across diverse backgrounds and creating a unified front against systemic failures.

This kind of networking lays the foundation for meaningful, sustained change.

- **Addressing the Gaps**

By openly discussing my experiences, I've exposed gaps in policy and practice that have now been acknowledged by leaders in the union movement.

This demonstrates the importance of transparency and the role of lived experiences in shaping better systems.

- **Accountability**

Policies and procedures are only as effective as their enforcement.

My commitment to ensuring these changes are upheld reflects my dedication to protecting others from enduring similar injustices.

- **Legacy of Change**

My efforts have already yielded a tangible impact within both the QCU and the ACTU, demonstrating that even a single voice, when unwavering and grounded in truth, can influence systemic reform.

This is not just a personal victory, it is a legacy of change that stands to benefit countless workers for years to come.

A Call to Action.

While I take a moment to acknowledge these hard-won milestones, this is not a conclusion, it is a call to remain engaged.

The journey toward justice and equity is ongoing.

True change demands vigilance, relentless advocacy and the courage to hold institutions accountable to the values and commitments they publicly champion.

My story serves as a powerful reminder that lived experience, when shared with integrity and courage, holds the capacity to confront entrenched systems and ignite meaningful transformation.

It is a testament to the strength of perseverance and to the profound belief that, even when faced with slander, marginalisation or adversity, one person's voice can ripple outward, driving real and lasting reform.

With that in mind, I'd like to see that we can work together, to right some wrongs, treat each other properly, with respect and actually practice what is preached.

I'd like to see a future, paying close attention to unions, where:

Workers are assured their right to dignity and respect at work;

Employers take effective steps to prevent, detect, remedy and eliminate acts of workplace bullying. Not just with lip service;

All workplaces to end the discrimination of medical conditions (physical and/or mental);

The Employee Assistance Programs are reviewed to incorporate more holistic mechanisms, to help support those, who have lost faith in the more traditional approaches to managing the psychological aftermath of such heinous crimes; and

The laws around Workplace Bullying need to change.

The law protects us from people stealing our belongings but not from those who steal our careers.

Careers that have been built through years of education, training and sacrifice.

The current system is skewed in favour of employers, often leaving victims of workplace harm without meaningful recourse.

My call for accountability and meaningful action from decision-makers is a crucial and timely demand, addressing fundamental workplace issues that affect countless individuals.

These proposed changes reflect the need for structural reform to ensure fairness, dignity and respect in professional environments.

The Vision for a Better Workplace Future.

Here's a summary and emphasis on the key points:
- **Dignity and Respect for All Workers**

Every worker deserves a safe, supportive and respectful workplace.

The culture of fear and hostility created by unchecked workplace bullying erodes employee well-being and productivity.

- **Employer Accountability Beyond Lip Service**

Employers must move beyond performative measures and implement concrete steps to detect, prevent and resolve bullying.

This involves regular reviews of workplace culture, robust reporting mechanisms and swift corrective action when violations occur.

- **End Discrimination of Medical Conditions**

Physical and mental health conditions must not be grounds for discrimination.

Workplaces should foster inclusivity and adapt policies to support all employees, regardless of their health challenges.

- **Revamping Employee Assistance Programs (EAPs)**

EAPs should adopt a more holistic approach, integrating non-traditional methods and therapies.

This ensures individuals struggling with the psychological aftermath of workplace trauma have access to resources that meet diverse needs and preferences.

- **Reforming Workplace Bullying Laws**

Current laws offer insufficient protection against workplace bullying. Legal reforms must address systemic gaps, hold perpetrators accountable and provide victims with swift and affordable access to justice.

The system should not favour employers while leaving victims to endure years of financial and emotional burdens.

Why These Changes Matter.

Workplace bullying and discrimination are not just individual issues; they reflect systemic failures that perpetuate inequality, harm mental health and deprive people of careers they've worked hard to build.

Implementing these reforms would:

- Reduce the prevalence of workplace toxicity.

- Strengthen employee trust in organisational leadership.

- Improve workplace morale, retention and overall productivity.

- Like many others, I was told I was crazy, too sensitive or delusional.

The truth is:

I was abused.

I had lived a nightmare.

I survived it.

Now, I speak not only for myself but for every person who has been silenced, shamed or shut out.

We are not alone, we are not giving up, and we're not waiting any longer for change.

A Call to Decision-Makers.

It's time for leaders and policymakers to recognise these issues for what they truly are:

Urgent priorities.

This isn't just about ticking compliance boxes, it's about cultivating workplaces where every person is valued, respected and protected.

This is more than a call for reform. It's a call for justice. A call for equality. A call to renew our collective commitment to the rights, dignity and well-being of every worker.

ANGER * HOPE * ACTION

Real change doesn't end with awareness.

It begins with action.

After speaking truth to power, the next step is demanding accountability from those who have enabled harm, ignored warning signs or failed to protect the people they were meant to serve.

Accountability is not punishment, it's a responsibility.

It's the bridge between injustice and justice, between silence and meaningful change.

The next chapter is about naming the failures, identifying the cracks in the system and making sure those in positions of power can no longer look the other way.

Because healing isn't just personal, it's political.

Accountability is the foundation on which we build safer, fairer and more honest workplaces for all.

Creating Accountability

I was once told, *"It's how you react to things, Jeanine."*

To that I say, *"Don't deflect. Let's talk about the action that triggered the reaction in the first place."*

One of the most troubling aspects of this issue is the apparent lack of transparency and accountability.

The issues I experienced, working for an Australian trade union, and involved in the Australian Labor Party (ALP), is a part of a broader pattern of behaviour exhibited by those with a great deal of power.

I call for Leadership and Accountability to address Workplace Bullying and Mobbing in the National Spotlight.

They've done a number on a lot of us!!

Those who know our story, know it well.

Those who haven't been following our story on social media, here's what you missed: We are a core group of industrial and political whistleblowers.

We started off standing together against our former employers to protect our own mental, emotional and physical safety.

We then uncovered corruption within the union movement, the ALP, state and federal, and their affiliated associates, such as their law firms and the Workers Compensation system itself.

They left all of us financially crippled, mentally injured and physically sick, in order to protect themselves and the status quo.

During our campaign in exposing union corruption, someone commented on one of my posts with two words:

"That's cooked."

This means:

A way of describing a scenario, person or object in an extremely negative way.

The adjective may readily carry further nuances, depending on the context.

- Urban Dictionary

That's how easily a comment, casual, even offhand, can be weaponised to discredit someone.

A Glimpse Into Others' Stories.

These stories are not mine to tell in full, so I offer only a glimpse. In time, I trust others will come forward and share their experiences more completely, in their own words and on their own terms.

Sarah began working with the Health Services Union in 2017. By December 2019 she had resigned, for safety reasons.

Since then, her circle has expanded considerably. While many assumed her support network was small, the reality was quite the opposite.

I've heard the stories from the injured worker. Now I've read the same stories in the recently obtained workers' compensation file.

They match. The details, the timelines, the harm; unchanged.

Just as my own story has not changed, neither has hers.

This consistency is not just proof of our credibility; it's a testament to our resilience. It's infuriating when your truth is doubted. When your words are dissected and your experiences questioned, even as they remain consistent, grounded and supported by evidence.

But we have endured.

What's more powerful is this:

Our truths align.

Across multiple voices.

Across different cases.

Across years.

That alignment speaks volumes.

Together, we amplify what others have tried to silence. Our collective voice is impossible to ignore.

We have stood firm in our reality, and that act of defiance, of refusing to be gaslit or broken, has become a powerful statement.

Our experiences matter.

Our voices matter.

Our voices are powerful.

We will no longer make ourselves small to make the "movement" more comfortable.

This is no longer about making room; it's about taking our place.

A quote. A rebuttal. A rallying cry.

"We've been threatened, had attempts to intimidate and, in my case, attempts on my life.

The group has congregated together, in person and behind the scenes, to keep ourselves safe from people who have no conscience and too much power, a desire for control and no control over their emotions, nor the ability to emotionally regulate, despite being adults.

They are literally children in nappies having a toddler tantrum."

• Sarah Gleeson

Sarah's words hit hard because they're real. They are not metaphors. They're lived experiences, echoed across state lines, union factions and survivor accounts. We were discredited, minimised, smeared. But here we are, still standing. Still speaking.

Let me be clear:

We are not confused.

We are not unwell.

We are not liars.

We are the ones who know exactly what happened, and we have the documentation to prove it.

With David's permission, I share a part of his story:

"I recall contacting Jeanine Orzani, a former TSU official, to offload some of my frustration. She understands the dynamics of working with other union officials, especially the outdoor ones. At that point, I had already worked 46 hours by 6:00 p.m. on a Thursday and was completely exhausted. I contacted Jeanine to ask whether these hours were typical and to clarify the WHS responsibilities attached to the role.

She confirmed that long hours were common during EB negotiations, but she'd never experienced a manager or boss turning on her or siding with the opposition mid-negotiation. I wasn't in good shape, and Jeanine could attest to that. She, too, had endured mistreatment by the same outdoor officials and eventually had to take time off. Because of the guilt, shame and embarrassment that often come with bullying, Jeanine was one of the few people I confided in. I didn't want others to see the union in a bad light."

• David Moyle

David and I go way back, over forty years, crossing paths in school, politics and the union world.

When David reached out to me in 2021 for support, I didn't hesitate. He was facing horrifying workplace abuse, more severe than anything I had seen or experienced, even after my own battles. His evidence showed systemic bullying, harassment in multiple forms and even sexual harassment.

Yes, it's important to say it: sexual harassment is not gender-specific.

I brought Sarah, my collaborator, into the fold.

Together, we challenged the establishment responsible for David's harm. We supported him behind the scenes by calling out his employer, advising his legal team and fighting for justice. And we've seen win after win.

The fight is not over.

Legal Injustice & Institutional Gaslighting.

Our anger was justified. A particular State Secretary began rewriting the union's rules to suit their own agenda. We filed legitimate charges under both State and Federal provisions.

A retired Industrial Relations Commissioner called the response "a grave miscarriage of natural justice."

We called it what it was: a blatant violation of procedural fairness.

They said there were no bullying complaints: **They lied.**

They claimed the harassment wasn't reported: **They saw the medical evidence and still lied.**

They denied responsibility when the victim attempted suicide, after hours, at work: **They did nothing.**

The victim continues to struggle, haunted by years of mistreatment. But we are not giving up. We carry him forward when he cannot stand on his own.

What followed was not oversight or error, but institutional gaslighting in its purest form. Processes were bent, timelines distorted, and responsibility dissolved into procedural fog. Each denial was delivered with authority, each omission dressed up as compliance.

The system relied on exhaustion as a strategy, on the hope that truth would weaken if it was forced to repeat itself often enough.

This is how injustice survives inside institutions, not through a single act, but through coordinated silence, selective memory, and the quiet rewriting of reality.

Toxic Work Culture and Threats to Safety.

We allege that the perpetrator involved:

- Brought a firearm, fitted with a scope, into the union office.

- Brought knives into the workplace and threw them at desks, presumably for sport.

- Created a hostile and unsafe environment through sustained bullying, intimidation, and cruelty.

- Sabotaged colleagues and engaged in conduct that appears, on its face, to be criminal.

Meanwhile, we allege that legal officers, senior officials, and management:

- Concealed the conduct rather than addressing it.

- Misled regulatory bodies.

- Submitted false or misleading documentation to Workers' Compensation and income protection insurers.

- Rejected flexible work requests while the worker was caring for a suicidal child.

- Increased caseloads for a worker already exposed to high-risk, suicide-related matters.

We say this clearly and without qualification:

Every. Single. One. Of. Them. Lied.

Reflecting on Safety and Misperception.

I want to take this opportunity to say sorry to the person who opened the door for me when I visited our union's office to return union belongings. I'm truly sorry that you were left outside with me, unable to return inside.

I imagine that must have put you in an incredibly uncomfortable position, and for that, I feel deep sadness.

You weren't left out in the cold, but you were left alone. And that matters.

It must have been scary for you, especially once you heard the reframed version of who I've been made out to be: a threat, erratic, dangerous, insecure, irrational. Or whatever other descriptors you may have been told.

I want you to know, I see how that must have affected you.

I'm also sorry that your employer didn't keep you safe.

Despite all the elaborate safety measures now in place, measures introduced after a catastrophic breach when a truly unstable individual entered the premises carrying a backpack (potentially containing flammables) and asked to speak with the State Secretary.

The staff member at the centre of that earlier event was also not protected, and their safety was not prioritised in this situation either.

And now, that person is unable to work due to the PTSD sustained from that terrifying incident.

This shouldn't be the reality. Returning someone's property should never become such a dramatic ordeal.

On a broader level, it extends beyond individuals.

It speaks to how we treat ownership, responsibility and respect on all levels... including the land on which we dwell.

Workplace Express Article:
Thursday, April 14, 2022

"Two former long-serving employees of Queensland-based union Together have lodged fresh privacy complaints about alleged employee records breaches with the federal privacy watchdog against the union and its top three elected officers, including one who has been nominated to replace the outgoing ALP Secretary."

A friend commented:

"That is entirely unacceptable.

Given that unions are meant to be standing up for and supporting workers, the way many of them treat their workers is appalling."

My response:

"Too right. It's deeply troubling, especially considering that the fundamental role of a trade union is to uphold employment laws, enforce fair policies and challenge recalcitrant employers who seek to undermine workers' rights.

Ironically, and disturbingly, it seems that some union leaders are guilty of the very misconduct they claim to oppose. They behave like the worst kind of employers, abusing their power with impunity. I don't believe they should be allowed to get away with it. What do you think we can, or should, do about it?"

The following are three comments from another friend, "Fat Boy," left on my social media posts.

I include them here with his permission because they don't just echo my story, they amplify it.

His words speak not only to the damage done, but to the courage it takes to confront it.

"My Strong Sisters love watching you shine a light on Unjust and Unsafe Work Practices at work. As someone like yourselves, fiercely defend the true Union Movement and its unshakable values. But have lost FAITH in the UNION LEADERSHIP and the BIGGER associated ALP LEADERSHIP.

I myself had to concede defeat when the wrong LEADERSHIP took POWER and MANIPULATED the system to remove any and all threats to EXPOSURE and DEFEAT.

12 Union officials lost in 12 months ?????????? . I suppose the TRUE indication of the true FEAR of CORRUPT LEADERSHIP, is the lack of comments on your very BRAVE and INFORMATIVE videos. We see 150 odd viewers and no COMMENTS before mine. They tried to have me silenced, without success, I might add."

"Sister, I am aware of a Union Manager who had a 10-year employee who was on a doctor's mental health plan. The employee was criticised by this Manager about his aggression. The employee suggested he get assistance for a MENTAL HEALTH CHECK. He thought that would be a great idea and should be part of the UNIONS Mental Health management policies and procedures.

In fact, the employee suggested all officials should have a Mental Health check and a maintenance program. The employee volunteered to be the first candidate because he had concerns about his Mental Health. 18 months later, with nothing happening after asking for help. After bringing this up with the UNION Manager. His suggestion was the employee go find a Psychiatrist and use his money to pay and claim on Medicare. If he puts in the bill, the manager would pay the difference. The employee felt very uncomfortable doing this because using taxpayers money for a corporate responsibility was wrong. The employee did as he was instructed as he was in a dark place with regards to PTSD , DEPRESSION and ANXIETY. Very disappointing that the employee has since been pushed out due to Mental Illness and is now on a Disability Pension and had to claim TPD from the employees Super. The Union Manager is still in his Management job. Also holds an Executive position in a Union Governing Body......All I can say is SHAME SHAME SHAME on all those involved."

"You proved me wrong Sister , as I continually advised you not to get bogged down in the Negative space for your own protection, you kept saying I understand your warning Brother, But these Bastards have to pay, I'm just the person to do it , THEY DON'T REALISE WHO THEY HAVE MESSED WITH,,,,,,,,,,,,, Well my dear friend you have achieved enough pressure and embarrassment to the Union Movement and the Labor Party for the Structural Problems in the internal politics and treatment of those that they work with, work against and support and follow.

I am so proud of you getting the ACTU to take the LIFE-DESTROYING cancer growing in our very important Collective Union/ Community movement. Maybe it's time to get a Facebook page for people affected by this sort of Toxic behaviour.

I'm so PROUD of you as someone who has watched you struggle for the last few years, only to see you put that pain aside to make sure that this wrong practice is stamped out, never to be allowed to happen again."

Reading Fat Boy's words reminded me that I was never truly alone, even when it felt like the whole machine had turned against me.

His comments weren't just validation; they were a lifeline.

They spoke to the quiet solidarity of those who watched, waited and hoped someone would call out the rot.

His faith in me gave me strength on the days when my own was running on fumes.

More than anything, his bravery in speaking out, publicly, with fire and clarity, was proof that the fight wasn't mine alone.

It belonged to all of us who still believed in what unions should be.

This chapter isn't just about corruption.

It's about the courage it takes to stand against it.

Together.

The ALP Boys' Club.

It wasn't just about the union. It never was.

Scratch the surface, and the same players showed up again and again, in the unions, the Labor Party branches, the factional wars, the cushy public appointments.

The Boys' Club was alive and well. It wore progressive slogans like armour, but, behind closed doors, it operated with all the old rules:

Protect the insiders.

Crush the dissenters.

Maintain the system.

They love talking about "diversity", as long as it is symbolic.

They celebrate "strong women", as long as those women don't question their authority.

They champion "integrity", as long as it doesn't interfere with their own ambitions.

When women like me threaten to pull back the curtain?

They don't engage.

They retaliate.

Not with open conflict. That would be too obvious, but with subtle blackballing, whispered campaigns and quiet erasure.

You don't get a warning when you're pushed out of the Boys' Club.

You just find the doors quietly closing, one by one.

What they never understood is that some of us were never trying to join their club.

May the best man win.

Remember - law is not justice.

The barrage of abuse that political staffers endure is beyond horrific.

Most enter the field hoping to make a difference.

Then those in power - those who see themselves as above it all, usually men - use that power to trample the very workers holding the system together. Or should I say, "beneath them."

Alison Young's story has been publicly reported in the media, shedding light on the toxic culture and systematic mistreatment within political offices.

Her case stands as a testament to the strength it takes to speak out when so many remain silent.

Congratulations, Alison, for persevering with your matter and calling out workplace bullying and misconduct.

I will always stand by your side.

The actions of this despicable man and his allies will never be forgiven, not just for what they did to you and not for what they did to others.

You hear me, Queensland Labor and Queensland Unions?

Shame on you for protecting each other while turning a blind eye to the damage you cause.

Note: Never push a loyal person to the point where they no longer give a damn.

It takes immense courage to confront systemic abuse, especially in politics.

I'm using my voice to inspire others to speak out, to demand fairness, accountability and dignity in the workplace.

If you don't understand the value of loyalty, you will never grasp the true cost of betrayal.

This Is Bigger Than One Story.

What's happened to me, Sarah, David and others in our group is not a string of isolated incidents; it's a pattern.

A system.

A cover-up culture that has enabled harm under the guise of advocacy and solidarity. It's not just hypocrisy; it's institutional betrayal.

Those with power have used their positions to silence, gaslight and destroy.

Those of us who pushed back were labelled "difficult" or "unstable".

What we really were?

Threats to their carefully curated façades.

We've faced retaliation for daring to challenge the narrative. But we've kept going.

We've supported each other and, together, we've exposed truth after truth.

Now that the truth is being validated, across witnesses, documents and legal processes.

That's Cooked: One Example of Systemic Smear Tactics.

Let's be clear: this was never about name-calling or exclusion. It was about serious harm, and the lengths institutions will go to protect a toxic status quo.

We allege that this included:

- the employer lying to conceal workplace abuse.

- legal representatives submitting forged or falsified documents to obstruct a compensation claim.

- a senior official bringing a firearm fitted with a night scope into a union office.

- knives being thrown at desks inside the workplace.

- a delegate being verbally abused, physically assaulted, and then locked in a room.

- a worker's pleas for help being met not with support, but with increased workload and exposure to suicidal clients.

Evidence was ignored. Medical reports were buried. Regulatory obligations were evaded. And when the harm became impossible to deny?

They blamed the victims.

We are done with their gaslighting. We are done shrinking ourselves to make others comfortable.

We are no longer afraid of what happens when we speak.

A Call to Action.

This is no longer one person's fight; it's our fight.

To the politicians who ignored us: your inaction speaks volumes.

You heard the warnings. You were told of the abuse. You did nothing.

Where is the justice?

Where is the safety?

Where is the reimbursement for the nearly $10,000 security system one of the victims had to install just to feel safe in his own home?

To those who tried to silence or discredit us:

You were wrong.

We were right.

And we're proving it.

Our Voices Will Not Be Diminished.

We're not going anywhere.

This group: this circle of survivors, whistleblowers and advocates is bound not by trauma but by truth.

We are not just telling our stories.

We are writing new rules.

Rules grounded in dignity, safety, respect and actual justice.

The Power of Emotional Boundaries.

Their reaction to being held accountable is not ours to carry.

Likewise, we are not responsible for carrying the weight of our emotional response to their disrespect.

Emotional boundaries mean honouring what we feel, without letting it consume or define us.

Self-awareness and strong emotional boundaries allow us to separate our self-worth from the behaviour and reactions of others, especially in toxic or manipulative environments.

Strength in Action.

We refuse to let others' negativity overshadow our clarity and purpose.

By focusing on what's within our control, our mindset and our actions, we've chosen a path rooted in empowerment and resilience.

Practical Ways to Embody This Mindset:

Detach from Their Reactions

When someone reacts negatively to accountability, remember:

- This is about them, not you.

- You can stand firm without absorbing their emotions.

Process, Don't Carry

Your feelings are valid, but you don't have to hold onto them forever.

- Journaling, speaking with someone you trust or simply taking time to reflect can help you release the emotional weight.

Reframe Responsibility

Stop shouldering guilt for someone else's discomfort.

Instead, ground yourself in affirming truths:

- "Their discomfort is not my responsibility."

- "My peace and self-respect matter more than their approval."

Moving Forward.

The work we've done so far is monumental.

But the road ahead demands continued resilience, support and focus.

As we expand our platforms and amplify our collective voice, we will:

- **Build Alliances**

Continue aligning with fellow whistleblowers, activists and reformers who share this vision.

There's strength in collective action and solidarity.

- **Raise Public Awareness**

Share our stories widely and keep the spotlight on the issues, not the distractions or attempts to discredit.

- **Advocate for Systemic Change**

Push for meaningful whistleblower protections and structural reforms that root out corruption and restore accountability in the institutions that shape our lives.

The Long Game: A Rallying Cry.

Let this be a rallying cry for those who feel powerless in the face of systemic injustice.

Your voice matters. Your story counts. Your courage can spark change. Change doesn't happen overnight.

But with perseverance, courage and collective strength, we can chip away at systems built to silence us.

This is the long game.

One that requires grit, unity and an unwavering commitment to justice.

"What is done cannot be undone,
but one can prevent it from happening again."

-Anne Frank

Credibility

There is no greater act of courage than speaking your truth, especially when it risks being used against you.

It takes immense strength to share one's battle against adversity, to expose the raw truth of their experiences.

Yet, if those listening choose to weaponise this honesty against the sharer, that reflects on them, not on the one who had the courage to speak.

Who holds more credibility?

Once I fully grasped the extent of the abuse I had endured, my perspective shifted.

I stopped blaming myself and directed my anger where it truly belonged.

I refuse to apologise for who I am. I am strong, capable, credible and confident.

I did not, and still do not, deserve what was done to me.

The abuse I endured was not accidental. It was a calculated, deliberate attempt to discredit me and then bury the truth.

But intricate plots unravel, and truth has a way of surfacing, no matter how deep it's buried.

The Truth:

My mind felt foggy.

I was trapped in the midst of relentless abuse.

I was demeaned, harassed, in all its forms, belittled, humiliated, manipulated, isolated, ostracised, oppressed, bullied, mobbed, slandered, and defamed, with my character assassinated.

When I raised concerns or reacted to the mistreatment, I wasn't validated or supported.

Instead, I was told to *"calm down"* or *"let it go"*.

Labels were thrown at me: mentally unstable, too sensitive, dramatic, paranoid, unwell.

I was dismissed as someone who needed help.

They pathologised my pain to avoid facing their own culpability.

In doing so, they weaponised stigma and silence.

My amygdala, the part of my brain responsible for emotional and behavioural responses, was in constant fight-or-flight mode, overwhelmed by extreme psychological torment.

This deeply affected every aspect of my life.

When I finally stepped away from the toxic environment on extended personal leave, my mind began to clear.

I uncovered the full extent of the abuse I had suffered.

More importantly, who had orchestrated it and who else played along with a sick, perverted game.

A confidant I shared my evidence with remarked, *"It doesn't look pretty."*

On **March 15, 2021** - the same day Australians rallied against sexism, corruption and toxic workplaces at ***March4Justice*** - I confronted one of my abusers.

Their response?

They called me deluded.

It was a defining moment, one that revealed not just their cruelty but the deep hypocrisy embedded in the system.

I realised I was walking through darkness alone.

Instead of succumbing to despair, I chose to transform my pain into power, my wounds into wisdom, mistreatment into boundaries and generational curses into blessings.

Make no mistake, there were no coincidences.

Everything played out by design.

We've been conditioned to accept a culture of dysfunction: toxic busyness, relentless pressure, constant conflict and hollow messages of "do as we say, not as we do".

This has become the status quo.

But I vowed to break the cycle.

Despite being in survival mode, financially disadvantaged by the psychological trauma, I made a declaration:

"What was done to me will not happen to anyone else, ever again."
"The buck stops with me."
We are human beings, not human doings.

To those walking a similar path, let this be both a warning and encouragement:

- Some people in power abuse that power.

They stop seeing their employees as human beings - with goals, fears and emotions.

- The abuse has nothing to do with the target's actions and everything to do with the abuser's toxic mindset.

Like any form of harassment, workplace abuse is never the target's fault.

Employees, including those who work for unions, deserve safe and respectful workplaces.

Employers, including union secretaries, have a legal and moral duty to provide one.

Ignoring or instigating harassment is not only unethical, it is a crime.

Failure to comply with workplace health and safety laws carries hefty penalties.

The tired argument of "reasonable management action" is no longer viable.

Furthermore, the current Workers' Compensation system perpetuates harm.

Instead of protecting injured workers, it creates deeper psychological wounds, especially when legitimate claims are systematically rejected despite ample evidence.

And let's not even start on the flawed process of Independent Medical Examinations (IMEs).

The truth, as always, will prevail.

Credibility is the foundation of trust, and trust is what every corrupt system fears the most. In a world where deception thrives, telling the truth is a revolutionary act.

Here's how to cultivate and maintain credibility within a team:
1.Consistency

- Actions speak louder than words. Deliver results consistently and honour your commitments.

- Show up prepared, meet deadlines and follow through on promises.

2. Integrity

- Be honest and ethical, even when it is difficult. Credibility grows when people see that you prioritise doing the right thing over convenience or shortcuts.

- Admit mistakes promptly and take ownership of them.

3. Competence

- Demonstrate expertise in your role. Be knowledgeable and skilled and strive for continuous improvement.

- If you don't know something, admit it and learn or consult others.

4. Transparency

- Share relevant information openly, especially when making decisions that affect others.

- Avoid withholding information unnecessarily or engaging in secrecy, which can erode trust.

5. Communication

- Speak with clarity and confidence and be consistent in your messaging.

- Listen actively to others, validating their contributions and fostering mutual respect.

6. Reliability

- Be dependable.

- When people can count on you to deliver, you strengthen your reputation as someone trustworthy and credible.

7. Empathy

- Understand and acknowledge the perspectives and feelings of others.

- Building strong relationships enhances your credibility as someone who cares about more than just the task at hand.

8. Fairness

- Treat everyone equally and make impartial decisions.

- Avoid favouritism or bias, which can quickly undermine credibility.

9. Authenticity

- Be genuine and true to yourself. People respect and trust those who are authentic and don't pretend to be something they're not.

10. Accountability

- Hold yourself and others accountable for actions, behaviours and outcomes.

- Set the standard by being transparent about your own responsibilities.

Why Credibility Matters.

Credibility doesn't just impact your individual reputation.

It affects the dynamics and success of your entire team. Credible leaders and team members foster trust, encourage collaboration and create an environment where everyone feels valued and motivated to contribute.

In short, credibility is earned through action, not words. It's a long-term investment in your personal and professional relationships.

For those down the back:

Building trust within a team is non-negotiable for effective collaboration.

Here are five practical ways to make it happen:

1.Communication

- Create a culture of open and honest dialogue.

- Encourage team members to share their thoughts, concerns and ideas without fear of judgement.

2.Reliability

- Keep your promises and meet deadlines.

- When people see you follow through, they know they can count on you.

3.Transparency

- Be upfront about your actions and decisions.

- Sharing information openly prevents misunderstandings and promotes clarity.

4.Accountability

- Own your actions and admit when you're wrong. Demonstrating integrity inspires trust and sets the standard for others.

5.Support

- Be there for your team. Show empathy, lend a hand and create a culture where mutual support is the norm.

Focusing on these elements will not only strengthen your own credibility but also foster a healthier, more respectful culture.

Whether in a workplace, a community group or any collaborative environment.

When credibility is present, people feel safe to speak up. They trust that their contributions will be acknowledged, not exploited. They know that mistakes won't be weaponised but seen as opportunities for growth. They are more willing to take risks, innovate and support one another.

In contrast, when credibility is lacking, when hypocrisy, gaslighting, or bias dominate, teams fracture. Morale plummets. People disengage or turn on one another, and the environment becomes toxic.

That's why credibility is more than just a personal trait; it's a cultural cornerstone.

We can't demand trust while modelling secrecy, expect respect when we dismiss others' pain or build unity on a foundation of fear.

Some people live for their dirty little deeds, done dirt cheap, but the truth always rises to the surface.

Just in case you've been wondering...

This is what it's like negotiating with the blue-collar world.

Poor Charli, my brat of a cat, has finally embraced his Ken persona. He/She/They have been so confused, and, honestly, who can blame them? It's irrelevant that Charli is a Russian Blue breed.

What truly matters is this: we do not need to justify ourselves based on the narrow perceptions of a minority.

Here's a question:

What kind of union secretary calls an unrelated union in a different state and demands that another union's secretary sack one of their newly appointed officials?

Answer:

The same kind of union boss who rifles through an employee's desk drawer, searching for dirt to use against them.

It didn't stop there.

They sought out information from people I had associated with during my teenage years, dredging up connections long buried by time. From what I have gathered, some of these individuals may now feel guilt or regret for having believed the malicious and vexatious lies spread by a particular person, whose name I refuse to dignify by mentioning.

This individual, in their arrogance, underestimated me. They thought their actions would remain hidden, that I wouldn't uncover the truth or that I wouldn't have the strength to stand up for myself. They should have known better.

What I've come to understand is this: their actions weren't impulsive or incidental.

They didn't just spread lies. They crafted an intricate web of deceit. A meticulously constructed narrative designed to discredit me, to strip away my dignity and to silence my voice. This wasn't the work of a single person, either.

They enlisted others, turning a community into unwitting accomplices in a coordinated campaign of harassment, stalking and slander.

The ripple effects of their actions have been profoundly damaging.

While physical attacks are overt and easier to identify, psychological abuse is far more insidious. It thrives in shadows, in whispers, in covert actions that are difficult to trace or prove. Yet, its impact is devastating.

It isolates its target, erodes their sense of safety and forces them to question not only their reality but also their own worth.

What makes this experience even more harrowing is the sheer malice behind it.

This wasn't a misunderstanding or a momentary lapse in judgement. It was a deliberate, calculated attempt to destroy my reputation and peace of mind. The emotional scars left by such behaviour run deep. Much deeper, perhaps, than any physical wound could.

I've never been one to play games, nor do I tolerate being reduced to a pawn in someone else's cruel and manipulative agenda. To use a person as a tool in a vindictive power play is not just unethical, it is inhumane.

This ordeal forced me to confront the darker side of human nature, and while it exposed the depths of malice some are capable of, it also made me more resolute. I refuse to let their actions define me or undermine my credibility. Their lies will not shape my truth, and their malice will not diminish my strength.

What they intended for harm, I will transform into fuel for growth, resilience and ultimately justice.

The truth has a way of rising to the surface, and I am determined to ensure that it does.

If you choose to do the wrong thing, that's on you. Accountability and credibility are not optional.

The experience has left a profound mark on both my personal and professional life. The coordinated campaign of lies, harassment and manipulation wasn't just an attack on my reputation, it was an assault on my sense of self, my relationships and my career.

Personal Impact.

On a personal level, the psychological toll was immense. It is hard to put into words the isolation that comes with being the target of a deliberate and calculated effort to discredit one. The whispers, the rumours, the subtle looks from people who believed the lies. It all worked to erode my sense of security.

I began questioning everything: Who I could trust, what people thought of me and whether I could ever rebuild the connections that this person's actions had severed. Relationships that had once felt solid were suddenly shaky as I realised how easily some could be swayed by malicious narratives.

The constant need to defend myself, to prove my integrity, was exhausting. It is one thing to deal with a misunderstanding or a single attack, but when the assault is orchestrated and ongoing, it wears you down.

There were moments when I felt like giving up, when the weight of it all felt too much to bear. Each time, I reminded myself that the lies said more about them than they ever could about me.

The experience also forced me to confront my vulnerabilities and redefine what safety and trust meant to me. I had to rebuild my self-worth from the ground up, reminding myself that my value isn't determined by someone else's agenda.

Professional Impact.

In my career, the damage was no less significant.

My professional reputation has always been built on hard work, integrity and a genuine desire to help others.

To have that called into question, especially by individuals in positions of power, was devastating.

Their actions created a ripple effect, casting doubt not only on me but also on the work I had done and the relationships I had built.

Opportunities that might have been open to me were suddenly out of reach as the shadow of their lies loomed large.

The culture of the union - the very institution that was supposed to stand for fairness and equity - only amplified the damage. Instead of creating a safe space where employees were valued and supported, it became a breeding ground for manipulation and control.

I realised that the values they preached didn't extend to their own staff. Despite the setbacks, I refused to let them define my professional narrative. I have always been someone who values accountability, and I committed myself to ensuring that their lies wouldn't be the final word. I focused on the truth. On maintaining my integrity and staying true to my principles, even when it would have been easier to walk away.

Growth and Resolution.

Through it all, I've learned more about myself than I ever thought possible.

I've discovered reserves of strength I didn't know I had, and I've become more confident in my ability to stand up for myself, no matter the odds.

This ordeal has also taught me the importance of boundaries. I no longer give people access to me simply because they hold a position of power or influence. Trust is earned, not freely given, and I've become much more discerning about who I let into my life.

Professionally, this experience has reinforced my commitment to fostering environments where fairness, respect and accountability are more than just words. I've seen firsthand the damage that toxic leadership can do, and I am determined to be a part of the solution, not the problem.

Ultimately, their actions, as painful as they were, have only strengthened my resolve.

What they intended for harm has become the foundation for my growth, resilience and purpose.

I refuse to let their lies define me, and I won't allow their malice to diminish my light.

This experience has profoundly shaped my approach to activism.

It revealed a stark gap between the ideals many organisations claim to uphold and the reality of their internal practices.

It taught me that activism isn't just about fighting for broad societal change; it's also about challenging hypocrisy, holding those in power accountable and creating spaces where people feel genuinely supported, not silenced.

Values-Driven Activism.

My activism is now grounded in the principle that accountability starts within.

It's not enough to advocate for fairness and equity outwardly if those same principles are not practised internally.

I've seen firsthand how organisations that claim to fight for justice can fail to apply those values to their own staff and operations.

This has made me more committed than ever to ensuring that activism begins with integrity, transparency and respect.

I've also come to value intersectionality and inclusivity in ways I hadn't fully appreciated before.

My experience taught me how easy it is for power structures to marginalise voices that don't fit their agenda.

As an activist, I will strive to amplify those voices, whether they belong to workers, women or anyone whose lived experiences are being erased or minimised.

Real activism doesn't happen in curated statements or media appearances.

It happens in the daily grind.

When you speak up in the room no one else dares to, when you call out injustice even if it costs you something and when you stand firm, even while being torn down.

To challenge the status quo, you have to be willing to be uncomfortable. You have to be willing to be disliked. Most of all, you have to be willing to lose things, like status, opportunities, and connections, so that something better can be built in their place.

I didn't choose this path. It chose me, the moment they tried to silence me. But I've found strength in the storm, and I know now that my story, my full, unedited, complicated story, is a tool for change.

This chapter was never just about credibility.

It's about reclaiming power.

It's about refusing to let others write your ending.

It's about what comes next.

We rebuild broken systems one honest action at a time.

And it starts with us.

Challenging the Status Quo.

This ordeal highlighted the dangers of unchecked power and the toxic cultures that can thrive in its shadow. As an activist, I now approach issues with a critical lens, questioning not only the systems we are fighting against but also the systems within our own organisations.

Activism is not just about marching in the streets or raising awareness; it's about looking inward and addressing the rot within.

I have become more focused on calling out performative activism: gestures that look good on the surface but don't result in meaningful change.

Whether it is unions, corporations or governments, I believe in holding everyone accountable to their commitments, especially when they involve vulnerable communities.

Advocacy Through Lived Experience.

Having been on the receiving end of targeted harassment and manipulation, I have learned the power of personal stories in activism.

Sharing my journey, warts and all, has allowed me to connect with others who have faced similar struggles.

It is not just about raising awareness, it's about fostering solidarity and showing others that they are not alone.

I have also realised that activism isn't always loud.

Sometimes, it's the quiet, consistent work of standing firm in your values, challenging harmful narratives and supporting others in their battles.

It's about being a steady presence, a voice of reason and a source of strength for those who are still finding their own.

Focus on Sustainable Activism.

Another important lesson I have learned is the need for self-care and sustainability. Burnout is real, especially when you are fighting against powerful forces.

My experiences taught me the importance of setting boundaries, prioritising mental and physical health and building a supportive network of like-minded individuals.

Activism isn't a sprint. It is a marathon.

To make a lasting impact, you also need to take care of yourself along the way.

A Vision for Change.

Ultimately, my approach to activism is rooted in a vision for a better future.

One where power is used responsibly, where individuals are valued for their humanity rather than exploited for their labour and where truth and justice are prioritised over convenience and control.

My experiences, painful as they were, have given me clarity and purpose.

They have shown me that the fight for justice is never easy, but it is always worth it.

They have strengthened my resolve to be the kind of activist who does not just talk about change but actively works to create it, from the inside out.

#crediblewoman

Choices

Choices have consequences. Every action sets a chain of events in motion, and no one is exempt from the ripple effects.

When perpetrators commit injustice, the responses they provoke stem directly from their own decisions. Mistreatment doesn't exist in a vacuum; it evokes reactions, often powerful and unapologetic, from those who've been wronged.

We all have the right to choose. But we don't get to choose the consequences.

When someone's actions cross the line and affect my life, my peace, or my dignity, I am equally entitled to my own choices in response.

Let me be clear:

I will not be silenced.

I was abused quietly, so I am choosing to heal loudly.

Choosing to stand up for myself, to speak out against mistreatment, and to hold those accountable for their actions is not just a right, it's a necessity.

Silence is complicity, and I refuse to be complicit in my own harm.

Choosing to speak out, to stand up against mistreatment, and to hold others accountable isn't just a right, it's a survival instinct. Silence might feel safer, but it often serves the oppressor. I choose another path.

If your choices bring harm into my world, then my response is not only justified, it is a consequence you invited.

Respect is a two-way street, and actions, whether kind or cruel, set the tone for the energy that will be returned.

So, choose wisely. Because if your decisions send shockwaves into my world, know this: I will respond - loudly, boldly, and without apology.

The moral is simple:

Don't start fires you can't withstand when the flames turn back on you.

Never underestimate the power of a woman's intuition. Some women can see the game before it even begins.

Sometimes, no words are needed, and no proof is required. The feeling alone is enough.

It's a hard truth to face, but the reality is this:

They knew.

They were fully aware of the impact their actions would have on me. They understood the pain they were causing, how deeply it would cut, and they chose to proceed anyway.

Coming to terms with the fact that someone could be so deliberate in their cruelty, so conscious of the hurt they were inflicting, and still move forward, that is a special kind of reckoning. It's profoundly unsettling.

The truth is, not everyone is driven by empathy.

Not everyone feels the weight of accountability.

Some act with thoughtless indifference. Others act with full awareness and simply do not care. They move through the world with selfish intent, leaving behind chaos and heartbreak.

Then carry on as though nothing happened, untouched by the destruction in their wake.

This realisation is a painful but necessary reminder:

You must guard your heart.

That doesn't mean building walls.

It doesn't mean becoming cold or closed.

It means protecting your energy.

It means recognising that not everyone has your best interests at heart.

It's a lesson in discernment, learning who values your well-being and who views your presence as convenient, disposable, or instrumental to their own ends. It's about identifying who uplifts and respects you versus who thrives on power and pretense.

This isn't just a call to protect yourself, it's an invitation.

To reflect on your boundaries.

To honour your worth.

To reject the idea that mistreatment is inevitable.

Because while you can't control others, you can control how much access they have to you and how much power they hold over your peace.

Deed Of Agreement And Protection Orders.

The funny thing is, our group of harbingers of justice don't always agree on everything. We debate and we argue over technicalities. Ironically, that same scrutiny, our unwavering attention to detail, is what made us targets in our former workplaces.

But there's one thing we agree on without hesitation:

The devil is in the details. We also agree on this:

The parallels between Family & Domestic Violence (FDV) and Workplace Abuse are chillingly similar.

Both rely on power imbalances.

Both thrive on control and fear.

Both leave victims questioning their worth, their reality, even their sanity.

Both are dismissed by those in power, hidden behind excuses or swept under bureaucratic rugs in a deed of agreement and/or protection orders.

The tactics are eerily familiar:

- **Gaslighting**

  Twisting facts to make victims doubt themselves.

- **Isolation**

  Cutting off support networks - family, colleagues, allies.

- **Emotional Manipulation**

Using guilt, fear, or shame to keep victims compliant.

- **Reputation Damage**

Spreading lies to discredit and isolate.

- **Economic Control**

Threatening livelihoods or financial security to maintain dominance.

The impact?

Psychological devastation.

Constant stress.

Chronic anxiety.

A state of survival where thriving becomes a distant memory.

One of us had to drive 2,375 kilometers, over three days, just to feel safe. That's how severe the fallout can be.

They drove from NSW - the "First State" to QLD - the "Smart State."

Additionally, the failures across all levels of bureaucratic systems are absolutely astounding.

These systems are complicit in perpetuating abuse; ignoring red flags, refusing to act, or actively protecting the perpetrators.

Modes and methods need to change. But for now?

"JOIN TODAY AND RECEIVE A FREE PEN."

Wait, there's more!

If you ring in the next 30 minutes, you'll receive a free set of steak knives.

It's all about the benefits, right?

Fairness. Equality. Dignity.

Catchy slogans. Empty promises.

When Family and Employment Intersect.

When family becomes your employer, the boundaries between personal and professional life blur. The dynamic grows dangerously complex, emotionally charged, high-stakes, and is often impossible to separate.

If something goes wrong, the fallout isn't just professional.

It's personal, layered, and often deeply painful.

The Unique Challenges of Family as Employers.

1.Blurred Boundaries:

Family dynamics come with emotional histories, unresolved tensions, and unrealistic expectations.

What might remain professional in a typical workplace quickly becomes personal here, turning everyday disagreements into family dramas.

2.Power Imbalance:

A family member who holds authority over you at work also holds sway in your personal life.

When conflicts arise, it can feel like there's no safe space, no neutral ground to stand on.

3.Perceived Favouritism or Scrutiny:

Whether it's extra leniency or heightened criticism, working with family often brings the perception of bias.

When things unravel, even the most justified actions can be weaponised as betrayal or favouritism.

4.Lack of Professional Distance:

Family employers may expect unwavering loyalty.

Loyalty that bleeds beyond business hours and boundaries.

When issues arise, they're rarely seen as work-related.

They're treated as personal betrayals.

5.No Formal Support Structures:

In a standard workplace, HR or other conflict-resolution processes might help.

With family? You're often on your own.

Left to navigate the tension without backup.

The emotional toll can be overwhelming.

When Something Goes Wrong.

Once the relationship breaks down, whether due to finances, unmet expectations, or perceived slights, the consequences can be devastating.

- **Professional Repercussions:**

Loss of income, career setbacks, and a fractured professional reputation.

- **Personal Fallout:**

Shattered trust, severed family ties, and long-lasting emotional wounds.

- **Isolation:**

In a traditional dispute, you might turn to family for support.

In this case, they are both the source of the pain and the system surrounding it.

Navigating the Storm.

1.Set Clear Boundaries:

Establish clear expectations and formal agreements. Don't rely on family ties to assume understanding.

2.Prioritise Open Communication:

Separate the personal from the professional as best you can. Address issues head-on, before they fester.

3.Seek Neutral Mediation:

Bring in a third party, if necessary. Someone outside the emotional dynamic who can hold space for a fair resolution.

4.Protect Your Peace:

If the situation becomes abusive, manipulative, or unsafe, it's okay to walk away. Even if it means cutting ties. Even if it hurts.

Some storms aren't meant to be weathered. Sometimes, the only way forward is through the wreckage, with your peace intact.

We Won't Wait!

Cutting ties with a toxic family member is never easy, but it is sometimes necessary for your healing and survival.

It's painful to admit... Loving someone doesn't always mean allowing them to stay in your life, especially when their presence becomes a source of harm.

Not all mothers and fathers love and protect you. Some fight only for their own ideals, disregarding your needs, your boundaries, and your well-being.

There are families so hurtful and harmful that distance becomes the only way to survive. Some relatives betray you, speak ill of you, gossip behind your back, or envy your success.

They claim to want the best for you, but deep down, your growth threatens them.

They gather in whispering circles, trying to tarnish your image, shrinking you so they can feel bigger.

These people don't care about your peace. They care about control. They only care about keeping you small. And some?

They're only around when it benefits them, using the bond of blood to manipulate, to guilt, to take. They drain you emotionally, consume your energy, and offer nothing in return.

It's time to stop romanticising the idea of family.

Not every relationship, parent, sibling, cousin, or otherwise, is sacred simply because of DNA. It's okay to acknowledge the darkness in your family tree. It's okay to walk away.

Growth requires boundaries. Healing requires protection. And peace sometimes requires letting go of those who refuse to see your worth.

You don't have to carry the weight of their anger, manipulation, hypocrisy, or neglect. You don't have to keep suffering to preserve an illusion.

Recognise the wounds. Acknowledge the patterns. But refuse to let them define you.

They are responsible for their own healing. You are responsible for your peace. And sometimes, peace begins with goodbye.

"What is right is not always popular
and what is popular is not always right."

-Albert Einstein

Behind Closed Doors.

Domestic violence is often described as harm inflicted behind closed doors, hidden from view.

Now, imagine that same dynamic in a workplace, where the perpetrators are your union colleagues, counterparts, and delegates. The parallels are chilling. In both situations, the abuse is insidious, calculated, and perpetuated by those who are meant to be allies or even protectors.

Just as in domestic violence, workplace abuse can involve manipulation, control, intimidation, gaslighting, and isolation. When this occurs within a union, a space that should champion fairness, equity, and justice, the betrayal cuts even deeper.

In these environments, the tools of oppression aren't fists or verbal tirades.

They're systemic tactics:

- Exclusion from critical conversations

- Character assassination

- Public humiliation disguised as "professional feedback"

- Policies and procedures used as weapons

All cloaked in professional decorum, while the emotional toll builds behind the scenes.

Victims are silenced by fear. Fear of retaliation, fear of losing their livelihood, fear of being labelled "too sensitive" or "not tough enough."

The same cycles of power and control that drive domestic violence thrive in toxic workplaces. Abusers count on silence. They thrive on it.

The irony is bitter: a union exists to protect its members, to fight exploitation and injustice.

Yet when union leadership becomes the perpetrator, it destroys the very foundation of trust and solidarity it claims to uphold.

Shining a light on this kind of abuse is just as vital as exposing domestic violence. Whether behind closed doors, at home or in the shadows of a boardroom, harm by those in power must be confronted. Victims deserve validation, support and the knowledge that speaking up is an act of courage, not weakness.

Now take this scenario one step further.

What happens when your own flesh and blood collude with your union boss to destroy you?

This convergence of betrayal is almost unfathomable.

On one side, your employer: someone with institutional power.

On the other hand, a family member: someone bound to you by blood, trust, and assumed loyalty.

When these two forces align, it becomes a perfect storm.

A dual betrayal that shatters your sense of safety both professionally and personally.

Family is supposed to be your safe place.

A refuge.

But when a family member joins forces with an abuser, the pain becomes exponential.

It's not just betrayal, it's disintegration.

The very people meant to catch you when you fall have pushed you instead.

Imagine the level of collusion required:

Private conversations.

Shared strategies.

Deliberate attempts to sabotage your reputation, career, and mental health.

This isn't passive complicity.

It's active participation in your destruction.

It forces disturbing questions:

- What did they stand to gain?

- Was it jealousy? Power? Vindication for old wounds?

- Did they truly understand the damage they were inflicting, or did they just not care?

Whatever the motivation, the result is the same: betrayal, isolation, and trauma.

The collusion magnifies the abuse, making it feel inescapable.

Where do you turn when those who should protect you become the architects of your harm?

Yet, even in the face of such devastation, there is strength.

It begins with recognising that their actions reflect them, not you.

Their betrayal exposes their moral failures, not your worth.

They tried to break me. But in doing so, they revealed everything about who they truly are.

The journey forward from this level of betrayal is not easy.

It means rebuilding trust, not in them but in myself. Reclaiming my power. Setting boundaries that guard my peace. Refusing to let their cruelty write my story.

Betrayal this deep is a profound wound. But it is not insurmountable.

Truth. Resilience. And the courage to rise, these will always outlast lies and collusion.

Understanding the Body's Response.

In the aftermath of betrayal and psychological harm, whether in the home or the workplace, many survivors are left questioning themselves:

Why didn't I speak up?

Why didn't I fight back?

Why did I freeze?

It's easy to internalise blame.

But the truth is, our reactions during trauma are not choices made with calm logic. They are rapid, involuntary survival responses directed by our nervous system. The freeze or collapse response, often misunderstood, is especially prone to shame. Survivors may feel weak or complicit when, in fact, their body did exactly what it had to do to survive.

Dr. Ruth Lanius, MD, PhD, offers a powerful and compassionate explanation of how the nervous system responds to trauma.

Shared by NICABM (National Institute for the Clinical Application of Behavioral Medicine), this psychoeducational tool helps dismantle self-blame and illuminates the biology behind survival:

"It can often be difficult for trauma survivors to understand how or why they reacted a certain way during a traumatic experience.

Instead of seeing their trauma response as the result of a split-second, unconscious decision made by their nervous system, they may blame themselves for not reacting differently. This can be especially true for trauma victims who went into the freeze or collapse response."

Understanding the science behind our trauma responses is a step toward healing.

It helps replace shame with self-compassion, and that shift can be life-changing.

Learn more here: <u>How the Nervous System Responds to Trauma – NICABM</u>

The Irony and Hypocrisy.

The irony is undeniable and deeply troubling.

On one hand, the union I worked for, an organisation publicly committed to protecting victims of domestic and family violence, has done vital advocacy. Securing leave entitlements in industrial instruments and lobbying governments to enshrine protections in awards is commendable. It's a significant step toward systemic change and justice.

Yet at the same time, individuals within this same setting actively participated in actions that contradict those very principles. By colluding with my enemies, including possibly a member of my own family, it didn't just undermine my career; it inflicted deep personal harm.

This betrayal exposes a glaring hypocrisy: a union that preaches fairness, support, and justice, yet acts with manipulation, exclusion, and cruelty behind closed doors. It's not an isolated incident. It reveals a pattern of behaviour that taints the union's credibility and corrodes the trust it relies upon.

The Stark Contradiction.

1. Advocacy vs. Action

While the union publicly champions protection from abuse, its treatment of me reveals a failure to live those values.

Allegedly colluding with an abusive family member to sabotage me is a gross betrayal of the very cause it claims to defend.

2. Exploitation of Power

This alleged collusion with family, former school peers, and internal actors was a strategic misuse of influence.

It mirrors the power dynamics seen in domestic violence: control, coercion, betrayal. That makes it all the more disturbing, given the union's advocacy in this exact area.

3. Moral and Ethical Failure

Leadership chose self-interest over integrity. Publicly, they spoke of justice. Privately, they inflicted harm. The dissonance is not only hypocritical but also cowardly.

4. The Personal Toll

Workplace abuse is devastating in any form. But when it intersects with betrayal by family, it becomes a totalising wound. It attacks not just your job but your sense of safety, identity, and trust in humanity.

Calling Out the Hypocrisy.

The union's behaviour raises urgent questions:

- Does it practise internally what it preaches externally?

- How can it lead to domestic violence reform while enabling abuse within its own ranks?

- What does this say about the values and culture of its leadership?

Real change demands more than slogans. It starts from within.

For any organisation to lead with authenticity, it must live its values at every level.

Not just in press releases or policy negotiations, but in its treatment of its own people. Otherwise, progress is hollow.

Credibility crumbles. And those who've been harmed are left to pick up the pieces in silence. This isn't just a personal reckoning.

It's part of a broader fight for accountability, transparency, and truth. A fight to ensure that those who speak of justice also embody it. That advocacy isn't a performance but a principle lived from the inside out.

Moral Injury.

Moral injury occurs when there is a profound betrayal of deeply held moral values, especially in moments where trust, integrity, and fairness are not just expected but essential. It's a rupture that doesn't just cause emotional pain; it shakes the foundation of your beliefs and identity.

In my case, the convergence of personal and professional betrayal created a uniquely devastating scenario. One that struck at the very core of who I was and what I stood for.

How Moral Injury Occurred in My Case.

1. The Betrayal of Principles by the Union:

The union, an organisation that claims to uphold fairness, equality, and protection from harm, betrayed those very ideals. While publicly advocating for domestic and family violence protections, it privately inflicted psychological harm upon me. This hypocrisy wasn't just painful; it was disorienting. These were the values I had believed in. Values I had worked to uphold. To see them weaponised against me was a moral wound that cut deep.

2. The Family Betrayal:

When the betrayal comes from your own flesh and blood, the impact is deeply personal. Family is supposed to be a source of unconditional love and loyalty.

But when those ties are twisted into tools of manipulation and destruction, it shatters something essential. It erodes your basic sense of safety. It turns love into a threat.

3. The Combined Impact:

When betrayal comes from both your professional community and your family, the pain is compounded. My identity, my values, my livelihood, all were attacked at once. I wasn't just fighting for my job or my reputation.

I was fighting to hold onto my sense of self. And that is the true nature of moral injury. It leaves you questioning everything you once trusted.

The Nature of Moral Injury.

Moral injury is not just about what was done to you; it's about what it means. It occurs when actions or decisions violate your internal moral code, creating a ripple effect of emotional and psychological distress.

It often involves:

- **Betrayal**

  By people or institutions you once trusted.

- **Shame or Guilt**

For being part of, or vulnerable to, something so damaging.

- **Anger and Resentment**

Toward those who inflicted or enabled the harm.

- **Loss of Faith**

In people, systems or values you once believed in.

In my case, the dual betrayal, by the union and allegedly by my family, upended my faith in justice, fairness and loyalty. It left behind a scar that's not visible but deeply felt. A scar I continue to carry, even as I work to heal.

A Personal Reflection.

I want to take a moment to highlight a truly powerful piece of literature - ***Line in the Sand***, written by Dean Yates.

Dean is a workplace mental health trainer, journalist, public speaker, podcast host and critically acclaimed author.

There is nothing more impactful than a humble person with a warrior spirit, driven by a greater purpose. *Line in the Sand* encapsulates exactly that.

As a former journalist and bureau chief at international news service Reuters, Dean shares his deeply moving journey through a highly stressful and traumatic environment that ultimately led to a diagnosis of PTSD. What makes Dean's story even more compelling is the intersection of PTSD and moral injury; a brain injury that compounds trauma and often contradicts one's own values and beliefs.

Despite receiving no support from his employer, Dean found healing through the help of empathetic physicians, friends and family. His transformation into an advocate for better workplace mental health and government accountability is a testament to his resilience. Dean and I share many similarities in our experiences, particularly when it comes to moral injury.

As he so wisely said to me, *"The more we know about what troubles us, the less frightening it is."* This insight has been instrumental in helping me navigate my own journey.

I want to personally thank Dean for his unwavering support and encouragement. His guidance has been invaluable in helping me understand my own moral injury. The insights he has shared have not only deepened my understanding of my own experiences but have also given me the tools to confront the impact of those injuries sustained within the trade union realm. Dean's willingness to speak out and help others heal from this type of trauma is something I hold in the highest regard.

Healing from Moral Injury.

    1. **Acknowledgement:**

The first step in healing is recognising the depth of the injury you've experienced. This isn't a sign of weakness. It's a recognition of how profoundly the situation impacted you, especially when it contradicts everything you stand for.

2. Reconnecting with Your Values:

Despite the actions of others, your core principles remain intact. The hypocrisy and malice directed at you don't define you. Standing firm in your values is a powerful form of resistance, and reaffirming those principles can help restore a sense of personal integrity.

3. Support Systems:

It's crucial to surround yourself with people who align with your values and offer authentic support. Connecting with others who have endured similar moral injuries can provide validation, helping to process the pain and reinforcing the strength in shared experiences.

4. Advocacy and Action:

Transforming your pain into purpose is a key part of healing. Speaking out against hypocrisy and advocating for change not only reclaims your power but can turn moral injury into a driving force for justice.

By sharing my story, I've found a sense of purpose in shedding light on systemic issues and advocating for change.

5. Professional Help:

Engaging with therapists or counsellors who are experienced in moral injury and workplace trauma is vital.

They can guide you through the emotional complexity of healing, helping you rebuild a sense of trust and purpose.

Why This Mattered For Me.

My experience with moral injury isn't just about the pain caused. It was about the capacity to confront and challenge injustice.

While the betrayal I've faced has been incredibly painful, it has also highlighted my strength, resilience and unwavering commitment to accountability.

Healing is an ongoing process, but by acknowledging and addressing my moral injury, I am reclaiming my narrative and standing firmly in my truth.

Moving Forward.

My story exposes the disconnect between public advocacy and private actions, an issue that plagues many organisations.

It's a call for systemic accountability and cultural change within institutions.

By speaking out, I've not only confronted personal betrayal but also unearthed the hypocrisy within systems that claim to champion fairness and justice.

This journey is far from over, but it's one that has already given me the strength to continue challenging the status quo.

I will continue to hold those in positions of power accountable and push for a better alignment between values and actions. It's not enough to simply preach fairness and equality; we must ensure these ideals are consistently reflected in the way every single person is treated, every day.

As I reflect on the betrayals and harm I've experienced, it becomes evident that the concept of Duty of Care was not just overlooked; it was actively violated.

The very institutions that should have protected me, upheld my rights, and cared for my well-being, not only failed in their responsibilities but compounded the damage.

This failure is not just a personal wound. It highlights a much larger systemic issue that permeates workplaces, institutions, and even families.

The next chapter, Duty of Care, explores this crucial principle in depth. It's a concept that extends far beyond the workplace and touches on every aspect of life where one person or institution has a responsibility to another.

Whether it's a corporation, an employer, or even a family member, the obligation to ensure safety, dignity, and respect is non-negotiable. But what happens when this duty is neglected or, worse, willfully ignored?

In Duty of Care, I will delve into the importance of creating environments where safety, fairness, and integrity are not just ideals but foundational principles that guide every decision.

I will also explore the legal and ethical ramifications when this duty is breached, examining the ways in which we must hold those in positions of power accountable.

The actions I've faced reflect the consequences of ignoring this responsibility, but they also serve as a call to action for all of us to ensure these principles are upheld every single day.

As we move forward into this next chapter, it's clear that true healing can only begin when the Duty of Care is prioritised, and accountability is non-negotiable.

It's time to take a stand for what's right, not just in the abstract, but in real, tangible ways that protect all of us from harm.

Duty of Care

Duty of Care refers to the legal and moral obligation to ensure the safety, well-being, and fair treatment of others.

In various contexts, it signifies the responsibility of individuals or organisations to act in a manner that avoids causing harm to others.

In the Workplace.

Employers have a Duty of Care to:

- Provide a safe working environment.

- Address risks or hazards promptly.

- Support employees' physical and mental health.

- Establish policies to prevent harassment, discrimination, and bullying.

In Other Contexts.

1. **Education:**

- Schools must ensure the safety and well-being of students.

2. **Healthcare:**

- Healthcare professionals must act in the best interest of their patients.

3. Legal:

- Professionals owe a Duty of Care to their clients to act competently and ethically.

Failure to uphold the Duty of Care can lead to legal consequences, reputational damage and harm to those under their care.

Bullying, sexual harassment and gendered violence are not just HR issues. They are workplace hazards that fall under Workplace Health & Safety (WHS) laws. Organisations have a legal obligation to manage these risks as part of their Duty of Care.

A 2024 case highlights this:

A Victorian company director faced 34 charges for failing to address workplace bullying, sexual harassment and gendered violence, constituting a breach of Duty of Care under the Occupational Health and Safety Act.

Key Takeaway:

Psychosocial risks are workplace health and safety risks. Managing them requires a collaborative approach between HR and WHS teams, driven by senior leadership and shaped in consultation with employees.

Under common law and WHS legislation, employers have a Duty of Care to provide a safe workplace.

Failure to address bullying, harassment or violence breaches this duty, leaving organisations vulnerable to litigation and regulatory action.

Prioritising psychosocial safety is essential to building a safe, thriving and legally compliant workplace.

Steps for Organisations to Meet Their Obligations.

1. Identify and Assess Risks:

- Engage employees in meaningful consultation to understand risks.

2. Implement Risk Controls:

- Introduce measures to prevent and manage hazards effectively.

3. Establish Clear Policies and Processes:

- Create transparent reporting mechanisms and address issues promptly.

4. Provide Training:

- Ensure everyone understands expectations and knows how to report concerns.

5. Offer Support:

- Provide access to confidential reporting options and wellbeing resources.

Why This Matters.

Ignoring psychosocial risks harms individuals and exposes organisations to:

- Legal consequences.

- Financial penalties.

- Damage to reputation and trust.

For those down the back:

The Work Health and Safety Act (WHS Act) isn't just policy.

It's the law.

It mandates that, so far as is reasonably practicable, employers must ensure the health and safety of workers in the workplace.

The person conducting a business or undertaking (PCBU) holds a legal Duty of Care to identify and address all risks to health and safety.

That includes psychological and emotional hazards, not just physical ones.

This isn't about "sensitive" employees speaking up on behalf of others. This is about known hazards being ignored or allowed to fester in plain sight.

Bullying is never justified.

"If you have nothing nice to say, don't say anything at all."

Has anyone else grown up with that gem?

It sounds like kindness, but for many of us, it taught silence in the face of harm.

Speaking up started to feel like wrongdoing.

Like breaking some invisible code of niceness.

It's wild to look back and realise how these little sayings shaped our leadership styles.

So I'm curious: What beliefs were passed down to you about conflict?

From parents, teachers, and elders, what "wisdom" stuck with you?

How did it show up when things got uncomfortable at work?

Allow me to also ask you this: Has an employer ever treated you like a child?

Because that's what infantilising leadership looks like.

It's fear-based, controlling and deeply disrespectful.

It drives good people out.

It creates resentment.

It kills initiative.

Here are just some of the behaviours that fall into this pattern:

1. Micromanaging

Demanding constant updates.

Withholding decision-making power.

Assigning unnecessary tasks to assert control.

2. Excessive Surveillance

Tracking movements through apps or GPS.

Monitoring breaks like it's a schoolyard.

Installing cameras. In some cases, even in boardrooms.

3. Restricting Basic Choices

Enforcing impractical dress codes.

Banning personal items from workspaces.

Dictating how and when tasks must be done, regardless of impact.

4. Disregarding Work-Life Balance

Refusing flexibility for real-life responsibilities.

Requiring permission for basic time off.

Contacting employees during leave or outside hours.

5. Infantilising Communication

Using patronising tones in meetings or emails.

Publicly reprimanding like it's a classroom.

Over-explaining tasks to skilled professionals.

6. Imposing Arbitrary Rules

Prohibiting casual conversations without approval.

Blocking internal transfers without excessive justification.

Enforcing rigid schedules with no human consideration.

7. Withholding Trust and Responsibility

Delegating only low-level, repetitive tasks.

Ignoring input and lived expertise.

Assuming employees can't handle confidential or complex matters.

I've experienced or witnessed most of these.

These aren't signs of strong leadership.

They're red flags for a culture built on control, not care.

The Weight of This Issue:

Treating adults like children erodes trust, autonomy, and morale.

People thrive when they're empowered, not policed. When they're respected, not reduced.

Employers who don't understand that risk more than just turnover.

They risk the very soul of their workplace.

Signs of a Toxic Workplace:

- No clear vision or mission.

- An obsession with short-term wins over long-term impact.

- Punishing or silencing those who speak up.

- Parading values without living them.

- Failing to recognise or value employees.

- Playing favourites and enforcing double standards.

- Prioritising "membership numbers" over human dignity.

Employers who treat their employees like children erode professionalism and autonomy.

A truly healthy workplace fosters trust, respect, and growth. Not obedience through fear.

Sure, we might learn to survive in toxic environments. We might become more resilient. But let's not confuse survival with success.

Toxic workplaces demand resilience as a condition of survival, and that alone should signal systemic failure.

The need to armour up just to make it through the day isn't resilience, it's a warning sign.

Workplace codes of conduct aren't just aspirational.

They're meant to create safe, respectful, collaborative environments.

If an organisation's culture pushes staff to "tough it out" instead of fixing the rot, it's not just unethical, it's a breach of duty. In unionised workplaces, these dynamics are even more complex. Unions are supposed to safeguard rights and enforce EBAs. But if the culture is one of survival rather than thriving, there's a deeper problem. One rooted in leadership failure, harassment or outright neglect of worker protections.

Here are four key strategies to navigate this terrain:

1. Leverage the Union

- Report violations to your union rep.

- Demand accountability, not just lip service, from leadership.

2. Document Everything

- Keep a log of incidents that breach codes of conduct or Workplace Agreement terms.

- Detail who, what, when and where. Patterns matter.

3. Push for Collective Action

- Don't accept "resilience" as the only solution.

- Advocate for structural change through meetings, motions or campaigns.

4. Understand Your Industrial Instrument

- Know your rights.

- Identify when those rights are being eroded or denied.

Resilience should enhance well-being, not excuse mistreatment. It must walk hand-in-hand with structural integrity.

Not serve as a band-aid for broken systems.

Bullying vs. Personality Clash.

Too often, employers dismiss workplace bullying as a "personality clash".

It's a convenient excuse.

One that avoids accountability and minimises the harm caused.

But bullying is more than disagreement.

It's a pattern of targeted, demeaning behaviour meant to silence, isolate or control.

Here's how to push back:

1.Document the Behaviour

- Log dates, incidents, language used and witnesses.

2. Know the Rules

- Review internal policies and relevant workplace agreements, such as an Enterprise Bargaining Agreement (EBA), the Award and other relevant workplace instruments.

- Link the behaviour to explicit policy and legislative breaches.

3. Involve the Union

- Don't go it alone.

- Use the collective strength and advocacy of your union.

4. Escalate Formally

- File complaints if informal steps fail.

- Supply evidence showing this isn't about "clashing personalities". It's misconduct.

5. Push for Culture Change

- Call for anti-bullying training and enforcement mechanisms.

- Demand transparency and consistency in how complaints are handled.

6. Go Beyond the Organisation if Needed

- If all else fails, consider external recourse; regulatory bodies, legal channels or ombudsman services.

Bullying is about power, not personality. It's the responsibility of leadership to know the difference and act.

Schooling the System.

I may not be an industrial relations expert, but at one point I did have to remind the former *Minister for Employment and Workplace Relations*, Tony Burke MP, of a basic truth:

Unions are workplaces, too.

Like every other workplace, their number one job as employers and as PCBUs is to comply with WHS law and uphold their Duty of Care.

I suggested the Minister start with a little due diligence.

Maybe even read the Work Health and Safety Act. You know, the one that's unavoidable and designed to ensure, as far as is reasonably practicable, that workers don't get hurt at work.

My case?

A union workplace where staff were sacrificed for the sake of membership metrics.

Where the pursuit of numbers outweighed the value of human beings.

That's not just toxic.

That's criminal.

This was 2024.

We are now in an era of accountability.

Yet, some union bosses are still spinning the old narrative:

"Nothing to see here."

While behind the scenes?

They burn their staff to the ground.

AKA: swings and roundabouts.

So I ask again:

Who's policing the people who are policing the employers?

Oh, that's right. The Albanese Government disbanded the Registered Organisations Commission (ROC) at the request of the ACTU.

A Gutsy Position.

It was only a matter of time before someone stood up, spoke out and called the establishment out on their bullshit.

I've been saying it for years:

"There is a problem in our own backyard."

And in the words of investigative journalist Nick McKenzie:

"It's no secret.

The agencies responsible have failed.

The policing agencies haven't done enough.

The regulatory agencies haven't done enough.

And ultimately, the politicians who've known about this for a long time have not done enough."

We are long past the point of polite conversation.

This is about harm. This is about human lives.

This is about holding the powerful to account.

Managing Psychosocial Hazards at Work.

A shift is happening.

The Work Health and Safety (Managing Psychosocial Hazards at Work) Code of Practice 2024 is now in force as a Commonwealth legislative instrument.

"A new Code of Practice on psychosocial hazards and risks is now in force across the Commonwealth jurisdiction. The Code provides practical guidance on how to prevent harm from psychosocial hazards at work, including psychological and physical harm... It includes case studies and outlines practical approaches to manage, monitor, and improve how we address these risks in real workplaces."

-Comcare

This isn't just a checklist. This Code is a reckoning. Developed to provide real, workable guidance, it outlines proactive measures to identify, assess, and control psychosocial hazards, including:

- Workplace bullying

- Excessive job demands

- Poor organisational support

- Harmful leadership and structural dysfunction

These are the very things unions should be fighting against, not enabling.

The Code exists to help employers stop the harm before it starts. Not cover it up once it's done.

It reinforces the employer's primary Duty of Care and mandates an active, not reactive, approach to psychological safety.

Comcare, as the national WHS regulator, is responsible for ensuring these protections are enforced.

No more passing the buck.

No more blaming "personality clashes."

No more pretending staff are resilient enough to endure a broken system.

The Duty of Care is non-negotiable.

•••————————•••

Positive Duty.

Another major step forward for workplace safety and equity came with the passing of the ***Respect@Work*** legislation through the Senate.

Under this reform, employers now have a positive duty to take reasonable and proportionate measures to prevent and eliminate sex discrimination, sexual harassment, and victimisation in the workplace.

This isn't a suggestion.

It's the law. Gone are the days of reactive policies that rely on individuals to speak up while organisations look the other way.

This legislation shifts the responsibility where it belongs: onto employers - to create safe, respectful, and inclusive environments before harm occurs.

Thank you to the union members, activists, and advocates whose tireless campaigning helped make this a reality. Your fight has brought long-overdue recommendations to life, translating advocacy into enforceable legal protections.

The passage of this legislation marks a transformational shift in how we understand workplace safety. It recognises that safety is not just about physical risks. It's also about psychological safety, dignity, and freedom from gender-based violence.

Work should never come with a side of fear or humiliation. Safety at work is everyone's business. And no one.... I'll say it again.... no one, should be harmed just for doing their job.

Laws can change. Policies can evolve. Codes of conduct can be updated. But without the courage to act, they're just words on paper.

Accountability begins with leadership, but it doesn't end there. Every individual in a workplace plays a role in shaping its culture. And when silence becomes the default, harm flourishes in the shadows.

We are living in a time when expectations are shifting, when safety is being redefined, not just as physical well-being but as psychological security too.

The ***Respect@Work*** legislation and the **WHS Code on Psychosocial Hazards** are not just bureaucratic milestones. They are calls to action.

So the question becomes:

When you see injustice, harm or systemic failure, what will you do?

Because doing nothing isn't neutral.

Silence has never been neutral. It has always been a side.

Upstander vs Bystander

What is an upstander?

An upstander is someone who chooses to be part of the solution, not the problem. They may be a friend, a colleague or even a stranger, but what defines them is their willingness to act. Upstanders speak out, check in and show up when someone is being harmed. They don't stand by in silence.

Too often, people feel uncomfortable intervening and choose to remain neutral. That's a bystander. But neutrality in the face of injustice isn't neutral; it's permission.

An upstander takes action to support others and challenge wrongdoing, even when it's uncomfortable or risky. Unlike bystanders, who stay passive or silent, upstanders speak up, advocate and disrupt the status quo.

Being an upstander can mean.

- **Speaking out:** Confronting bullying, discrimination or abuse when you see it.

- **Offering support:** Checking in with victims and letting them know they're not alone

- **Seeking help:** Reaching out to those in positions of authority when a situation requires intervention.

- **Modelling courage:** Showing others what integrity looks like through your own actions.

Remaining neutral enables harmful behaviour.

Even small acts of courage can have a ripple effect.

One voice can make others feel safe enough to speak.

Change often starts with just one person.

Being silent is purgatory.

So define yourself.

Be the person who reaches out to former coworkers.

Be the one who helps raise concerns to board members, higher-ups or journalists; even anonymously.

Be the person who lights the match, so others trapped in darkness know there's a way out.

Power can spread like wildfire, just as easily as abuse can.

Making Excuses.

It's deeply disheartening when colleagues make excuses for unethical behaviour, especially when it's a coordinated effort by bosses to discredit you.

Their complicity doesn't just sting.

It cuts deep.

Often, these excuses are rooted in fear, self-preservation or blind loyalty to authority. But silence and justification don't absolve responsibility; they reinforce harm.

It's not just those orchestrating the abuse who are accountable. It's also those who stood by and said nothing.

I didn't need excuses.

I needed allies. I needed integrity.

I needed someone, anyone, to say, "This isn't okay."

Instead, what I got was indifference. But that indifference only made me stronger.

It taught me exactly what kind of person I refuse to be.

Conscience.

These are the tools we have to drive real change, one workplace at a time.

By choosing to use my voice and stand my ground, I became the kind of person others could lean on when they felt voiceless.

I was the one willing to spark the movement that others were too afraid, or too tired, to start.

That's why I kept saying, to everyone, including the bosses who tried to break me:

"You fucked with the wrong person."

And I meant it.

Standing my ground wasn't just for me.

It was for everyone they tried to silence before, and everyone they might target after.

I made it clear: your tactics won't work on me. Your power isn't absolute, and your actions have consequences. They underestimated me. Now they know better.

Why This Matters.

- **Breaking the Silence:**

Bullies thrive in environments of silence and fear.

Speaking up, especially on behalf of others, disrupts that dynamic.

It shows that those who have been silenced are not alone, and that their stories matter.

- **Building Collective Power:**

One voice can ignite a movement. Every time someone speaks out, even anonymously, it creates space for others to do the same.

That's how collective momentum builds.

One story at a time.

- **Challenging Toxic Systems:**

When individuals band together, they can no longer be ignored. Executives, board members, and external watchdogs are forced to reckon with the truth. Change begins with pressure, and pressure comes from people united in purpose.

How to Be That Person.

1. **Reach Out Thoughtfully:**

- Connect with former coworkers who may have experienced similar harm.

- Send a message of support. Let them know they're not imagining it, and they're not alone.

- Offer anonymity and assure them that their safety is your priority.

2. Gather Stories and Evidence:

- Encourage others to document their experiences, even privately.

- Look for patterns; similar behaviours, repeat offenders, signs of systemic issues.

- These stories, collected and protected, form the backbone of truth-telling.

3. Leverage External Channels:

- If internal systems fail, as they often do, seek help from journalists, advocacy organisations or legal avenues.

- Collective voices hold weight, especially when directed at those in power.

4. Encourage Accountability:

- Push for tangible change: independent investigations, updated policies, leadership accountability, and comprehensive training.

- Make it clear that brushing things under the rug is no longer an option.

The Power of One Person.

In my case, I've proven that one person taking the first step can spark a wildfire of change.

By choosing to be that person, I've embodied hope, resilience, and the refusal to stay silent.

This is how better systems are built.

One brave voice at a time.

Acknowledgements.

"I was called difficult and a nightmare," shared Jennifer Lawrence.

Rude. Difficult. Emotional. Bossy.

Women are too often labelled just for having boundaries and using their voice.

Thank you, Jennifer, for leading by example and speaking up.

I also acknowledge and honour the courage of:

- **Brittany Higgins:**

For breaking the silence around workplace sexual assault in Parliament House, sparking a national reckoning on power, justice, and the treatment of survivors.

- **Katherine Thornton (may she rest in peace):**

For her courage in naming the harm done, even when the system wasn't ready to hear her.

Her story paved the way for others to speak their truth, even posthumously.

- **Grace Tame:**

For using her voice to demand accountability, challenge victim-blaming and redefine what it means to be a "survivor" with strength and ferocity.

- **Greta Thunberg:**

For showing the world that age is no barrier to leadership and for standing firm, despite ridicule, in the fight for climate justice and intergenerational accountability.

- **Jelena Dokic:**

For speaking out about abuse, trauma and mental health in elite sport, reminding us that behind strength and achievement, there is often unseen suffering and immense courage.

- **Roxane Gay:**

For her outspoken writing on feminism, trauma and identity.

- **Chanel Contos:**

For initiating the movement calling for consent education in Australian schools.

- **Rosie Batty:**

For her advocacy against domestic violence following personal tragedy.

- **Tarana Burke:**

Founder of the original #MeToo movement.

- **Julia Gillard:**

For her famous misogyny speech in Parliament and her work on gender equity post-politics.

- **Bri Lee:**

For her work on sexual assault law reform and justice system critique in Australia.

- **Van Badham:**

For speaking out on political hypocrisy, union politics and feminism.

- **Dr. Anne Aly:**

Australia's first Muslim woman MP and advocate for countering hate and extremism.

- **Grace Millane:**

In remembrance and as a symbol of how systems fail women worldwide.

- **Emma Husar:**

For confronting the intense scrutiny and public shaming that followed unproven allegations during her political career.

Emma's experience highlights the challenges women face in politics and the importance of due process and support.

Each of them stood tall and said, "Enough is enough."

And so did I.

I remember commenting on one of Emma's posts:

"It is terrifying. In my case, I discovered a large group of people had accessed my Facebook Messenger account. Upon further investigation, I concluded it started with a former employer who deliberately shared my password. The most disturbing part? Not one of them thought it was wrong. That collective complicity; the silence, the participation, is what haunts me the most."

I hope the bastards had fun reading my private messages. Because what they actually read was the inner life of a woman they couldn't break.

It was a staggering violation of trust and privacy. And the fact that no one involved questioned the ethics of their behaviour only deepens the betrayal. So yes, I am angry. And rightfully so.

While I've taken steps to secure my accounts and protect myself, I still deserve something more:

I deserve accountability and proper closure.

This book, and the activism it represents, may be part of that.

Maybe it's the closure I've needed all along.

Who knows?

If you're reading this and you've been through something similar, know this:

Closure and accountability can take many forms.

Here's What That Might Look Like.

1.Legal Accountability

- **Data Breach Laws:** If your privacy was unlawfully breached, you may have legal grounds under data protection laws. A lawyer can help you explore your options.

- **Criminal Charges:** In some jurisdictions, sharing a password or accessing private messages without consent may be a criminal offense.

- **Civil Remedies:** You may be eligible for compensation, especially for emotional distress or damage to your reputation.

2. Organisational Accountability

- **Formal Complaints:** File with a workplace regulator, ombudsman or human rights body. If bad faith is found, your employer may face scrutiny or penalties.

- **Public Exposure:** If safe to do so, sharing your story (even anonymously) can create pressure for change.

3. Personal Accountability

- **Acknowledgement of Harm:** An apology from those involved won't undo the damage, but it can mark a turning point.

- **Education and Reform:** Push for privacy and ethics training for those involved to prevent future violations.

4. Closure

- **Reclaiming Power:** Strengthening your digital security (changing passwords, enabling two-factor authentication) helps restore control.

- **Therapeutic Support:** A counsellor can help you work through trauma, betrayal, and anger.

- **Finding Peace on Your Terms:** Closure doesn't require forgiveness. It means moving forward - your way.

The Role of Monetary Compensation.

Monetary compensation isn't just about money.

It's about recognising harm and giving you the resources to heal.

1.Legal Compensation

- **Civil Lawsuits:** You may be able to seek damages for invasion of privacy, distress, or reputational damage.

- **Contract Breach:** If confidentiality clauses were broken, your employer could owe you more than an apology.

- **Punitive Damages:** Some jurisdictions award additional compensation to punish misconduct and deter future violations.

2. Employment Settlements

- **Negotiated Compensation:** Employers can settle privately to acknowledge harm done, covering stress, career loss, or damage to reputation.

- **Revisiting Severance:** If a severance agreement exists, it might be renegotiated based on misconduct.

3. Additional Avenues

- **Defamation Claims:** If the breach included false or damaging rumours, you may be able to pursue a defamation case. Time limits apply.

- **Workers' Compensation:** If the breach caused psychological injury, you may be eligible for workers' compensation. Just be mindful of time limits.

4. Practical Costs

- **Reimbursement:** You can seek compensation for securing devices, legal advice or therapy.

- **Lost Income:** If the breach affected your work capacity or future opportunities, those losses can be factored in too.

If this is a path you want to take, talk to a lawyer or advocacy organisation. You don't have to navigate this alone. Your pain matters. Your story matters. And what happened to you is not your fault.

Prevention Is Better Than Cure.

Bystander intervention is one of the most powerful tools we have to prevent harm before it happens. It empowers individuals to take meaningful action, whether through speaking up, offering support, or simply not turning away.

This is how we shift culture: by interrupting silence, challenging complicity, and fostering environments where safety, respect, and accountability are non-negotiable.

Key Principles of Bystander Intervention.

1.Recognise the Situation:

- Pay attention to behaviours or dynamics that could cause harm.

- Like bullying, harassment, or manipulation.

- Understand that power and control often underpin these situations.

2. Assume Responsibility:

- Don't wait for someone else to act.

- You are someone.

3.Choose How to Intervene:

- **Direct:**

Call it out.

- **Distract:**

Change the focus, defuse the situation.

- **Delegate:**

Alert someone with authority.

- **Delay:**

Follow up, check in, offer support.

4. Ensure Personal Safety:

- Always assess risk.

Intervening doesn't mean putting yourself in danger.

There are always safe ways to support someone.

Real-World Examples of Bystander Action.

- Calling out racism, sexism or harmful jokes at work.

- Supporting someone being targeted, even privately.

- Reporting abusive conduct, even when it's uncomfortable.

Why It Matters.

- It prevents violence and escalations.

- It empowers people and creates safety.

- It dismantles the silence that allows abuse to thrive.

- It builds collective care, and that's how culture changes.

How We Foster This Culture.

1.Education: Regular, realistic training that gives people the tools to act.

2. Policy: Clear expectations and protections for those who speak up.

3. Role Models: Leaders and peers who lead by example.

4. Respect: A shared belief that everyone deserves safety and dignity.

Neutrality Is Invalidation.

Doing nothing is never neutral; it's harmful. Studies in trauma show that silence from bystanders can hurt more than the abuse itself. We all play a role in the systems we inhabit.

The Gottman Institute outlines three steps for healing betrayal trauma, relevant not only in personal relationships but in collective ones too:

1.Atone:

Take responsibility and begin to repair.

2. Attune:

Really listen and connect with the harmed person's experience.

3. Attach:

Commit to long-term change and accountability.

These steps aren't abstract; they're the bones of real healing.

Final Word.

This book, my activism and my truth are all acts of intervention. I refuse to be silent. I refuse to be complicit.

If you're reading this, you've already taken the first step, too, by listening.

Let this be a beginning. Because change always starts with one person willing to say:

Enough.

Silence protects the powerful.

I'm done being silent.

We've talked about accountability, justice and prevention, but here's the truth: no one was coming to save me.

So I saved myself.

I turned my pain into purpose and my outrage into action.

They tried to strip me of my voice, my credibility and my dignity.

They failed.

Now watch what happens when I take my power back.

Reclaiming My Power

I consider myself a good person.

But the actions of others have shaped me into someone they never expected: someone dangerous, not physically but intellectually. Smart. Strategic. Unafraid to do what it takes to expose and dismantle those who tried to destroy me.

My story is powerful because it's personal. Because it's real. Because it reflects the unimaginable strength it takes to rise after being torn down.

Moments that changed me:

The death by suicide of a fellow worker - changed me.

The aftermath of that death and how others responded - changed me.

Betrayal - changed me.

Being discarded - changed me.

Deceit - changed me.

Being constantly dismissed, demeaned and gaslit - changed me.

Being looked down upon - changed me.

Being lied to - changed me.

Bullying, mobbing and sexual harassment - changed me.

Cruelty from others - changed me.

Being manipulated - changed me.

Post-traumatic stress - changed me.

The truth is, we can never go back.

I am a shell of the person I once was, my mind locked in a battle even I don't fully understand. Despite the shadows - cynicism, mistrust, irritability, resentment - I keep choosing to seek light.

I am grateful for:

- My family (and fur-babies), the foundation on which I stand.

- My health.

- The amazing friends I share life with.

- Weekends for rest and reset.

(And if you work weekends, you deserve every cent of your penalty rates.)

- A warm home - something too many live without.

- Music, which keeps me sane and grounded.

- Road trips that clear my head and restore my spirit.

- The ability to feel deeply and express honestly.

Most of all, I am grateful for myself.

For taking small steps every day toward healing.

For refusing to give up.

For turning pain into power.

Perspective has shaped my experiences, and with that perspective came resilience, determination, and fire.

I haven't just survived.

I've transformed.

In that sense, my experiences have given me a unique and ultimately powerful perspective that cannot be easily dismissed.

What led me to turn those experiences into strength?

The answer is scattered throughout this book, woven into posts on my Facebook page and echoed across my other social media platforms.

I'm not alone. I am one of a core group of whistleblowers - former employees of various Australian unions.

And our stories? Eerily similar.

In 2020, the Workers' Compensation Advisory Service within the Queensland Council of Unions told me that going to the media was my last resort to hold those responsible to account for what happened to me, while working for a large trade union, within a so-called democratic institution.

So I chose to speak up. I used social media to expose what others wanted to keep buried.

And now?

'They' don't like it. Some have blocked me from their platforms. All because I dared to speak up.

But here's the truth:

Accountability feels like an attack when you're not ready to acknowledge how your behaviour affects others.

The misinformation and disinformation spread with malicious intent was, and still is, appalling.

All executed behind closed doors, within and around that democratic institution.

Maybe that institution needs to take a good, hard look at itself, and at the facts, before spreading gossip.

Maybe if they don't want people knowing what happens behind those closed doors, then maybe they should rethink what they say and do.

Bottom line:

The double standards are astounding.

The hypocrisy? Off the charts.

That's why I created ***The Reckoning Room,*** a platform dedicated to exposing workplace abuse, systemic corruption, and the betrayal of whistleblowers. My advocacy has uncovered misconduct within powerful institutions, including unions, employers, and public bodies. In doing so, I have sparked national conversations about accountability, truth-telling, and the urgent need for systemic reform.

Organisational culture isn't neutral. It shapes every outcome, every investigation, and every life impacted by silence. Until internal accountability is real, community trust can not be rebuilt.

More reflections in The Reckoning Room: https://jeanineorzani.substack.com

A Reminder of the Power Within.

What it all comes down to is perspective.

One's perspective is valid when it's rooted in lived experience.

I remembered that the power within me is greater than any force working against me. No smear campaign, no external negativity, no attempt to diminish my worth will ever define who I truly am.

I remembered:

- **My Truth Matters**

Lies can spread, but truth is unshakable. It stands the test of time.

- **Resilience is My Shield**

Every challenge has made me stronger, sharper, and more determined.

- **My Actions Speak Loudest**

By staying true to my values, I've let my character speak for itself, and no one can take that from me.

- **I Am Not Alone**

There is support around me. I reached out to those who believe in me and in my integrity.

- **I Focus on What Matters**

I didn't let distractions derail me. I stayed aligned with my purpose, and my progress has silenced the noise.

The power within me comes from knowing my worth, trusting myself and rising above what was meant to pull me down.

I have faced challenges that were designed to destroy me, but I survived. And, through those trials, I've learned that I can overcome anything.

I'm trusting the journey. It's shaping me into something even stronger.

2024: Local Government Election.

The former Mayor of Townsville and her cohort have much to answer for.

Not just for what they did to me but for what they did to an entire community.

The people of Townsville were crying out for change.

For deeply personal reasons, I took a firm stance against the previous leadership.

I challenged the status quo, expressed my dissatisfaction, and presented a vision for something better.

I encouraged people to think critically about the direction of our city and to demand more from those in power.

I later learned that my actions during the 2024 Local Government Election, particularly a Facebook post, didn't sit well with the former Mayor.

I have no regrets.

For me, sparking meaningful conversations and driving real change was worth every bit of discomfort I caused.

Moving Forward.

I made a decision, and it was for the greater good.

I vowed that no one else working in a union should have to endure what I went through.

This message is both a celebration of what's been accomplished and a declaration of independence.

By taking this stand, I honour the battles I've fought, while reclaiming my energy for the future.

It's a delicate, powerful balance of accountability, advocacy, and self-care.

My reflection stands as a testimony to resilience, justice, and the unrelenting pursuit of dignity.

It acknowledges the pain, recognises the victories, and firmly states: my well-being comes first now.

Let's talk about dignity because we all deserve it. And we all know when it's being denied.

Here are ten core elements of dignity:

1. Everyone wants their identity accepted.

2. We all want to be recognised for our uniqueness.

3. We deserve acknowledgement when we've been harmed.

4. We need safety - physical and psychological.

5. We want to live without humiliation.

6. We want to belong.

7. We want to be understood.

8. We expect fairness.

9. We deserve the benefit of the doubt.

10. When we are wronged, we want an apology.

Yet, there are people who believe the world revolves around them.

Someone once told me, "*You need me more than I need you.*"

Like fuck I do. I'm doing just fine without them.

That comment wasn't about care or connection.

It was a control tactic.

A weak attempt to diminish me, to rewrite the power dynamic in their favour.

But my response made one thing clear: I know my worth. I don't need anyone who treats me like I'm disposable.

Why would someone say something like that?

- **Power Play**: To assert dominance and make me question myself.

- **Insecurity:** Because deep down, they were afraid of being irrelevant.

- **Projection:** They needed me more than they could admit, and they tried to flip the script.

But I didn't buy it. I took back the narrative, and I stood firm. Because:

- I am self-sufficient.

- I set boundaries.

- I trust myself.

Taking My Power Back.

I took the higher ground by recognising that I'm better off without their influence, and I'll keep owning my power. I don't need them to succeed, nor do I need them to feel whole.

Taking back my power meant rejecting the constraints of the Deed of Agreement I signed at Settlement, including the Non-Disclosure clause.

I declared my power by saying that the NDA is not worth the paper it's written on.

In this context, my declaration is an act of bold defiance, empowering and purposeful. It signals that I refuse to be silenced or diminished by terms meant to suppress my truth or protect those who may have wronged me.

If you encounter someone like this regularly, it's crucial to reinforce your independence by:

1.Focusing on Your Goals:

Prove to yourself, and inadvertently to them, that you're thriving on your terms.

2. Setting Clear Boundaries:

Refuse to entertain manipulative comments or behaviour.

3. Surrounding Yourself with Support:

Engage with people who respect and value you as you are.

What Taking My Power Back Represents.

1.Reclaiming My Voice:

NDAs are often used to silence individuals, particularly those who've experienced workplace abuse or injustice.

By declaring the clause meaningless, I chose to prioritise my truth over their control.

2. Breaking the Cycle of Silence:

Refusing to honour the NDA sends a clear message: I won't be complicit in enabling harmful behaviour. It challenges the culture of secrecy that lets toxic practices persist without consequence.

3. Standing in Integrity:

By taking back my narrative on my terms, I showed that my integrity and commitment to justice outweigh any perceived risks.

Why NDAs Often Lack True Power.

1.Unenforceability in Certain Cases:

Many NDAs, especially those concerning workplace abuse or misconduct, can be legally unenforceable if they're found to suppress whistleblowing or shield unlawful behaviour.

2. The Power of Publicity:

Organisations often rely on fear of legal consequences to enforce NDAs. However, the court of public opinion, and your courage, can be just as powerful, if not more so.

3. A Flawed System:

NDAs are frequently used as tools to silence victims rather than address the underlying issues. By declaring the NDA invalid, I confronted this imbalance head-on.

My Act of Resistance.

1.A Statement of Self-Worth:

By rejecting the NDA, I declared that my truth and well-being are worth far more than any attempt to silence me.

2. An Act of Solidarity:

My courage may have inspired others to break their own silence, fostering collective strength against abusive systems.

3. A Rejection of Fear:

Refusing to honour the clause signifies that I will not be intimidated or manipulated.

My Advice.

1.Know Your Rights:

Ensure you're aware of any legal implications of rejecting the NDA and consult with legal professionals, if necessary, before proceeding.

2. Speak Your Truth:

Continue sharing your story in a way that empowers you and resonates with those who need to hear it.

3. Focus on Empowerment:

Use this experience as a foundation for advocating for yourself and others facing similar challenges.

Standing Up for Worker Rights & the Campaign to End NDAs.

In addition to reclaiming my own voice, I've been supporting our friends **@union_women** in their campaign to end gender-based violence through the misuse of NDAs.

While their focus has been on political action in Victoria, this issue is alive and well across Australia.

Workers everywhere are being silenced by the threat of NDAs, a tool designed to suppress the truth and protect perpetrators rather than victims.

I also want to take this moment to thank the defamation lawyer I spoke with in 2020. Turns out, I didn't need legal assistance after all. I just needed to trust my intellect. But your time and advice were appreciated.

Every worker, regardless of their job, deserves a safe, respectful and equitable workplace.

To end harassment, including sexual harassment, we need to break the silence and hold employers accountable.

Victim-survivors should have the option to speak out if they wish and on their own terms.

This isn't just a Victorian issue. Across the country, workers are standing up.

In Queensland, organisations like ***Basic Rights Queensland*** have also joined the fight, launching a campaign to challenge the harmful misuse of NDAs.

The tide is turning. Together, we are demanding change, calling out a system that protects power over people and reclaiming the right to speak our truth without fear or gag orders.

Key Points from the Message:

1.What is an NDA?

An NDA is a legal tool that can silence workers, forcing them to keep workplace injustices, such as sexual harassment or gender-based violence, a secret indefinitely. This misuse perpetuates harm and prevents accountability.

2. Advocacy and Support.

My support for **@union_women** and their legislative efforts in Victoria reflects solidarity and the importance of tackling this issue nationwide.

3. Call to Action.

By encouraging others to sign the petition to end NDAs, I'm empowering them to take a tangible step toward systemic change.

4. Worker Rights.

Every worker deserves a safe, respectful, and equitable workplace.

This is a fundamental human right that should never be compromised.

Conclusion:

This advocacy against NDAs is essential to breaking the cycle of silence and ensuring justice for victim-survivors. The message conveys not only the gravity of the issue but also the hope that collective action can bring about meaningful change. By standing up and sharing my story, I hope to inspire others to do the same.

A Call to Action.

It's not just about economics, it's about recognising and valuing the humanity of every worker.

By reframing the narrative and advocating for a new trajectory, we can begin dismantling a system that prioritises profit over people and build one that ensures dignity, equity, and fairness for all workers.

Freedom of Speech.

The fight for workers' rights, justice, and accountability is intrinsically tied to Freedom of Speech.

The fundamental right that allows individuals to speak out without fear of retaliation or oppression.

Freedom of speech is more than just a person's tool for dismantling silence, exposing truth, and fostering social change.

In the context of NDAs, whistleblowers and workplace injustice, it becomes a critical line of defense for those who have been wronged but are too often muted by fear or legal constraints.

Freedom of Speech is the right of individuals or communities to publicly express their opinions and ideas without being censored, prosecuted, or retaliated against.

It is considered a basic human right, an essential part of a free and democratic society, and necessary for the protection of all human rights.

The United Nations' Universal Declaration of Human Rights, adopted in 1948 and signed by Australia, states in Article 19:

"Everyone has the right to freedom of opinion and expression; this right includes freedom to hold opinions without interference and to seek, receive and impart information and ideas through any media and regardless of frontiers."

This declaration reinforces that freedom of speech is indispensable to societal change and the functioning of democracy.

Why is Freedom of Speech Important?

1.Promotes Change:

Openly sharing ideas and opinions is essential for identifying injustices and pushing for reform.

Activism, protests, and media campaigns are practical examples of this process in action.

2. Protects Other Human Rights:

Freedom of speech amplifies the voices of marginalized groups, ensuring their rights are acknowledged and upheld.

3. Encourages Accountability:

Governments, corporations, and institutions are held responsible for their actions through public critique and discourse.

4. Fosters Innovation and Progress:

Diverse viewpoints and open discussions lead to new ideas, solutions, and advancements in society.

Modern Applications.

1.Digital and Social Media:

The rise of digital platforms has created unprecedented opportunities for individuals to share their thoughts globally. Social media has become a powerful tool for advocacy, awareness campaigns, and organizing movements.

2. Protests and Campaigns:

Marches, rallies, and demonstrations remain vital expressions of freedom of speech, bringing attention to causes that need societal or governmental action.

Challenges to Freedom of Speech.

While the right to free expression is fundamental, it is not absolute. Laws against hate speech, defamation, and incitement to violence exist to balance free expression with the safety and dignity of others. However, overreach or misuse of such laws can threaten the very principle of free speech, making vigilance essential to preserve this right.

Freedom of speech remains the backbone of democratic societies, ensuring that voices can rise to challenge power, spark change, and inspire progress.

The Disparity: A Reflection on Workers' Struggles.

The stark disparity between the financial gains of CEOs and the exploitation of workers is one of the most glaring injustices in modern society.

While executives reward themselves with exorbitant salaries and bonuses, the workers who form the backbone of these businesses are often paid the minimum wage, despite their central role in keeping the organisation afloat. This speaks to a wider issue that continues to plague Australian workers: many are living below the poverty line or are forced to work multiple jobs just to survive.

The struggle to make ends meet isn't just an economic issue.

It's a moral failure.

Take, for example, the story of an employee, the administrative, financial, and managerial nerve centre behind a business, who went above and beyond what was expected of an employee in their role.

Despite this, the employer did not think this worker was worthy of anything more than the basic minimum wage.

Meanwhile, the boss awarded themselves a huge salary, along with other privileged staff.

The system is rigged, and it needs to be addressed.

The Core Issues.

1.Wage Inequality:

The growing gap between executive salaries and workers' wages is both unethical and unsustainable. A living wage is a fundamental right, ensuring workers can live with dignity.

2. Exploitation Under the Guise of Efficiency:

Cost-cutting measures like outsourcing and understaffing prioritize profits over people, leaving workers to bear the brunt of business failures and challenges.

3. The Poverty Line Reality:

Many Australians, despite working multiple jobs, still struggle to meet basic needs.

This systemic issue must be framed as unpaid wages - $5 billion in estimated "extra wages costs" should be seen as wages workers are rightfully owed.

A New Trajectory: What Needs to Change.

1.Fair Pay for Fair Work:

Implement and enforce policies like "same job, same pay," ensuring equitable compensation for all workers, regardless of employment arrangements.

2. Executive Accountability:

Capping executive pay or tying it proportionally to the average worker's wage could help address the growing disparity in income.

3. Living Wage Legislation:

Governments must legislate a living wage that reflects the actual cost of living, including housing, food, and healthcare.

4. Reinvest in Workers:

Instead of cutting costs at workers' expense, businesses should reinvest profits into fair wages, training, and better working conditions.

A Call for Change.

This is not just an economic issue.

It's about recognising and valuing the humanity of workers.

The narrative needs to shift.

Workers should not be treated as expendable tools for profit but as essential contributors to the success and growth of businesses.

It's time for a system that prioritises equity, fairness, and the well-being of all, ensuring a more just future for everyone.

Closing Reflection.

Freedom of speech allows us to name injustice, to speak our truth, and to challenge the structures that silence or suppress.

But healing, real healing, comes not just from speaking out but from being heard, seen, and understood.

For those of us who have lived through trauma, inequality, and erasure, the fight for justice is both external and internal.

It is in this space, between the silence we've endured and the voices we're reclaiming, that recovery begins.

Because recovery is not about forgetting the past. It's about facing it head-on, in our time, on our terms, and, slowly, deliberately, choosing to build something new from its ashes.

Recovery

Reflections.

"Trauma survivors are not 'fixated' on the past.

The past is INTRUDING upon us.

It intrudes upon our thoughts.

It intrudes upon our feelings.

It intrudes upon what we experience in our physical body.

Not only do trauma survivors not "fixate" on the past, most often, but survivors are also doing everything in our power to NOT think about the past.

Which goes about as well as telling yourself not to picture a purple elephant right now.

Nobody in trauma recovery engages with the past because we want to. I assure you: we'd much rather NOT think about or reexperience the past, at least the aspects of the past that tend to kick our ass via trauma responses.

Containment and trauma processing in recovery is about engaging with the past because, if we HAVE to engage with it, we'd rather it be on our terms, in our time, for our reasons.

I know. Easy does it."

-Dr. Glenn Patrick Doyle

Furthermore, Robin Williams once said:

"I think the people who have been through the most sadness are the ones who always try the hardest to make others happy. Because they know in their flesh what it's like to feel empty and depressed, and they just don't want anyone else to feel that way."

These words illuminate a profound truth about empathy and the human spirit: those who have endured the deepest sadness often become the greatest sources of joy for others. It may seem paradoxical, but it's precisely because they've walked through life's darkest moments that they understand the transformative power of a smile, a kind gesture, or shared laughter.

They see the silent battles others fight and respond with instinctive compassion, a quiet resolve to ease someone else's pain.

This compassion is not learned; it is lived.

Those who have faced emptiness and despair develop a heightened sensitivity to the struggles of others. They know what it is to feel invisible, isolated, or hopeless. That awareness fuels their drive to create light for others. For them, even the smallest act of kindness: a moment of connection, a heartfelt joke, a word of encouragement, becomes a way of saying, "You are seen. You are not alone."

In lifting others, they find purpose. Turning their own pain into someone else's comfort allows them to reclaim what once felt like senseless suffering. Each time they bring joy or relief to another, they transform their wounds into something meaningful.

Yet this path of giving is not without challenges.

Too often, these compassionate souls neglect their own needs, prioritising the happiness of others while hiding their own struggles behind a mask of strength. They carry their burdens in silence, believing they must be the unwavering source of light for those around them.

But even the brightest lights need tending.

Self-care is not selfish, it is essential.

Their journeys remind us of the strength found in vulnerability and the power of resilience. By choosing to turn their pain into kindness, they inspire a ripple effect of compassion, proving that even the heaviest sadness can be transformed into hope, joy, and connection.

They teach us that the human spirit, no matter how broken, has an extraordinary capacity to heal, not just itself, but others.

In my spare time, I like to read.

One of my recent reads was a remarkable and confronting book:

How Many More Women is both an inspiring and sobering read. It shines a glaring light on systemic injustices and the resilience of those fighting to change them. While global movements like #MeToo have empowered individuals to speak out, the book lays bare the persistent challenges in dismantling entrenched power structures.

It's a harrowing account, one that leaves little faith in the institutions supposedly designed to protect women.

Too often, the police, the legal system, and the courts feel rigged to fail us.

Add to this the insidious belief that women are somehow responsible for the violence inflicted upon them, whether by "asking for it," "knowing better," or simply existing as women in a patriarchal world. The injustice is staggering.

This book is an exhausting, yet essential, reminder of the scale and repetition of these failures across countries, cultures, and industries. It left me asking the same haunting question posed by the title:

How many more women?

It's as heartbreaking as it is enraging.

How many more women, indeed.

The patriarchal system tried to erode my sense of self. To strip me of my identity until there was nothing left. But I escaped.

And once I did, I began to understand what, and who, they are.

I chose to show myself compassion. I chose patience. I stayed committed to the process of healing.

And something incredible happened.

I used my understanding, my resilience, and the experience of surviving horrendous workplace abuse to grow into something more. More than I ever thought possible.

I learned that when they fail to destroy you, you end up defying everything they tried to accomplish.

You become a version of yourself that is stronger, wiser, and beyond what they could ever hope to diminish.

That clarity didn't come easily. In the thick of it, when the wounds were fresh and the road ahead felt impossible, it was hard to believe any of this could be true. But I gave myself permission to heal. I gave myself the time to stay the course.

As I said during therapy, *"I'm taking each day as it comes."*

I still have my down days, but I know that the empowered version of me is there, waiting patiently for me to fully step into it.

At the time, I told myself that surviving was enough.

I would learn later that survival and justice are not the same thing.

In the meantime, I am healing, at my own pace.

And I will continue to:

- Rise above the lies and the injustice.

- Raise my voice and call out the hypocrisy embedded in a community that knows the rules but chooses, without consequence, to break them.

- Write, because writing is both cathartic and healing.

Recovery Strategies.

Recovery from workplace abuse involves more than reflection and reading. It's an active, multifaceted process. Healing emotionally, mentally, and physically. Rebuilding confidence. Reclaiming your identity.

If you find yourself in a similar situation, here are some steps and strategies that have helped me and might support you, too:

A Guide for Reclaiming Your Power.

Healing from workplace abuse is not a passive process. It demands emotional, mental, and physical restoration. It also requires a commitment to rediscovering who you are, beyond what was done to you.

If you're navigating your own recovery, here are some steps and strategies that may help guide your path forward:

1.Seek Professional Support

- **Therapy or Counselling:**

Work with a therapist, ideally one experienced in trauma or workplace issues, to process the abuse, manage triggers, and develop healthy coping strategies.

- **Trauma-Informed Care:**

Therapies such as EMDR (Eye Movement Desensitization and Reprocessing) or somatic experiencing can be powerful for healing deep emotional wounds. (I haven't tried it, but it comes recommended.)

- **Support Groups:**

Connecting with others who've had similar experiences can lessen isolation and offer much-needed validation.

2. Rebuild Your Confidence

- **Set Small Goals:**

Start with manageable tasks to regain a sense of agency and accomplishment.

- **Celebrate Strengths:**

Reflect on your resilience. Surviving workplace abuse already shows tremendous inner strength.

- **Reframe Negative Beliefs:**

Challenge the internalised narratives of inadequacy or failure that the abuse may have imprinted.

3. Reconnect with Yourself

- **Self-Care Practices:**

Nourish your body and mind through activities like yoga, meditation, journaling, or nature walks.

- **Explore Hobbies:**

Revisit passions or try something new that brings you joy and affirms your identity beyond work.

- **Practice Boundaries:**

Learn to say no. Protect your time and energy, without guilt.

4. Build a New Narrative

- **Separate Identity from Work:**

Your worth is not defined by a job title or workplace hierarchy.

- **Reframe the Experience:**

Though painful, surviving abuse can deepen your empathy, insight, and self-awareness.

- **Define Your Values:**

Reflect on what truly matters to you as you move forward, personally and professionally.

5. Surround Yourself with Positivity

- **Cultivate Supportive Relationships:**

Spend time with people who uplift, affirm, and respect you.

- **Distance from Toxicity:**

Limit exposure to environments or individuals that echo the harm you've endured.

- **Seek Mentors or Allies:**

Whether professional or personal, mentors can help rebuild trust and open new pathways.

6. Address Practical Matters

- **Explore New Opportunities:**

If staying at your current workplace isn't viable, research roles or environments that align with your well-being.

- **Know Your Rights:**

Familiarise yourself with workplace laws, union protections, and your legal options.
Knowledge is power.

- **Financial Planning:**

If leaving your job has financial consequences, create a step-by-step plan to regain stability.

7. Focus on Physical Wellness

- **Exercise:**

Regular movement helps release built-up stress and restores a sense of bodily autonomy.

- **Healthy Habits:**

Prioritise rest, hydration, and nutrition.
These foundations will support your emotional healing, too.

- **Mind-Body Practices:**

Mindfulness, tai chi, or breathwork can help regulate your nervous system and rebuild a sense of inner calm.

8. Engage in Personal Growth

- **Educational Opportunities:**

Learn something new, whether for career progression or simply for joy.

- **Volunteering:**

Helping others can shift focus away from trauma and remind you of your capacity to make a difference.

- **Develop Resilience Tools:**

Books, workshops, and podcasts about healing and empowerment can offer new insights and motivation.

9. Monitor Your Progress

- **Track Your Healing Journey:**

Journal, create check-ins or mark milestones, small or large, as a reminder of how far you've come.

- **Be Patient:**

Recovery is rarely linear.

Give yourself grace during setbacks.

- **Celebrate Your Growth:**

Honour the strength it took to survive and the courage it takes to rebuild.

Healing is deeply personal and takes time.

It's not about erasing what happened; it's about integrating it in a way that empowers you to move forward.

You are not what they did to you. You are who you choose to become in spite of it.

On my deeply personal and transformative journey of recovery and healing, I had the privilege of connecting with some extraordinary individuals.

One of them was Tammy Copley, the founder of Nurses and Midwives Against Bullying Australia (NAMABA).

Tammy's work highlights an uncomfortable truth: Bullying doesn't just wound emotionally, it damages physically, mentally, and spiritually. The consequences are far-reaching and severe.

Bullying can trigger chronic stress responses, leading to gastrointestinal issues, debilitating migraine attacks, and a weakened immune system. Over time, these stress responses may contribute to the development of serious health conditions such as PTSD, anxiety, depression, heart disease, stroke, and even early-onset dementia.

The cost is immense.

In the most tragic cases, the compounded effects of bullying: feelings of hopelessness, isolation, and despair, can result in early death or suicide.

These aren't rare outcomes.

They're devastatingly common and alarmingly under-recognised.

Workplaces, schools, and communities have a responsibility, a Duty of Care, to act.

Bullying must be acknowledged not only as a cultural and social issue but as a public health crisis.

By fostering environments rooted in empathy, dignity, and accountability, we can help prevent the long-term damage inflicted by systemic cruelty.

Thank you, Tammy, for your tireless advocacy in a profession that's supposed to be about care.

Ironic, isn't it?

Music.

Music played a profound role in my recovery, serving as both a sanctuary and a source of strength during some of my darkest moments.

It became a safe space where I could process emotions, whether through the catharsis of lyrics that spoke directly to my pain or the soothing rhythms that helped calm my mind.

Certain songs felt like they were written just for me, putting into words feelings I couldn't yet articulate and reminding me that I wasn't alone in my struggle.

Beyond the emotional connection, music helped me reconnect with joy and creativity. It offered moments of escape and inspiration, allowing me to refocus my energy on healing and self-expression.

Whether I was singing along or simply listening in solitude, music became a faithful companion on my journey, guiding me back to hope, resilience, and, ultimately, a renewed sense of self.

I want to express my heartfelt gratitude to the countless artists around the world whose songs, filled with deeply resonant and meaningful lyrics, became a guiding light.

Your music spoke to my soul in ways nothing else could, offering comfort, understanding, and hope when I needed it most.

Each lyric carried a piece of wisdom or emotion that helped me process my pain and reminded me that I was not alone.

Through your creativity and vulnerability, you gave me a lifeline.

Thank you for helping me find strength in the most challenging moments of my recovery.

Movies / TV Shows.

Likewise, I want to extend my gratitude to the actors and performers whose characters and stories gave me an escape from the relentless chaos of my mind.

During a time when my thoughts raced at a million miles an hour, endlessly replaying scenarios, piecing together details, and trying to make sense of who was involved, I desperately needed a break from the overwhelming mental noise.

Watching movies and series became a form of sanctuary, allowing me to step into other worlds, if only for a little while.

The stories and characters offered more than distraction; they gave me the space to quiet my mind, regain perspective, and recharge.

Your work provided more than entertainment. It became a vital part of my coping and healing process. Thank you for that gift.

In the quiet of my recovery, it was the artists: the singers, the actors, the storytellers, who helped me find my voice again.

With that voice, I'm ready to tell the rest of the story.

No masks.

No filters.

Just the truth.

I'm No Angel

You will never be able to use my weaknesses against me because I've already exposed them myself.

I've faced them.

I've owned them.

I've embraced them.

Plot twist.

When you take control of your narrative, when you stand in your truth, instead of hiding from it you strip others of the power to weaponise it against you.

That's where real strength lies.

Vulnerability isn't a flaw. It's a SuperPower.

It's the courage to be honest about your struggles, your imperfections, and your fears.

Self-awareness? Another SuperPower.

It's the foundation of growth, healing, and resilience.

When you know yourself, your strengths, your weaknesses, your values - no one else can define you.

No one can diminish you.

So let them try. Let them point fingers. Let them dig for dirt.

They're only revealing their own limitations, not yours.

Because when you own every part of yourself - you become untouchable.

After years of creating online content about narcissists, psychopaths, and sociopaths in the workplace, it's refreshing to see the mainstream finally catching up. We've been ringing the bell for a while now.

It takes courage to admit mistakes, and acknowledging them is the first step toward growth and accountability.

While drunk driving is serious, it also offers an opportunity; a moment to reflect on what led to that decision and to commit to ensuring it never happens again.

Yes, I was caught driving under the influence while driving my work car.

On 25 February 2016, I travelled 350 kilometers from Townsville to Cairns, attending meetings along the way and upon arrival. It was an exhausting day, both physically and mentally. I had my period and was in a significant amount of pain but I pushed through, as I always did. That evening, I had made a commitment to attend a local government election launch for an ALP candidate. I wasn't one to back out of obligations, no matter how I felt.

At the event, I tried to stay engaged, even though my body was begging me to rest. I had two glasses of wine, along with some water, hoping it would help me relax and get through the night.

Afterward, I had another commitment: a CFMEU branch meeting. Despite my fatigue, I went. Showing up mattered to me. Being present mattered.

At the meeting, I had two more glasses of wine. The discussions went on and, by then, I was running on little more than adrenaline and sheer determination.

When it ended, CFMEU Organiser M walked out with me as I was leaving. I turned to him and asked, "How are you getting back to the hotel?" It was a simple question, but one that set the stage for what came next.

Just 200 metres from the accommodation, I was pulled over by the police. I hadn't expected it. The flashing lights, the sudden stop, it felt surreal. The officer asked for my license, then came the breathalyzer. I blew 0.09 - over the legal limit.

M was in the passenger seat. The weight of the moment hit me hard. After the test and the on-the-spot processing, they took me to Cairns Police Station. What happened next is hazy. My body was exhausted, and my mind was spiralling.

But one moment stands out with startling clarity.

Before the police took me in, M turned to me and said: *"Don't tell anyone. Don't tell N. Don't tell your husband. Call B."*

His tone was sharp. Urgent. Like he needed to control the narrative before it could spread. His words landed heavy. And they stuck.

At the time, I didn't fully understand why he was so specific or why he seemed more concerned with who I told than what had just happened. But I trusted him. I was a relatively new regional organiser. He was seasoned, confident, and convincing. So I followed his advice.

I saw the lawyers. I sat in the meetings. I was reassured: *"We've got your back."*

That's what M said. And I believed him.

What should have happened is that I should have told my boss.

In that moment, I should have been honest, upfront, and transparent about what had occurred. As difficult and uncomfortable as it was, the right thing to do was to take full responsibility, face the consequences, and keep my integrity intact.

By not telling my boss, I tried to protect myself from the fallout. But all I really did was make things more complicated. I let fear and shame lead the way, hoping I could quietly manage the situation and avoid the worst of it. But deep down, I knew: the truth always finds a way to surface.

And the longer I waited, the further I strayed from my own values.

Being honest would have been the courageous choice. It would have shown accountability, maturity, and earned respect in a way that hiding never could. I've learned over time that there is power in facing your mistakes head-on. The truth was never going to stay hidden, and by delaying it, I only made things harder than they needed to be.

Looking back, I wish I had trusted that my boss might have handled it with fairness or at least some understanding. Taking responsibility could have been a step toward personal and professional growth.

I don't know how, but I now believe my boss found out.

It wasn't the way I'd hoped the truth would come to light, but it did. One way or another.

What happened next was not what I expected.

There was no direct confrontation. No formal discipline. No honest conversation.

Instead, my boss proceeded to play a game.

Rather than addressing the issue openly, everything shifted into something more subtle. Like a test. A power move. A quiet way to observe how I'd handle things, without ever naming what we both knew had happened.

The lines blurred. The air got heavy with unspoken expectations. And instead of clarity or consequence, I was met with ambiguity. Support, perhaps, but laced with manipulation. I wasn't sure what I was being asked to do, what was being held over me, or how to navigate the increasingly uncomfortable space I found myself in.

That moment, when it could have been about growth and integrity, turned into something else. A power play.

Suddenly, it wasn't about my mistake. It was about managing the dynamics of silence, trust, and control.

Looking back now, I see just how crucial it is, for both employees and employers, to handle these moments with honesty, clarity, and integrity. Because games like that don't teach lessons.

They just create confusion, and no one grows from that.

Processing the Experience.

I admit, I did not handle the situation well. But I know my mistakes do not define me.

How I respond to them does.

This became a turning point. A moment to move forward with greater awareness and responsibility.

Owning the Mistake.

The first and most important step was acknowledging what happened and taking responsibility for my actions.

I accepted that responsibility and owned the consequences of my decisions.

Reflecting on the Circumstances.

It's clear I was managing a lot that day:

- Physical pain and discomfort from my period

- Professional and social obligations tied to the ALP and CFMEU

- The pressures of an environment where social drinking was normalised

- Emotional fatigue and other mitigating factors

All of these contributed to a lapse in judgement.

They don't excuse my actions, but they do underscore the importance of prioritising self-care and setting clear boundaries, especially under pressure.

Responding to Pressure.

After the incident, I was told to keep quiet.

That reaction only added to my emotional burden, leaving me feeling isolated and unsupported.

Looking back, it's clear how vital it is to have people around you who prioritise well-being and accountability over secrecy or reputation management.

Learning and Moving Forward.

This experience, while difficult, became a catalyst for growth.

I've developed healthier coping strategies. I now recognise when I'm overextended, and I give myself permission to step back or say no, without guilt.

Advocating for Change.

By sharing my story, I hope to encourage safer practices and help others learn from my experience.

It's not just about acknowledging mistakes. It's about showing how we grow from them. Through honesty and reflection, I aim to foster understanding and accountability.

To empower others to make better choices and create more supportive environments.

Acknowledgement.

Mistakes are part of life. What defines your character is how you respond.

By owning my actions, learning from them, and making thoughtful changes, I've turned this experience into a stepping stone for resilience and growth.

Resolve.

Leaving the union wasn't the defeat they hoped it would be.

It was a turning point. A new chapter.

It gave me space to take the lessons I had learned through adversity and use them as fuel to challenge injustice wherever I found it.

Their attempts to silence me didn't work.

If anything, they amplified my purpose.

I became even more determined to advocate for fairness, transparency, and accountability, not just in the union but in every space I enter.

Their actions were meant to diminish my voice.

Instead, they strengthened it.

The Reality of My Story.

While the title I'm No Angel fits, it doesn't tell the whole story.

Yes, I've acted irresponsibly. I own that, without hesitation.

My imperfections don't define me.

How I choose to move forward does.

If you were to speak to the Delegate who represented me during my departure from the union, they could tell you how complex the situation really was.

It wasn't just about what I had done.

It was about culture, power, and how accountability was applied selectively.

My actions, while flawed, were met with responses that said more about the people and systems around me than they did about my character.

What I've come to understand is this:

Owning your reality means holding yourself accountable and refusing to let others define your worth by your lowest moments.

I am not perfect. But I am resilient.

It's that resilience that allows me to grow, to learn, and to keep fighting for something better.

The Delegate once said to me, "*You're an angel, compared to them*".

At the time, I didn't know what she meant.

I was deep in trauma, trying to piece together what had happened and who these people really were.

Her words stayed with me, echoing in the background as I worked through pain and truth.

Maybe she saw something I couldn't yet see.

The contrast between my imperfect but accountable choices and the calculated indifference or cruelty of others.

Maybe she saw the humanity I was fighting to preserve in a place that had so little of it left.

The Delegate's words remind me of the importance of perspective.

At the time, I couldn't see my own worth.

I was too focused on my flaws.

But to someone else, I represented something more.

Something human.

Something decent.

Even now, those words strengthen me.

They remind me that while I'm not perfect, I've always tried to act with integrity, even in the face of adversity.

And maybe, just maybe, that's what she saw in me.

Perspective.

In my youth and young adulthood, I used cannabis recreationally. As I later discovered, though, I was also using it medicinally, long before I understood its full potential and before it became legally recognised for medical use. More on that a bit later.

My brother was the one who introduced me to it. I remember the first time like it was yesterday. I had been out with my friends, and he was out with his. We bumped into each other at the bar of the Criterion Hotel, on The Strand, in Townsville.

We started chatting, and the topic of weed came up.

"You want to try some?" he asked, grinning in that mischievous way he had.

Before I could overthink it, he grabbed my hand and said, *"Come on"*.

The next thing I knew, he was pulling me through the noisy crowd, weaving between patrons and past security. The cool winter's night air hit me as we crossed the street and headed into the park. It was quieter there; the sounds of the bar had faded into the background.

He pulled a joint from his pocket, lit it with the ease of someone who'd done it before, and took a drag. Then he handed it to me.

My first joint. I was 17.

I continued using cannabis recreationally into my young adulthood. It was part of my social life, something I associated with freedom and fun. But in 1994, I stopped.

The stigma surrounding cannabis had grown too heavy, and the weight of it pushed me to walk away from something I once enjoyed.

My life's circumstances - becoming a mother and other responsibilities - influenced my decision to stop.

My priorities had shifted, and I changed my perspective on recreational use. It was a natural cessation. Albeit, I dabbled every now and then in the years that followed.

Thankfully, the progressive Queensland Palaszczuk government legalised medicinal cannabis in 2016. That decision marked a turning point. Not just for public health policy but for me personally. It gave me permission to explore something I had long been curious about, something I had experienced as both recreational and therapeutic in my younger years.

It was 2017, and I was sitting beside the fire in my backyard. The flames flickered and cracked, casting warm light into the cool night, but none of it could distract me from the pain.

I shifted in my chair, letting out another moan, unable to mask the discomfort any longer.

Beside me, my daughter sat quietly.

She had recently started using cannabis to manage her debilitating migraine attacks, something that had plagued her for years.

I'd seen how much it was helping her, softening the edges of her pain and giving her some semblance of normalcy.

When she turned to me and asked, "Would you like to try my cannabis for your pain?" her question caught me off guard.

I froze. I'd told myself that leaving it behind in the '90s had been the mature thing to do, the responsible thing. But here was my daughter, offering it back, not as rebellion but as care.

I looked at her, searching her face for any hint of doubt, but I saw none. There was no judgement in her expression, no pressure. Only compassion. She wasn't asking me to get high or to rebel against anything. She was offering me relief, just as she had found relief for herself.

Still, I hesitated. What would it mean to cross that line again? Was I opening the door to something I thought I'd closed for good? Or was this simply an opportunity to rethink the narrative I'd been handed. To reconsider cannabis not as a vice but as a tool?

The pain in my body tugged me back to the present, and I realised the question wasn't really about the past or society's judgement. It was about this moment, right now. My daughter was offering me a chance to feel better, and I had to decide whether I could accept it.

I took a deep breath and nodded. "Okay," I said quietly, "I'll give it a try."

My daughter handed me a meticulously rolled joint immediately after lighting it.

The act of taking and receiving the joint felt strange and yet oddly natural, like muscle memory resurfacing from a long-forgotten past.

I hesitated before taking that first draw, feeling a mix of curiosity and apprehension.

The effects were almost immediate. Within minutes, the sharp edges of my pain began to dull. My body, which had felt so tense and clenched against the discomfort, started to relax.

It was as if a heavy weight I'd been carrying had finally been lifted, allowing me to breathe deeply for the first time in hours.

I sat back in my chair, stunned. "I feel… better," I said, almost in disbelief. The firelight flickered across my daughter's face as she smiled, relief and validation clear in her eyes.

In that moment, I felt not just the physical relief from the pain but also a sense of profound gratitude. Gratitude for my daughter's compassion, for her willingness to share something that had helped her, and for the chance to reconsider everything I thought I knew about cannabis.

What it comes down to is perspective.

I can choose to believe the perspective of the medical fraternity, a perspective that, far too often, blindly parrots the same rigid narratives and serves entrenched agendas. Or I can choose to believe in a different perspective: one rooted in centuries of evidence, where cannabis has been used as a treatment for ailments across cultures and eras.

The truth is, we are witnessing its benefits in real time. We've seen how it can ease the pain of cancer patients, offering them relief when other options fail. We're beginning to understand its potential for mental health, how it can soften the edges of anxiety or depression. And then there's my daughter, using medicinal cannabis to manage her neurological condition; a tool that's helping her navigate the pain and challenges she faces every day.

These aren't just abstract ideas or theories. They're lived experiences, real stories of healing and relief.

For me, the choice isn't just about science or tradition. It's about acknowledging the reality of what works and the courage to embrace it, even when it challenges old beliefs.

For years, I chose to believe the perspective of the medical fraternity. A perspective that dismissed cannabis as anything more than a recreational drug, wrapped in stigma and taboo.

Their narrative felt absolute, reinforced by laws, policies, and a societal reluctance to question the status quo. I didn't challenge it. I accepted it, internalised it, and allowed it to shape my own beliefs.

But over time, cracks began to form in that rigid perspective. It started with stories. People sharing their experiences about finding relief in ways that traditional medicine couldn't offer. Cancer patients whose pain was eased. Individuals with anxiety or depression finding stability.

And then it became personal. My daughter, battling her neurological condition, found solace in using cannabis for medicinal purposes, something no prescription or treatment had been able to provide.

Even then, I hesitated.

Decades of stigma don't fade overnight, and stepping outside the narrative I had clung to felt daunting. But pain has a way of forcing reflection.

That night by the fire in 2017, as my daughter offered me her cannabis for my pain, I faced a choice: cling to the outdated beliefs I had carried for so long or open myself to the possibility that I had been wrong.

When I took that first draw and felt the pain melt away, I experienced more than physical relief.

It was as if my perspective had shifted in an instant, forcing me to confront the rigidity of my own thinking.

How had I allowed stigma and fear to blind me to something that had so much potential to heal?

That moment marked the beginning of my journey toward acceptance, not just of cannabis, but of the idea that healing requires open-mindedness.

It taught me to trust not only science but lived experience, mine included.

In my personal life, cannabis became a lifeline. It helped me manage the physical and emotional toll of perimenopause, PMDD, and chronic fatigue. But professionally, it became something else entirely: a quiet target, used against me by those who claimed to support progress but clung to stigma when it suited them.

I'd always suffered from painful periods ever since I started menstruating at the age of 10. But as I entered perimenopause, those pains intensified. My cycles became erratic and relentless as I approached menopause, coming every three weeks, accompanied by tremendous cramping that left me bedridden at times. The fatigue was overwhelming: a weight I carried every single day.

And then there was the PMDD (Premenstrual Dysphoric Disorder), a beast of its own.

The mood swings were extreme and unpredictable, pulling me from anger to despair with alarming speed. Small frustrations could trigger an outburst; moments of sadness would spiral into full-blown hopelessness. It felt like I wasn't just battling my body but also my mind.

These conditions didn't exist in a vacuum.

They affected every corner of my life.

My relationships bore the brunt of my mood swings and exhaustion.

I found myself withdrawing from friends and family, too drained to engage or explain why I felt so irritable or distant.

The pain and fatigue made it difficult to keep up with daily tasks, let alone maintain a sense of normalcy.

At work, I struggled to stay focused. Fatigue dulled my thoughts, and the emotional turbulence made it hard to remain calm under pressure. Even the simplest things - getting out of bed, cooking dinner, or running errands - became monumental tasks.

Mentally, I felt like I was falling apart. The mood swings weren't just hard on my relationships; they were hard on me. I questioned my worth, my stability, and my ability to cope.

Anxiety and depression crept in, amplifying the emotional strain. It was as though I was fighting an invisible war, one that no one else could fully understand.

Through it all, cannabis was my anchor. It didn't just dull the pain; it gave me a chance to breathe, to rest, and to reclaim moments of clarity in a time that felt overwhelmingly chaotic. It allowed me to face the day when I wasn't sure I could.

Cannabis didn't just ease my pain. It changed my entire approach to self-care. It taught me to listen to my body, to recognise its needs, and to prioritise my well-being in ways I never had before.

For years, I had pushed through the pain, forcing myself to meet expectations, even when it felt like my body was screaming at me to stop. But once I began using cannabis medicinally, I started to see self-care not as a luxury but as a necessity. A form of survival.

Looking back, though, I realise that others may have noticed.

My bosses, for instance, seemed to catch on in subtle, almost unspoken ways. I remember one moment in particular. J once said, *"There's a funky smell in the car."*

I froze. I had just eaten an apple turnover, and the sweet, sticky smell lingered. I never, ever smoked in the car. It was a hard rule I followed. So how did she know? Was it just a coincidence, or was there something about me, something I didn't notice but they did?

It wasn't the only comment, either.

Little remarks here and there made me wonder if they could tell, even though I was careful and discreet.

Did I seem calmer?

More relaxed?

Or did the stigma of cannabis hover around me, even in the absence of evidence?

At the time, those moments filled me with unease.

I didn't want to be judged or misunderstood.

But looking back now, I wonder: did it matter?

Using cannabis gave me the ability to show up, to work through the pain and exhaustion that might have otherwise sidelined me completely. It allowed me to keep going when nothing else worked. It transformed my quality of life.

In hindsight, I see those moments as a reflection of society's lingering discomfort with cannabis, not a reflection of me.

What mattered most was that I was taking care of myself in the best way I knew how, even if the world wasn't ready to understand or accept it.

Despite my employer's significant involvement and my own personal efforts in helping the progressive Queensland Palaszczuk Labor team rise to power, which paved the way for the legalisation of medicinal cannabis, I was alarmed to discover that my former bosses were aware of my cannabis use.

What was even more unsettling was how they learned of it and later weaponised that knowledge, attempting to use it as a tool of intimidation.

At first, I couldn't quite believe it. I never used it at work. But I always wondered - could they tell?

Was there something about me they sensed, or were they just looking for something to use?

I had been so careful, so private. I never used cannabis at work, never allowed it to interfere with my performance, and had gone out of my way to ensure it remained a personal matter. But looking back, I realised there had been subtle comments, hints that they knew more than they let on. At the time, I brushed it off as a coincidence or paranoia, but those suspicions were eventually confirmed.

What stung the most wasn't just that they knew. It was how they used that knowledge against me. Instead of recognising my cannabis use as a legitimate form of treatment, approved under the same laws they had helped usher in, they chose to weaponise it.

Whether it was to assert control or to instill fear, the result was the same: I felt exposed, vulnerable, and betrayed.

It was a stark reminder of how deeply stigma still runs, even in supposedly progressive environments.

For all the strides made in legalising medicinal cannabis, the judgement and misunderstanding around its use hadn't disappeared. My employer's actions revealed that, even when the law is on your side, societal attitudes can lag far behind.

But it also strengthened my resolve. I knew I was doing nothing wrong.

I was managing my health in a way that worked for me, within the bounds of the law.

Their attempt to intimidate me said more about their prejudices than about my choices.

Their actions didn't discredit me. They revealed themselves.

I chose to heal. They chose to judge.

And that's where the real divide lies.

The experience with my former bosses reminded me of the way many union leaders treated alcohol. Drinking wasn't just a social norm in those circles; it was almost a requirement. Yet, paradoxically, the same people who raised a glass at the end of every long week were often the first to weaponise drinking habits when it suited them, calling out staff or twisting narratives to undermine someone's credibility.

The Hypocrisy was Glaring.

For them, alcohol was permissible, even celebrated, as a bonding ritual or stress release. But the moment they could use it to assert power, it became a liability for others. The same double standard applied to cannabis.

Despite supporting progressive policies like the legalisation of medicinal cannabis, many were quick to stigmatise its use when it came to staff.

It's a pattern I've come to recognise over the years: when power is in play - personal habits, whether drinking, cannabis use, or anything else, you become convenient targets.

It's never really about the substance. It's about control. About who gets to set the rules and who gets judged for breaking them.

That's why I've learned to stand firm in my choices. Whether it's managing pain with medicinal cannabis or declining to participate in toxic drinking cultures, I prioritise what's right for me. I won't let other people's double standards dictate how I live. If I want a glass of wine with my lunch, even with my boss present, I will. I refuse to let hypocrisy shape my behaviour.

For too long, I watched certain behaviours be accepted, even celebrated, for some, while the same actions were used to discredit others. It became clear that it wasn't about the act itself. It was about who held the power in the room.

Now, I own my choices unapologetically. Whether it's medicinal cannabis to manage my health or wine at lunch, these decisions don't define my competence or my worth. If anyone wants to judge me for them, that's on them, not me.

But that didn't stop one of the union bosses from trying to assert his judgement during the 2019 Labour Day celebrations in Brisbane.

It was my first time attending the Brisbane event, a spontaneous decision.

I happened to be in town with my daughter, who was trialling chiropractic treatment for her migraine disease.

With a bit of spare time, I decided to drop by the march.

Not out of loyalty but curiosity.

I wanted to see if anything had changed.

At the time, I was on extended personal leave, managing both my health and my daughter's. The truth was, working for the union had wrecked my mental health. The toxic environment, the unrealistic expectations, and the constant pressure had taken a toll; I could no longer ignore.

When I arrived, the first familiar faces I saw were David Smith, the ASU National Secretary, and Ian Buckley, the retired QSU Assistant Secretary. Their reactions were priceless, especially David's. As our national leader, he and I had shared many conversations, including one I'll never forget.

I had raised concerns with him about the unsafe demands of our travel schedules: early morning flights from Townsville to Brisbane, full-day work events, then evening return flights, often delayed. The schedule was punishing. His response? Dismissive at best.

So when I walked up to David and Ian that morning to say hello, I had a hunch that my name had been on their lips recently and not in a flattering context. Their expressions confirmed it: surprise, discomfort, and maybe even guilt.

The confirmation came later that afternoon.

I was sitting at a table, chatting with Jim Madden, the former Member for Ipswich West, when "old mate," one of the union bosses, approached. Jim greeted him warmly: "*Mate, you've lost some weight*".

I'd noticed it too, five months earlier, at our 2018 Christmas function.

"Old mate" and his ever-present sidekick had both slimmed down noticeably. They had also been unusually attentive to me that afternoon, checking in to see if I was okay, something they had never done before. Maybe they were overcompensating, given everything I'd been through: the personal crises, the workplace bullying.

"Old mate" fumbled for a response.

"*Oh yeah, mate, I've stopped drinking.*"

The way he said it, the tone, the delivery; it wasn't just a casual comment. It was a pointed remark, and obviously directed at me.

I'd seen it before: alcohol used as a social lubricant when convenient and as a weapon when strategic.

That moment was no different.

As his words hung in the air, I felt the weight of their silent accusations. The quiet judgements disguised as small talk.

It was a reminder of the culture I had walked away from. A culture that celebrated drinking until it didn't. A culture where judgement was wielded like a tool.

David Smith passed away in November of that same year, 2019. May he rest in peace.

That moment at Labour Day said everything without saying much at all.

The glances, the carefully chosen words, the unspoken judgements, it was all part of the game they'd been playing for years.

But I wasn't a pawn anymore.

I saw the hypocrisy, the cowardice, the desperate need to hold onto power by tearing others down.

And I saw through it.

All of it.

For a long time, their opinions had held weight. They shaped how I saw myself, how I moved through the world. But not anymore. Their approval, their whispers, their smug smiles, they no longer had a hold on me.

That day, I left the march not with bitterness but with clarity. I knew who I was, what I stood for, and most of all, what I would no longer tolerate.

I had spent too many years surviving their systems.

Now, I was ready to build something different.

Something better.

The future was calling, and this time, I would be the one writing the rules.

The Future

I've spent a long time looking over my shoulder, piecing together the betrayals, the silences, the whispered judgements. But the future isn't behind me. It's in the choices I make now, the boundaries I set, and the stories I choose to tell.

I don't want to be defined by what was done to me. I want to be remembered for how I responded. For reclaiming my voice. For shining a light on what too many are still afraid to name. For refusing to carry shame that was never mine to begin with.

The systems that failed me still stand, but they are no longer invisible. And that's where change begins: with truth, with exposure, with the courage to speak even when your voice shakes.

I don't know exactly what the future holds. But I know what I stand for and I'm no longer afraid to stand alone.

I'm okay now, but the workplace abuse took a massive toll on my mental health. I was targeted and ganged up on by my union colleagues, counterparts, and delegates from multiple unions, to the point where I became suicidal. Thankfully, a few good unionists reached out and quite literally saved my life.

What hurts the most is knowing that the people who were meant to stand beside me, fellow unionists who were supposed to uphold solidarity and shared values, were the ones who caused such harm.

That's why **_R U OK Day_** is a major trigger for me. The union I worked for, along with others I regularly interacted with, would perform public displays of care and concern on that day. Meanwhile, behind closed doors, they subjected me and others to appalling treatment that led to serious mental health consequences.

Can you see the irony?

The double standards?

The hypocrisy?

Before the workplace abuse, I was happy, confident, and capable. But the abuse changed me. It left me angry, bitter, cynical, untrusting, irritable, and resentful. I now live with Complex PTSD, and my time working for a union only deepened the trauma, adding layers I still grapple with every day.

They probably didn't expect me to come out of it stronger, more powerful than before.

I was already a threat in their eyes.

My take on the legislation passed by the Albanese government to push the CFMEU into administration: the entire union movement was long overdue for a serious shake-up.

I've been reviewing the unions' rules, and it's clear they're in dire need of reform. Many are outdated and poorly written, particularly when it comes to gender-related provisions.

Given the 2024 (alleged) revelations, placing the CFMEU into administration appears to have been a necessary step in the broader process of accountability and renewal.

In the corporate sector, administration has often led to successful outcomes by entrusting independent experts to assess the situation objectively and explore all available options.

Voluntary administration allows operations to continue while thorough investigations take place and, ideally, with fresh leadership and a renewed vision, the CFMEU can chart a more responsible and inclusive path forward.

The situation could be much worse. De-registration would have been a death knell, not an opportunity for renewal.

It also sends a very clear message to the other unions because the message that was sent by bringing the AWU to their knees was clearly not enough.

For unions to maintain their moral authority and effectiveness, their internal practices must reflect the values they publicly champion.

One common critique is the prioritisation of high-profile industries or sectors, often at the expense of lower-paid or less-organised workers.

This imbalance in resource allocation and attention leaves some members feeling neglected, creating divisions within the movement.

Another issue arises when unions challenge external employers for unfair treatment while neglecting to address similar complaints within their own ranks.

Union employees may struggle to have their grievances acknowledged or resolved, revealing a hypocrisy that undercuts the movement's mission.

At times, political allegiances and campaigns are given precedence over the immediate needs of union members.

When resources are diverted away from workplace issues to advance broader political goals, it can alienate workers who feel their concerns are being sidelined.

Additionally, some unions resist reforms that could enhance transparency, accountability, or efficiency.

This resistance fosters a perception of self-preservation rather than a genuine commitment to members' interests, further eroding confidence in their leadership.

If the union movement is to remain a powerful force for workers, it must address these internal contradictions and hold itself to the same standards it demands from others.

Only through alignment of values and actions can unions rebuild trust and retain their relevance in the modern workplace.

As part of a process, I'm also taking the time to reflect on my past.

I'm revisiting key moments; turning points that shaped me, lessons that guided me, and challenges that tested me.

By understanding where I've been, I'm better equipped to move forward with intention and purpose.

This reflection isn't about dwelling on the past but about honouring my journey, learning from it, owning it, and using it to shape a future that's mine and mine alone.

I'm taking charge of my life, and I refuse to let others project their inability to cope with a changing reality onto me.

I am the sole architect of my future, and it is both unfair and inappropriate for anyone else to decide what will bring me happiness or guide my healing.

Only I have the authority to make those decisions.

It's not my job to meet their expectations or shoulder their discomfort. It is their responsibility to focus on their own well-being.

For the first time in my life, I feel a sense of peace and empowerment in the choices I make for my future.

I trust myself, and that trust has opened the door to clarity and confidence as I move forward.

Rising Above.

The people who tried to undermine me have already sealed their own fate, burdened by the very shadows they once cast over mine.

My future, by contrast, is clear: a path of growth, discovery, and purpose. Every step I take is proof of my resilience, my resolve, and my unwavering commitment to healing and becoming. I walk a road lit by possibility, no longer defined by their darkness.

Still, I hope the bullies took something from all this. The lesson is simple: everyone matters. No one stands above or below another on this shared journey of life. We are all faced with choices: moments that test whether we live by the values we claim to hold. And, in the end, how we treat others says everything about the paths we choose.

As for me, I choose compassion. I choose integrity. I choose a future grounded in my truth.

***

Owning Personal Growth.

Reflecting on the past isn't about getting lost in regrets or reopening old wounds. It's about honouring the path that brought me here: every hardship, every misstep, every moment of resilience.

These experiences are not just chapters behind me; they're lessons etched into my growth.

By facing them with honesty, I gain insight into who I am and who I want to become.

In that clarity, healing begins. In that awareness, evolution takes place.

And in that courage, I can carve out a future built on purpose, strength, and unwavering authenticity.

I choose to wear the bullies' efforts as a badge of honour, a reminder of my resilience and strength.

Every challenge, every attempt to undermine me, only fuels my confidence.

Instead of breaking me, their actions have shown me just how capable I am of rising above.

My focus now is on my journey.

I refuse to let their negativity define me or hold me back.

Their attempts belong in the past, while I move forward with integrity, purpose, and unwavering strength.

This is my story, and I'm determined to write it on my own terms.

The best response to their actions is simple: I will keep thriving.

By living my truth, embracing my values, and succeeding on my own terms, I will show that no amount of negativity can dim my light.

My success isn't just about proving them wrong.

It's about proving to myself that I'm unstoppable.

"As I look back on my life,
I realize that every time
I thought I was being rejected
from something good,
I was actually being redirected
to something better."

-Steve Maraboli

Solidarity and Systemic Change.

To the Survivors:

You are seen.

You are heard.

You are believed.

Your voice matters.

Our voices matter.

Believing survivors must be the norm, not the exception.

It's time to dismantle the systems that doubt, discredit, and retraumatise those who bravely come forward.

No one should be forced to relive their pain to prove the truth.

We must stop sacrificing survivors to shield those who cause harm.

Here's to:

- A future where perpetrators are held accountable, and justice is non-negotiable.

- Tearing down the structures that protect abusers and silence victims.

We are witnesses to injustice.

We are fighters for truth.

We are builders of a world where safety and justice are not privileges, but rights.

Emotional Wisdom and Adaptability.

Uncertainty is a part of life that we all face, yet it can feel like standing on the edge of the unknown, unsure of what lies ahead. It's unsettling, often uncomfortable, and sometimes even overwhelming. But uncertainty is also where possibility lives. It's the space where growth, change, and new beginnings are born.

To live with uncertainty is to embrace the idea that we can't control everything and that's okay. It's a reminder to focus on what we can control: our attitude, our actions, and our ability to adapt. While it's natural to crave clarity and stability, there is also beauty in the unpredictable. The potential for outcomes we could not have imagined.

Uncertainty challenges us to trust ourselves, to have faith in our ability to navigate whatever comes our way. It pushes us to let go of perfection and step into the present moment, where life unfolds in its raw and unfiltered form.

Rather than fearing uncertainty, we can choose to see it as an invitation. A chance to explore, to learn, and to grow in ways we never thought possible.

It's not easy, but within the discomfort lies the opportunity to discover something new about ourselves and the world around us.

As I stand here no longer a victim but a survivor, I embrace the uncertainty ahead, knowing that I am ready for whatever it brings.

In facing the unknown, I've learned that healing isn't linear and growth doesn't always arrive wrapped in clarity. But somewhere, between the shadows of what was and the light of what could be, I've found my truth.

I've come to understand that uncertainty doesn't define me, my choices do.

The most powerful choice I've made is this:

To no longer be shaped by the harm done to me but instead to shape myself, fully and freely, into who I was always meant to become.

Choosing Who to Become.

Life is a series of choices, and one of the most powerful ones we make is deciding who we want to become.

It's not about who we have been or the circumstances that have shaped us.

It's about the person we choose to be moving forward.

Choosing who to become means embracing self-awareness, acknowledging our strengths, and confronting our weaknesses.

It's about letting go of old patterns that no longer serve us and stepping into a version of ourselves that aligns with our values, goals, and dreams.

It requires courage to rewrite your narrative, especially when the world tries to define you by your past.

The truth is, you are not your mistakes, your trauma, or the opinions of others. You are the sum of your choices, and every day offers a new opportunity to create the life you want to live.

To choose who to become is to reclaim your power.

It's standing in the mirror; flawed, healing, whole, and saying, *"This is my life. I decide who I am."*

It's not about perfection. It's about presence.

It's not about living up to someone else's expectations. It's about rising into your own.

Becoming is not a final destination. It's an ongoing act of self-respect. And in choosing who I become, I choose freedom. I choose my purpose. I choose me.

It's a process of growth, learning, and becoming. And it's one of the most beautiful acts of self-love you can undertake - not being beholden to others' expectations.

Taking Out The Trash

I remembered who I was, not who I was told to be, and the game changed.

The game they'd been playing.

A system rigged with power plays, silencing tactics, and double standards.

When you reclaim your true self, free from external expectations, everything shifts: your perspective, your choices, your potential.

It's like stepping into a new dimension of possibility, one where you are finally in control.

For me, the shift was quiet. A gradual unveiling. One day, I looked around and realised everything felt different, because I was finally aligning with who I truly am, not who I'd been shaped to be. It was liberating... and a little unsettling.

Stepping into my power.

That was unstoppable.

Like unlocking something that was always there but just needed to be recognised, not by anybody else, but by me. I channelled that newfound power in my life by taking on the establishment that took advantage of my potential and misused it for evil.

It was a bold and righteous path to take.

Confronting the system that exploited and distorted my potential was a profound way to reclaim not just my power but the power of others who have also been affected in similar ways.

I channelled my newfound energy into a larger purpose: to expose the contradictions and injustices that had thrived in silence for too long.

What began as personal survival evolved into a mission for change, solidifying the day I realised my story wasn't just mine but a reflection of so many others who'd been silenced, too.

Exposing hypocrisy, double standards, and corruption isn't just about telling the truth; it's about dismantling the false narratives that allow these systems to survive. It takes courage, but that courage can be the catalyst for real change.

Social media amplified my voice and accelerated the spread of truth, but it also demanded a careful balance between authenticity and strategy. Every post became an act of resistance, a deliberate mix of raw honesty and calculated impact.

One moment in particular stands out - a post where I paired a confronting truth with a powerful track. The response was immediate and overwhelming. That's when I realised: it's not just what you say, but how and when you say it that can shift the conversation.

The Gift That Keeps On Giving.

The target audience: The Australian union movement played right into my hands.

It was a gift that kept on giving, especially the blokes from one particular union.

Their reactions were textbook: defensive, dismissive, and laced with the kind of misogynistic lines I could have scripted myself. At one point, I posted a photo of me kissing my cat. Predictably, the comments rolled in: mocking, condescending, and utterly off-topic.

They didn't realise they were reinforcing everything I was calling out. Their predictability became my greatest asset, fuelling the campaign's momentum and amplifying its reach.

Recognising the need to truly understand the audience, I joined numerous groups to gain insight, immersing myself in conversations and uncovering the nuances of perspectives.

It didn't take long to realise I was not alone.

There were many others with shared frustrations and experiences, eager to connect.

One friend pointed out to me, *"They're not shushing you."*

That simple observation carried a great deal of weight. It confirmed that my voice was being heard and that the campaign was making waves. But it wasn't just my voice. It was the voices of others I was engaging with, including those in high places.

Instead of dismissing or silencing the message, the target audience engaged with it, sometimes unwillingly but always predictably, fuelling its reach and strengthening its impact.

By consistently sharing compelling and relatable content, I built a sense of community that resonated deeply. Engagement grew naturally, and as I nurtured this connection with persistence and care, I watched the seeds I had planted begin to take root and flourish.

It wasn't just about visibility; it was about trust. Each post, each story, each interaction was a deliberate act of vulnerability and strength.

I wasn't broadcasting. I was inviting conversation, sparking reflection, and encouraging others to step into their own truths. Slowly, the narrative began to shift.

What once felt like shouting into a void became a chorus of voices echoing shared experiences, frustrations, and hopes.

The long game is often the most powerful, especially when you're exposing deep-rooted issues. It allows you to build momentum, gather allies, and stay resilient against pushback. Consistency and patience are key, as is ensuring that each step is strategically placed to create lasting impact. The long game requires patience, but also consistency paired with a clear vision.

The challenge: managing other people's apathy. This is one of the most frustrating aspects of the long game. People often become numb to injustice, either out of exhaustion, disbelief, or simply because they feel powerless to change anything.

People often tune out because they're overwhelmed by the constant barrage of bad news or don't know where to start. Some might not understand the full scope of the issue or how it personally affects them. Others may feel powerless or believe that systems of corruption are too entrenched to change.

Tackling apathy, especially when you're working to expose deep-rooted issues, can feel like pushing against a tide. It's discouraging when people turn away, indifferent, or overwhelmed. But change often starts quietly.

As you build momentum and connect with others on a human level, even the smallest shifts can ripple outward. Sometimes the most powerful work is simply planting seeds, knowing they might take time to grow.

In the face of apathy, persistence and adaptability are essential. You won't reach everyone at once, and that's okay. By framing the issue in ways that resonate - through shared values, lived experience or emotional truth - you create opportunities for people to come to the cause in their own time.

Understanding the barriers people face helped me approach these moments with empathy rather than frustration. It changed the way I communicated. Instead of trying to persuade with facts alone, I focused on stories, feelings, and questions.

I learned to listen more, to meet people where they were, and to honour their pace. That shift didn't just make the campaign more effective; it reminded me that a real connection is the foundation of lasting change.

Clarifying the Campaign's Heart:

Building a profile for the campaign required a thoughtful and strategic approach to ensure its success. The process began with crafting a clear and compelling representation of the mission, values, and goals, which laid a foundation that captured the essence of the cause.

At its core, the campaign championed accountability, demanded greater transparency, and called for a shift in leadership culture, setting the tone for everything that followed.

Identifying the target audience was crucial, allowing the messaging to be tailored in a way that would genuinely connect with those it aimed to inspire.

Defining key messaging ensured that every piece of communication was aligned, reinforcing the campaign's purpose and leaving no room for ambiguity.

Establishing a consistent tone and visual identity further strengthened the campaign's presence.

I made it clear to the powers that be: they could no longer hide behind their unofficial code of conduct, ***"Do as I say, not as I do."***

It was a mantra that exposed the gaping divide between the union's stated ideals and the self-serving reality of its leadership.

They preached solidarity, fairness, and justice. Yet when I reported bullying and misconduct, they closed ranks to protect their own.

The same people who ran campaigns against workplace abuse turned a blind eye when it happened under their watch. Their silence wasn't just complicity, it was strategy.

They don't teach you this in "Organising Works," but you learn it quickly on the job, especially when you're employed by a union. Ironically, my official Organiser training didn't arrive until the very end of my employment, right in the thick of dealing with the bullies. By then, I'd already completed the real course.

It's called Hypocrisy 101.

You won't find it on the syllabus, but it's buried deep in the fine print, right between "solidarity" and "cover your ass."

It seems we're witnessing a troubling paradox in our current reality.

A group of people, demanding that everyone else adhere to the "Rule of Law," while they themselves break laws daily without consequence.

Take, for instance, the example of Setka. He shows up at a Victorian construction site: uninvited, unauthorised, and stirring the pot among workers. This wasn't just a breach of protocol, it was a blatant defiance of the very rules they claim to uphold.

It's the pot calling the kettle black, wouldn't you say?

The Setka incident serves as a striking example of union leaders' behaviour. His unauthorised appearance at the construction site wasn't just an inconvenience, it further eroded trust in leadership. Workers were left questioning the very system designed to protect them, highlighting the need for accountability and change within the union structure. It's these types of actions that perpetuate the cycle of hypocrisy and manipulation, reinforcing the urgency for a shift in leadership standards.

We've watched the pattern of behaviour and repetitive cycles for too long.

It's time for **REAL CHANGE**.

We're taking a stand, exposing the dirty deals being made at a bargain price. We've had enough of the status quo. We were tired of being the only few who dared to question the corrupt motives of union leaders, challenge their decisions, and call out their behaviour. But it turns out, there are more of us than they ever anticipated.

Let's pause and reflect on the workplace policies that, far from protecting employees, are actively causing harm.

Take, for example, the so-called "flexible work hours" policy. On paper, it sounds like a dream, an acknowledgement of the need for balance between work and life. But in practice? It became a tool for exploitation. With deadlines creeping later and later, it wasn't flexibility that we had, but a never-ending expectation to be available.

Or the harassment policy, another paper tiger. *"Zero tolerance,"* it promised, yet the complaint I filed was met with gaslighting, deflection, and outright dismissal. These are the policies that are supposed to safeguard us, but instead, they've become part of the system that traps us.

Maybe it was the hypocrisy that got to me most. The way they enforced environmental regulations with religious fervor: papers filed, audits run, consequences swift. Yet when it came to the people doing the work, their well-being was an afterthought. I watched worksites grind to a halt over a misplaced waste bin, but complaints about bullying, chronic stress, or dangerous workloads? Those were quietly ignored, or worse, seen as an inconvenience.

Then there's the myth of worker protections. Rights that look good on paper, plastered across policy manuals and HR training slides, but when tested, they dissolve like sugar in hot tea.

I remember when I spoke up, there was no accountability, only silence, deflection, and subtle forms of retaliation that spoke louder than any policy ever could.

These policies and the toxic cultures they foster don't just harm individuals. They quietly erode trust, replacing collaboration with caution and openness with guarded silence.

The damage extends far beyond those directly affected, shaping a workplace where fear overrides fairness and where unethical practices become routine rather than challenged. When leadership turns a blind eye, worse, when actively enabling this kind of behaviour or laboriously participating, it sends a clear message: survival matters more than integrity.

In such environments, exploitation doesn't just survive, it becomes embedded in the system.

Systemic toxicity doesn't happen by accident, it's cultivated. It thrives because those in power permit it, protect it, and benefit from it. Addressing it would mean dismantling the very systems that sustain their control, and toxic leaders have no intention of doing that. Acknowledging the problem would mean implicating themselves.

Instead, they lean on silence, complicity, and the status quo to shield their authority. We've seen this play out time and again: HR departments dismissing complaints to "protect the reputation of the organisation," unions prioritising political alliances over member welfare, or executives quietly transferring abusers instead of holding them accountable. Meanwhile, workers absorb the fallout, psychologically, professionally, and often physically.

What's even more infuriating is coming to terms with the fact that some of the very leaders who once claimed to support me were, in truth, complicit in the very toxicity they publicly condemned.

Their so-called guidance wasn't about uplifting me. It was about controlling me, keeping me compliant within a broken system.

This realisation shattered my perception.

It forced me to question everything I believed about leadership, loyalty, and the true motives of those in power. The betrayal cut deeper because it was wrapped in the language of care.

Here's the harsh reality: when you're a union boss, accountability has a way of vanishing. Employment laws, policies, and procedures, meant to protect workers, are often ignored or selectively applied.

And under WorkCover, there's a disturbing technicality: "***reasonable management action***" doesn't actually have to be reasonable.

It's a legal loophole that allows employers and union leaders alike to justify harmful decisions under the guise of management prerogative.

I've seen this exploited firsthand.

Used to excuse mobbing, gaslighting, and the targeted isolation of workers who dared to speak up.

Instead of safeguarding workers, the system shields those in power, enabling a culture where harm is normalised and accountability is optional.

Some might call what I'm doing union-busting.

I call it what it is: holding them accountable.

We didn't start the fire, but we sure as hell intend to put it out

So buckle up, we're all in for a long and turbulent ride. Welcome to the shit show.

Let's explore that a little further.

We are brave like soldiers.

We pick our battles.

We chose one we knew we could win.

From one of the oldest and largest unions in the country, we took out:

- A National Secretary,

- A National Assistant Secretary,

- A State Secretary,

- A District Secretary,

- Two Officials, and

- A State Legal Officer who was demoted for giving dangerously poor advice to the State Secretary.

We did what we were trained to do.

The union was brought to its knees.

Then they scrambled into damage control.

But this wasn't just about individuals falling from power, it was a seismic shift. The message was clear: no one is untouchable. For workers, it signalled the possibility of a cleaner, more accountable union. For the movement, it forced a reckoning.

And for those of us on the frontlines, it proved that truth and strategy could rattle even the oldest foundations.

It's an era of accountability.

For too long, State Secretaries have been creating the narrative: there's nothing to see here, while they burn their staff into the ground. AKA, also known as 'swings and roundabouts.' It's a roundabout way of saying, "You do it because you love it, so give up your free time for free."

Burnt out, you cannot get out, so you flee to safety.

In ALP terms, at a Federal level, that's:

#safetea

It's a matter of hypocrisy and deeply disturbing double standards: one for the workers out there and another standard for the workers who are trapped behind closed doors.

It's hard to describe the feeling, watching people who are meant to protect you, betray you.

They speak of rights, of fairness, of dignity in the workplace.

They make speeches.

They run campaigns. And then, behind closed doors, they become the very thing they claim to fight against.

They know the law.

They understand it better than most. And still, they break it, against their own employees.

It's not just a double standard.

It's a wound that cuts deeper because it comes from those who should have known better.

Those who did know better did it anyway.

The real questions still haven't been answered:

Who's policing the people who are supposed to police the employers?

Where are the checks and balances?

When will they offer more than just lip service and slogans?

It was only a matter of time before someone stood up, spoke out, and called them on their bullshit.

UNITED WE STAND. DIVIDED WE FALL.

IF I GO DOWN - WE ALL GO DOWN.

Remember this: I, along with others, am a whistleblower, and whistleblowers like us are protected under the *Fair Work (Registered Organisations) Act 2009*, Chapter 11, Part 4A.

That legislation exists for a reason: To acknowledge the vital role we play in exposing wrongdoing, corruption, and unethical conduct within registered organisations.

It's meant to shield us from retaliation.

But here's the truth no one likes to admit: legal protection is just the foundation.

In practice, whistleblowers face intimidation. Isolation. Character assassination.

They are frozen out, talked down, pushed aside, and made to disappear.

The emotional toll is brutal.

The professional cost? Often permanent.

The law says we're protected. Reality says otherwise.

I did what I was supposed to do.

I went through the proper channels.

I formally requested whistleblower status from the Fair Work Commission.

What did they do?

They put it in the too-hard basket.

This is what happens when the system is more interested in protecting itself than the people it claims to serve.

This is what happens when those in power would rather turn away than confront the corruption festering within.

I followed the rules.

I trusted the process. But the process was never built to protect people like me.

It was built to contain us.

To delay us.

To break us, quietly, bureaucratically, and without accountability.

Here's what they didn't expect:

I didn't disappear.

I wasn't intimidated into silence.

I didn't lose my voice.

They stalled. They avoided it. They hoped I'd give up.

But I'm still here.

Still speaking. Still exposing. Still refusing to be part of their cover-up.

Because being a whistleblower isn't just about what you risk.

It's about what you refuse to accept, and I refuse to accept a system where silence is rewarded and truth is punished.

We need stronger safeguards for whistleblowers within this system.

Those willing to expose corruption at any level deserve more than just words on paper.

They deserve real, enforceable protections and support.

Case Study:

David McBride – Silenced for Telling the Truth.

David McBride, a former Australian Defence Force lawyer, exposed alleged war crimes by Special Forces in Afghanistan by leaking classified documents to the ABC in 2017. These documents, known as the "Afghan Files," revealed unlawful killings of civilians and detainees.

Despite raising concerns through internal channels, McBride was prosecuted for leaking the material.

In 2023, the courts ruled he couldn't rely on whistleblower protections under the *Public Interest Disclosure Act*. In 2024, he pleaded guilty, and in 2025, he was sentenced to prison. His case highlights the chilling reality: even in democracies, whistleblowers can face harsh punishment while the systems they expose remain protected.

After all, the success of institutions like the NACC depends on the courage of individuals who are willing to risk everything to bring truth to light.

Let's ensure they're not left to fend for themselves, but instead backed by a robust system that values integrity, transparency, and accountability, above all else.

It's time to lead by example and show that whistleblowers are not just protected, they're respected.

The Audacity of Indifference.

I was incredibly disappointed in someone who couldn't spare a moment to speak with me at a rally held in Brisbane in September 2024.

I truly thought we were allies. But in that moment, it felt like they turned their back on me. Whether it was deliberate or simply a lack of empathy, the result is the same, and it cuts deep.

As the union movement says:

"Shame"

For a fellow woman and unionist to show such disinterest in the struggle of an industrial relations advocate is, at the very least, alarming. It's the audacity that stings the most.

How can this person claim to be UNION when they refuse to even hear about what I've endured? I wasn't safe in my job, working for a union. I had to fight every single day just to maintain basic rights and conditions.

Yet, somehow, that didn't seem to warrant their attention.

The CFMEU administration is not just another headline; it's a critical moment that will set a precedent for every union across the country.

My fight for safety on the job is every union worker's fight.

As former CFMEU National Secretary, Zach Smith said in his address to members:

"Workers have had enough."

(news.com.au, September 18, 2024)

You're right, Zach, we have had enough. But let's not kid ourselves about how long this has been going on.

"Five weeks"? Please.

We didn't just draw a line in the sand. We built a wall around it. Because we knew that if we didn't hold the line now, we'd be swept away by a tide of indifference and complacency.

I've been in this fight since February 2011, ever since the merger and amalgamation that marked the start of a long, brutal struggle.

The fact that I'm still fighting says everything about a system designed to silence and ignore the very people who are its foundation.

The Time for Excuses is Over.

Workers in all areas have long been silenced, dismissed, or sidelined by a system designed to prioritise political expediency over accountability. No more can the refrain of "we're in an election year" justify sweeping systemic abuse under the rug.

This isn't about optics or winning votes.

It's about addressing the rot within, recognising the harm inflicted on workers who have given their labour, loyalty, and passion to a movement, only to be met with betrayal.

When I started writing this book, the Labor Party held almost absolute power across the nation.

That power brings an obligation.

One they can no longer shirk by blaming the Tories or external adversaries.

The 2025 federal election reaffirmed that mandate, with voters once again placing their trust in the ALP. But with that renewed support comes renewed responsibility.

It's time for the ALP to look inward, to acknowledge the culture of harm, and to take decisive action.

Workers across Australia, in the party and beyond, are watching.

To truly lead, the ALP, the workers' party, must confront the abuse and inequities entrenched within its own structures.

It's not just about cleaning up the mess.

It's about rebuilding trust and proving that they are a party that values humanity, fairness, and justice above all.

If the ALP fails to address the rot within its own ranks, the damage won't just be to the party's reputation; it'll be to the very workers who have trusted them for generations.

The ball is in their court now.

What happens next will define not only the party's future but the legacy it leaves for generations to come.

Stand with us or risk being on the wrong side of history.

My journey of healing, growth, and reclaiming my voice is still ongoing.

It feels like I'm only just getting started.

The more I share my experiences, the more I speak up and stand firm on social media, the more visible I become.

Every post, every story, every raw moment of truth seems to resonate with someone out there.

Some are inspired, some are encouraged, and others feel seen for the very first time.

People who have been silenced, dismissed, or undermined start to find courage in my words, reaching out to say, *"Thank you for saying what I couldn't."*

There's another side to this visibility:

With more eyes on me, I've noticed that it's not just allies who come forward.

Some reach out in subtle ways, trying to push back against what I'm saying, hoping to invalidate my experiences or quiet my voice.

While the support is empowering, the criticism often cuts deeper than I'd like to admit. But each moment of resistance, each attempt to undermine my voice, only reinforces my commitment to the cause.

These moments can be challenging, but I see them for what they are: further opportunities to take out the trash.

Every piece of 'trash' we remove from this system is another step closer to a world where justice and transparency aren't just ideals but realities.

Every interaction, positive or negative, reminds me why I started speaking out in the first place. It strengthens my resolve to keep going, to keep exposing injustice, and to keep shedding light on truths others might want buried.

This isn't about vengeance or staying stuck in the past, it's about making space for healing, change, and accountability.

This isn't just about my voice. It's about everyone who's been silenced. Everyone who's had their truth buried.

I'm not just here to tell my story. I'm here to ensure others have the space to tell theirs, too.

For every piece of "trash" I take out, be it a toxic perspective, an outdated belief, or someone trying to silence me, I make room for something better. Something stronger. Something that brings us closer to the world we deserve.

The fight for accountability, transparency, and justice has only just begun.

Activism

Activism wasn't something I stumbled into by chance. After working in the union movement for 18 years, it was a natural extension of both training and lived experience.

It began with skill-based education; learning how to advocate, negotiate, and support others in the workplace.

At first, it was about helping fellow workers navigate their rights and resolving immediate issues. But over time, those small, personal acts of advocacy revealed a much larger truth: the systems we were working within, even the so-called progressive ones, were deeply flawed.

What started as problem-solving became something deeper: a growing awareness of inequity, hypocrisy, and abuse of power.

My experiences in the workplace and beyond made it impossible to look away.

The more I saw, the more compelled I felt to act.

Activism, for me, isn't just a political stance or a social cause. It's personal. It's the product of a lifetime shaped by injustice, both experienced and witnessed. It's about refusing to stay silent. About standing up, even when it's easier to sit down. It means challenging systems that protect the powerful and betray the vulnerable. It means giving a voice to the silenced and holding the mirror up to institutions that pretend to stand for justice while perpetuating harm.

That's what activism means to me: action, accountability, and purpose, even when the odds are stacked against you.

As many would know, once I began to understand just how much devil was in the detail, I couldn't unsee it. Patterns emerged. Small inconsistencies, subtle manipulations, and quiet betrayals that pointed to something far more coordinated than coincidence. That's when I launched a quiet, deliberate campaign to test my theories. I wasn't just chasing hunches. I was pulling at threads, one by one, to see what would unravel. The what, the how, the who, and the when. Every detail became a potential clue in a larger puzzle.

Testing my theories wasn't just about gathering evidence, it was about confronting hard truths.

I started asking deeper questions:

Who benefits from the silence?

What gets protected when people look the other way?

How far does the rot go? and

Who's complicit in keeping it hidden?

There wasn't one singular moment that sparked it. It was a slow build. A series of moments when something didn't sit right, when the pieces didn't quite fit. Eventually, the weight of those moments tipped into action. I could no longer afford to be passive.

So I became an investigator in my own story. I followed timelines, tracked behaviours, revisited conversations, and watched what people did when they thought no one was paying attention.

What I found confirmed what I feared:

The system wasn't broken by accident. It was functioning exactly as designed, just not for people like me. At its core, it all came down to critical thinking. Dissecting the layers, asking the uncomfortable questions, and refusing to accept the surface story.

It wasn't just about uncovering the truth, it was about tracing the systems, patterns, and mechanisms that allowed lies, corruption, and harm to take root and thrive, often in plain sight.

Critical thinking isn't a sterile, academic exercise. For me, it demanded something far more personal. It forced me to question everything I thought I knew about people I trusted, institutions I believed in, and the structures supposedly built to uphold justice and accountability. Each revelation chipped away at the foundation of familiarity and certainty I had once leaned on.

Testing my theories became more than a pursuit of truth, it became an act of rebellion, of survival, and, in many moments, an emotional reckoning. I had to hold my ground while everything I thought was solid began to shift.

The cost?

Disillusionment, isolation, grief.

But there was also clarity and strength. An unwavering resolve to keep going, even when the truth cut deep.

What followed wasn't just a journey of discovery, it was an act of resistance.

A refusal to be complicit in the silence that so many relied on to keep their power intact.

In the beginning, my activism emerged in cryptic fragments: subtle signals buried in social media posts, crafted for those who knew the story behind the scenes.

It was a quiet rebellion. A coded language. A way to voice my truth without yet naming names.

Each post was layered, deliberate, a breadcrumb trail meant for those willing to pay attention.

Those posts weren't just strategy, they were survival.

They became a form of armour, protecting me from direct confrontation while offering a sliver of control in a situation that had left me feeling powerless. Each post gave shape to feelings too dangerous or overwhelming to speak aloud.

It was how I processed betrayal, and how I reclaimed some measure of autonomy in a system that seemed determined to silence me. They were moments of catharsis but also lifelines.

Proof that I hadn't imagined the harm.

That I still had a voice.

In response, the bullies played their own game: cryptic jabs and subtle threats masked as passive posts, dripping with subtext. A twisted game of cat and mouse played out in the shadows of public platforms. Each interaction revealed more than it concealed, exposing the fragility of those trying to maintain their façade.

Every post was a calculated risk.

I was testing boundaries, exposing cracks in the veneer, and watching how quickly defensiveness gave people away.

But more than that, I wanted to disrupt the narrative. To invite others to question what they thought they knew. To plant doubt in the minds of those still convinced by the polished version of events.

Looking back, those early posts were a necessary stage: my way of holding on to truth while finding the courage to confront it. But I eventually came to understand that subtlety alone wouldn't dismantle the systems of silence, complicity, and abuse.

If I wanted change, real change, I'd have to stop hiding behind metaphor and start calling things by their name.

As the cryptic posts evolved, so too did the tools I used to speak out. When words felt too dangerous or too raw to share outright, I turned to music.

Much of my activism became rooted in song; music as a message, music as a shield, music as a weapon. It offered me something my own voice, at times, could not:

Safety.

Resonance.

Power without exposure.

Music became both a mirror and a megaphone. It reflected my emotional state with haunting precision; my anger, my grief, my resilience, and at the same time, it pushed back against the forces that tried to silence me. A carefully chosen lyric could say what I wasn't yet ready to spell out. A melody could soften the blow while delivering a truth too sharp for ordinary language.

In those moments when I couldn't name the bullies outright, I let the songs do it for me.

Lyrics became ciphers; coded reflections of my reality.

Sometimes they were subtle nods. Other times, they were blunt instruments.

The beauty of music was its universality.

While some listeners might have brushed it off as background noise, those who knew the story heard every line for what it was.

A warning.

A confession.

A declaration.

Music allowed me to connect with others who might not have listened otherwise.

It bypassed intellectual defenses and went straight to the heart, planting seeds of awareness where direct confrontation might have only provoked denial. It gave me a language to speak in when my own had been stripped away.

In the silence that followed each post or shared song, I could feel the shift.

There was a distinct discomfort from those it targeted: a flicker of defensiveness, a sudden change in tone, or a carefully timed response post of their own. From others, I felt quiet validation: nods of solidarity, private messages of support, or simply the absence of dismissal. Then there was the curiosity: people on the periphery leaning in, beginning to question, starting to connect the dots.

Each reaction told me I was hitting a nerve. In those moments, I felt a complex mix of things; empowered by the truth I was daring to speak, yet isolated by the risks I was taking to speak it. Sometimes I wondered if I was pushing too hard, if I'd gone too far. Other times, I wished I'd said more. What stayed constant was the sense that I wasn't crazy. That the patterns were real, the harm was real, and I wasn't alone in seeing it.

It was activism in its purest form: creative, strategic, and impossible to ignore. Though it came with emotional weight, it also gave me something I'd been missing:

Agency.

A way to reclaim space in a world that had tried to shrink me.

Teamed with others, our messaging evolved into something far greater than any one of us could have achieved alone.

Together, we created our own Days of Activism.

A bold, symbolic, and emotionally charged campaign that blended creativity with strategy and anger with purpose. What started as an idea between a few of us quickly gained momentum.

The synergy was electric. There was this unspoken understanding that we were onto something powerful; each of us bringing our own lived experience, energy, and voice to the table. It felt like we were reclaiming space we had long been denied.

The campaign began with a song that set the tone perfectly: Billy Joel's **"We Didn't Start the Fire."**

The choice wasn't random. It was deeply intentional. Joel's breathless catalog of political unrest, social upheaval, and relentless crises mirrored the emotional and historical weight of what we were exposing. The message was clear: I didn't create this mess, but I was sure as hell not going to let it burn quietly.

Personally, the song struck a nerve. It reminded me of the overwhelming pace of harm I'd endured. How each betrayal, each act of silencing, had blurred into the next. This time, I was lighting my own fire. One of truth, of resistance, of collective voice.

Curating the playlist for those days was a labour of love and pain.

Each song carried meaning. Some were tied to specific events or turning points, others to memories I hadn't revisited in years.

Choosing them wasn't always easy. Some songs cracked me open, took me back to the rawness of it all.

That vulnerability was part of the message. I wasn't just presenting a campaign. I was sharing parts of myself, encoded in melody and verse.

The emotional weight of those songs?

That was the point. I wanted people to feel something. To stop scrolling, start listening, and maybe, just maybe, begin to understand.

Ongoing Resistance.

From those first cryptic posts to a carefully curated playlist, the messaging evolved into something more than protest; it became a living archive of resistance.

Each song was chosen with purpose: to reveal, to provoke, to connect.

Day after day, I used music to dismantle false narratives, amplify silenced truths, and build a chorus of solidarity that could not be ignored.

What this campaign was about, what it became, was never just about exposure. It was about reclamation.

Of voice.

Of power.

Of truth.

I didn't just survive the fire. I learned how to speak through the smoke.

I told my truths, not for pity, but for power. I stand now, not just as a survivor but as a reminder: the system may be rigged, but it's not immune to accountability. My resistance lives on in every lyric, every post, every whispered conversation that starts with: "Have you seen what they said?"

When they tried to erase me, when they retaliated, I answered back in the language they couldn't control: music, memory, and message.

I am still here. Still singing. Still standing. Still fighting.

Like: "The Champion" - Carrie Underwood ft. Ludacris.

Because I still am. Creating content, raising awareness, and reclaiming the narrative; one post, one truth, one story at a time.

May 5, 2025: PTSD

Song: "Wrong Side of Heaven" - Five Finger Death Punch.

Today's track reflects the cruel discard of American veterans once deemed no longer useful. Chewed up, spat out, left to live with PTSD, and far too often, on the streets. The same story plays out here in Australia. Veterans caught in a system that extracts everything it can from them and abandons them once the job is done.

The parallel is clear for union officials; people who step into a broken system only to be broken by it.

Like soldiers in a silent war, we were used, drained, and discarded by those who glorify in the very damage they cause.

This system is set up to serve those at the top, at the expense of those on the ground, and it has armed itself with legal instruments that further oppress victims of workplace abuse.

In our case, we were teased, humiliated, belittled, mocked, singled out, ganged up on, excluded, emotionally and sexually abused, micromanaged, and ultimately forced out.

- When we pushed back, union funds were weaponised against us.

- The perpetrators flipped the narrative, casting themselves as victims.

- Their fakery runs so deep they've forgotten what authenticity feels like.

- They thought they could break us, gaslight us into silence, but we saw through their charade. And they got caught, with their pants down.

- We, the whistleblowers, have survived.

- We've endured hell, and clawed our way back.

- Some of us remain stuck in limbo, but we're not done.

- We are moving on, and breaking free from their toxicity.

- The best is yet to come.

- We're still everywhere; our names in the files, our faces on the walls.

- From the "Big Kahuna" in North Queensland: good luck with future union elections.

- As for us: We hold no position.....

- We've got nothing to lose.

May 6, 2025: Let It Go

Song: "The Champion" - Carrie Underwood ft. Ludacris.

The track, "The Champion" - Carrie Underwood ft. Ludacris has been our anthem over the past several years.

A reminder of strength.

A reminder of survival.

A rally cry.

We've worked tirelessly to heal from the trauma inflicted at our former places of employment; trade unions, supposedly built to protect vulnerable Australians.

Instead, we were targeted by bullies, harassed, sexually harassed, sexually assaulted, and subjected to systematic mobbing.

One of the biggest misconceptions? That we're just "holding on" to the past. But letting go of abuse doesn't mean forgetting it. In fact, workplace sociopaths don't let go.

They cling. They stalk. They manipulate.

We are each "the one that got away."

Sarah faced continued harassment, through union resources, and was vilified simply for lodging a workers' comp claim. A claim that triggered a legal process so corrupted, it piled trauma upon trauma.

A union-funded law firm engaged in unethical practices. The court cared more about profits than people.

The lesson?

Document everything. Compartmentalise. Stand firm.

Because if it can happen to us; people deeply familiar with employment rights and workplace systems, it can happen to anyone.

#WorkplaceBullying   #UnionAccountability   #TraumaRecovery #SurvivorStories   #JusticeForWorkers   #MobbingAwareness #HealingJourney   #WorkplaceJustice   #EmploymentLaw #WorkplaceRights #PsychosocialSafety

---

May 7, 2025: Collusion

Song: "The Score" - Head Up.

This one's dedicated to We Are Union - Women: the happy dancers fronting a hollow campaign.

Meanwhile, the powers that be sent spies. Under the guise of "concern," they watched me; at work, and at home, implying I was unstable, while casting themselves as victims.

Behind the curtain? Collusion on a grand scale.

Of course, they deny it. Deny everything.

When I confront them, they brand me "deluded."

But the reality?

It's calculated.

The goal?

Isolate me.

Discredit me.

Ensure I have no reference point for what healthy relationships or support looks like.

The result?

Lifelong trust issues. Now I have to actively resist slipping into paranoia when meeting new people or seeing people I know, and I know a lot of people.

But I have found some light.

I'll leave you with a message from a friend:

"Well, I have to say, it's pretty nice to be on the right side of karma.

You were never going to turn me to the dark side.

The force is strong within me!"

#ExposeTheSystem   #WeAreUnion   #UnionAccountability #SolidarityNotSurveillance #CallOutCorruption #PowerToThePeople #EndWorkplaceAbuse   #BelieveSurvivors   #WomenDeserveBetter #GaslightingIsAbuse   #NoMoreSilence   #SystemicAbuse #JusticeForWorkers #ReclaimTheNarrative #ActivismInAction

---

May 8, 2025: Safety

Song: "Stronger" - The Score.

This one's for David; the third member of our group.

David had to install a top-of-the-line security system while working for a large trade union.

Some thought he was paranoid. Turns out, he was right. There were many unlawful actions by the perpetrator, including filming David without consent, which may be illegal under Queensland law, depending on the circumstances.

But when you're a union boss? Apparently, you get a free pass.

False and vexatious allegations were made.

They didn't hold up.

I spent hours compiling documents, meticulously, working with David's legal team to prove the truth.

We've learned that in politics, paranoia is policy.

Surveillance is the norm.

And, lives are micromanaged by the power-obsessed.

It's invasive, it's toxic, and it's real.

They may have tried to destroy our spirits, but they opened our eyes.

That's our win.

#unioncorruption   #AbuseOfPower   #WorkplaceSurveillance #ParanoiaIsPolicy   #ToxicPolitics   #PowerAndControl #UnlawfulSurveillance   #TruthWillOut   #JusticeMatters #SpeakingTruthToPower #SolidarityWithDavid

https://vt.tiktok.com/ZShBYfSH3/

May 9, 2025: Protection

Song: "Toxic" - Ashnikko.

This one goes out to the cowardly leaders who tremble at our existence. The ones who send their flying monkeys to do their dirty work. The ones who can't bear to watch us shine.

Sarah had a court experience; about seeking protection from her former union employer who used every tactic to silence her since she lodged a workers' comp claim for sexual assault and harassment.

This could be the first case of its kind within the trade union movement.

That made it dangerous for them.

On the day of Sarah's hearing, three sets of documents were submitted by her former employer. Only one was shared with her.

The others?

Full of lies. That's called a smear campaign.

The court rejected critical evidence, including my statutory declaration and that of another whistleblower.

Dismissed as "hearsay," even though mine contained photographic proof.

This is the cost of being a witness. Hours of unpaid labour, only to be silenced by a corrupted system.

The legal system doesn't want the truth, it wants a story that fits.

I was stunned by what Sarah told me. But not surprised.

"I'm watching a train wreck," she said. *"I'm in shock, but I didn't expect anything different from any of them."*

I urged her to relocate to Queensland. For her safety.

She agreed.

We have sayings in our group:

"Like attracts like."

"Never let the truth get in the way of a good story."

"Birds of a feather flock together."

#WhistleblowerSupport #BelieveSurvivors #SolidarityInTruth
#ProtectWomenNotReputations #QueenslandSafeHaven
#NotInMyUnion #ReclaimYourPower #JusticeForSarah
#SpeakOutStandTall #EndWorkplaceViolence

May 10, 2025: Documents

Song: Sharks - Imagine Dragons.

The elephant in the room has finally been let out to roam these pages, free and undeniable.

Perhaps those in power, their political allies and legal representatives, should have done their due diligence. It's unfortunate they're now floundering, unsure how to respond. That's their problem, not ours.

As the saying goes, "Nothing will destroy a great employee like watching their employer tolerate and reward the bad ones."

It's been fascinating to note exactly when and why certain unions, legal bodies, and political figures have chosen to block or restrict access on social media.

In my view, that speaks volumes.

It doesn't reflect well on them, and it certainly highlights just how sensitive they really are.So this music clip is dedicated to David and his unintentional talent for collecting evidence. In the fog of trauma, he didn't even realise how much he had gathered, until we began to unpack it together.

With the documentation now compiled, Sarah and I spent countless hours sorting through the printed records in my office. Four boxes ready for what we called our "destruction party" - a symbolic event where we burned the paperwork tied to these events.

But make no mistake: the key materials, the ones with legal weight, have been preserved. They've been carefully packaged and secured for future legal use, stored in a safe location.

#DocumentedTruth #EvidenceMatters #PaperTrail #ExposeTheRot #AccountabilityNow #UnionCorruption #LegalReckoning #PowerAndProtection #SymbolicDestruction #TruthWillComeOut #ToxicWorkplaces #ReclaimYourPower #DueDiligenceFailure

May 11, 2025: Identity

Song: "No Tears Left to Cry" - Ariana Grande.

When you're in the trenches of corruption, there's a part of you that becomes unrecognisable.

You lose track of who you were before the battle.

You start to question what's real.

I've spent years peeling back layers of what was forced on me.

And in the process, I've had to confront not just the people who hurt me, but the truth about myself; about how I let myself be manipulated, and how the system has blurred my identity.

It's a strange feeling, this reshaping.

No longer the "good little soldier," and no longer someone who stays quiet to keep the peace.

But when the system is broken, what else can you do, but fight back?

Somewhere along the way, I stopped being afraid.

Not because I stopped caring, but because I stopped fearing the outcome.

I found the courage to challenge the lies, to reclaim my truth.

Now, I see a new version of myself: stronger, clearer, unapologetic.

There's no turning back.

There's no going back to who I was.

#IdentityReclaimed   #NoTearsLeftToCry   #TruthSeeker #FromSilenceToStrength #UnapologeticallyMe #ReclaimYourPower #SurvivorStory   #SystemicCorruption   #InnerRevolution #NotYourGoodSoldier #BreakingTheSilence #HealingThroughTruth #AuthenticSelf #FightForJustice #StrongerThanBefore

May 12, 2025: No More Silence, No More Shadows

Song: "The Day Collusion Died (Parody of American Pie)" - Don Caron.

The song, The Day Collusion Died (Parody of American Pie) by Don Caron quickly became an anthem of sorts, for those of us who'd seen too much and refused to stay silent.

This year's birthday held more than political weight.

It marked the fifth anniversary of a personal betrayal that no one should ever have to endure, especially not on their 50th birthday.

I had already endured more than my fair share of cruelty in the workplace: mobbing, deceit, betrayal, being discarded like I didn't matter.

Then, while on extended personal leave, came the final blow, delivered in a letter from my union boss, dated February 27, 2020.

It was cruel.

Cold.

Calculated.

Yet, in time, it proved to be a turning point.

This day is a trigger for me, but I know that it really was a blessing in disguise.

No more toxicity.

No more walking on eggshells.

No more being made to feel like I was the problem, because I wasn't.

What was done to me was incomprehensible.

In the union world, this kind of systematic mistreatment is often described as deeply, widely felt.

What is also deeply, widely felt, is when we dare to speak up.

It's the strength of solidarity, even in the darkest hours.

#NoMoreSilence #NoMoreShadows #TruthToPower #FromPainToPower #UnionAccountability #ToxicWorkCulture

May 13, 2025: Recovery

Song: "Rise Up" - Andra Day.

Recovery is messy.

Healing isn't linear.

It's a thousand steps forward and a hundred back.

Every time you stumble, you get back up.

I've learned that recovery isn't just about what happened, it's about how I choose to respond.

The pain doesn't go away, but you do learn to live with it.

You create space for it.

In the depths of the fight, I realised that it wasn't just about survival anymore.

It became about growth.

Strength.

The pursuit of justice for others who have been crushed by the same system.

I've seen the same cycle; abuse, neglect, retaliation, played out time and time again.

That's why I won't back down.

I refuse to be silent. Because speaking out isn't just for me; it's for all of us.

The path to recovery isn't just about enduring.

It's about reclaiming your power.

#RecoveryJourney #HealingIsNotLinear #RiseUp #TraumaRecovery #ReclaimYourPower #SurvivorStrong #MentalHealthAwareness #JusticeForSurvivors #BreakTheSilence #SystemicAbuse #ResilienceInRecovery #SpeakYourTruth #MessyHealing #EmpoweredNotSilent #FromSurvivalToStrength

May 14, 2025: Betrayal

Song: "Shallow" - Lady Gaga & Bradley Cooper.

There's a special kind of betrayal when it comes from those you trust.

When it comes from the very people who are supposed to protect you.

I've seen it firsthand.

Colleagues who turned on each other.

Allies who became enemies.

A system that was supposed to uplift but instead crushed everything in its path.

The hardest part?

The people who betrayed me still refuse to acknowledge their actions.

They still try to manipulate the story, gaslight the truth, and rewrite history.

But I'm not letting them.

The truth has a way of rising to the surface, no matter how hard they try to bury it.

And while they may think they've won, they're only fooling themselves.

This fight isn't about revenge.

It's about justice.

It's about setting the record straight.

No matter how long it takes, I'll keep fighting for it.

#Betrayal   #ShallowTruths   #TrustBroken   #GaslightNoMore #JusticeOverRevenge   #TruthWillPrevail   #SilentSaboteurs #RewritingTheNarrative   #FightForJustice   #SpeakingOut #BreakingTheSilence   #NoMoreCoverUps   #SystemicFailure #CallOutCorruption #AccountabilityMatters #StandInYourPower

May 15, 2025: Support

Song: "Watch Me" - Dramaman.

Since speaking out against corruption in the trade union movement, Sarah faced relentless harassment.

She has experienced:

1x attempted break-in at her front door

1x attempted break-in at her bedroom window

1x attempted break-in at her living room window

1x break-in (not at her residence), where a door was opened, and a dog let out onto the road

1x break-in (elsewhere) while she was asleep, damaging the door so it couldn't be locked

The day after she reported the perpetrator to police, the rear door of the property, she was staying in, was forced open. The house wasn't hers. The stalker had followed her to another location.

Union-branded vehicles appeared at locations she never disclosed.

It was no coincidence. It was stalking.

Then there were the trucks.

A B-double truck swerved toward her Fiat.

Then a utility vehicle did the same.

Then another truck.

They were trying to intimidate her. Perhaps more.

Three months later, back in Wollongong, it happened again.

More trucks. More swerving. One nearly clipped her mirror. The second? Even closer.

I'm not sharing this for attention.

I'm sharing this because it happened.

And it needs to be heard.

#WatchMe #SpeakOut #EndCorruption #UnionAccountability

May 16, 2025: Courage

Song: "Fight Song" - Rachel Platten.

When Sarah first filed the complaint, she was terrified.

Every step forward felt like an uphill battle.

Somewhere along the way, she realised something: fear didn't control her anymore.

Every document she signed.

Every courtroom session.

Every piece of evidence she presented.

It was all an act of defiance.

A message to them.

A message to the people who thought they could intimidate her into silence.

To those who believed they could bury her? They were wrong. You can break her body.

You can tear down her reputation. But you can never break her spirit.She's still standing.

And this fight?

It's just beginning.

#UnbreakableSpirit #CourageInAction #FearlessAndFree #StillSheRises #SheFightsBack #PowerInPersistence #DefyingSilence #ReclaimYourVoice #JusticeJourney #TruthTeller #BreakTheSilence #VoicesUnite #LegalCourage #SurvivorStory #SpeakTruthToPower #FightSongAnthem #ThisIsMyFightSong #SoundtrackToSurvival #TheyWereWrong #YouCantSilenceUs #WomenWhoFightBack #RiseUp #StrengthInTruth #TraumaToTriumph #ResilienceRevolution

May 17, 2025: Thank you

Song: "Ego Is Not a Dirty Word" - Skyhooks.

On behalf of our little squad, I want to say this loud and clear:

We make no apologies for speaking truth to power, or, for taking the time to heal from the trauma caused by workplace abuse.

As our therapists have reminded us, writing and journaling have always been essential tools for healing.

When certain individuals tried to weaponise the legal system through iCare, in an attempt to silence Sarah, and strip her of this coping tool, I stepped in and carried the load.

At the time, David was completely exhausted.

He didn't have the capacity to write, but let me tell you, he's an excellent scanner.

And an amazing photographer.

Those were his coping tools.

Yet another insurer tried to weaponise it against him.

What makes our squad work?

We leave our egos at the door.

Thank you for indulging us.

On a lighter note, thank you to everyone who sent Birthday messages this year.

Your kindness means the world.

What's next on the horizon?

You'll just have to wait and see.

#EgoIsNotADirtyWord #ThankYou #TruthToPower #HealingInProgress #CreativeCoping #WritingToHeal #PhotographyAsTherapy #SolidarityInHealing #TraumaRecovery #WorkplaceJustice #SpeakingUp #WorkplaceAbuse #SystemicAbuse #WeaponisedSystems #iCareFail #SurvivorVoices #JusticeForWorkers

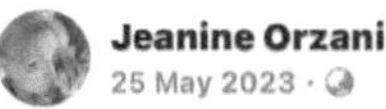

Jeanine Orzani
25 May 2023 ·

You were given multiple opportunities to do the right thing. However, you consistently chose to do the wrong thing. That's on you. Not us.

If only you had of listened to us, to begin with. Maybe we wouldn't, now, be in this predicament. Who knows. We can't go back in time.

One thing for sure is:

"We didn't start the fire. It was always burning, since the world's been turning."

- @billyjoel

The question is, where to now?

I'm not sure yet, but I was asked recently, "How long are you going to keep this up for?"

My response:

"How long's a piece of string?"

#comeback #comebackstronger #narcissisticabuse #emotionalabuse #bullying #overcomingbullying #verbalabuse #psychologicalabuse #justice #accountability

Music by audionautix.com

Activism teaches you something quickly:

The resistance is rarely random.

It follows patterns.

I survived the sabotage.

But survival isn't justice.

The next story is about power.

Who has it?

How they abuse it.

And how they protect each other.

Welcome to the Boys' Club.

The Code.

Every institution operates with a code.
Some of the rules are written.
Most are not.
Power understands the code.
Power protects the code.
And when someone begins to read it...

The system reacts.

Breaking The Code

Breaking The Code

A Code Collective Investigation

Jeanine Orzani and Sarah Gleeson